IMPACT
CALIFORNIA SOCIAL STUDIES

U.S. History
Making a New Nation

RESEARCH COMPANION

Mc Graw Hill Education

Program Authors

James Banks, Ph.D.
Kerry and Linda Killinger Endowed Chair
in Diversity Studies
Director, Center for Multicultural Education
University of Washington
Seattle, Washington

Kevin P. Colleary, Ed.D.
Curriculum and Teaching Department
Graduate School of Education
Fordham University
New York, New York

William Deverell, Ph.D.
Director of the Huntington-USC Institute
on California and the West
Professor of History, University
of Southern California
Los Angeles, California

Daniel Lewis, Ph.D.
Dibner Senior Curator
The Huntington Library
Los Angeles, California

Elizabeth Logan Ph.D., J.D.
Associate Director of the Huntington-
USC Institute on California and the West
Los Angeles, California

Walter C. Parker, Ph.D.
Professor of Social Studies Education
Adjunct Professor of Political Science
University of Washington
Seattle, Washington

Emily M. Schell, Ed.D.
Professor, Teacher Education
San Diego State University
San Diego, California

mheducation.com/prek-12

Send all inquiries to:
McGraw-Hill Education
303 East Wacker Drive, Suite 2000
Chicago, IL 60601

ISBN: 978-0-07-899398-5
MHID: 0-07-899398-9

Printed in the United States of America.

3 4 5 6 7 8 9 LWI 22 21 20 19 18

Letter from the Authors

Dear Social Studies Detective,

Think about the United States of America. Why did different groups of people decide to settle in the territory that would become the United States? When those regions came together, how did the economy, the politics, and groups of people change? In this book, you will find out more about how a territory became a nation. You will think about what it meant to become an independent United States—and what it means to be an American.

As you read, take on the role of a detective. As questions come to your mind, write them down. Then analyze the text to find the answers. What piques your interest? Take notes as you read. You will use your notes as you share what you learned with your classmates. Look closely at all the text—photos, maps, time lines, and historical documents will bring the history of the United States to life!

Enjoy your investigation into the world of social studies where you will explore how a group of territories became the United States, a place full of women, men, and children who came from many places to form a growing and diverse country!

Sincerely,

The IMPACT Social Studies Authors

Declaration of Independence

Contents

Reference Sources

Chapter 1

The Land and People Before Columbus

 Where and How Did American Indians Live Before the Arrival of Europeans?

Chapter 2

The Age of Exploration

 ESSENTIAL EQ QUESTION

What Happened When Diverse Cultures Crossed Paths?

McGraw-Hill Education

Chapter 3

A Changing Continent

 How Did European Settlements Impact North America?

Chapter 4

The Road to War

Why Would a Nation Want to Become Independent?

McGraw-Hill Education

Chapter 5

The American Revolution

 ESSENTIAL EQ QUESTION What Does the Revolutionary Era Tell Us About Our Nation Today?

McGraw-Hill Education

Forming a New Government

 How Does the Constitution Help Us Understand What It Means to Be an American?

McGraw-Hill Education

Chapter 7

Life in the Young Republic

ESSENTIAL EQ QUESTION

How Were the Early Years of the United States Transformative for the Nation?

Chapter 8

The Westward Expansion

 What Does the Westward Expansion Reveal About the Character of Our Nation?

McGraw-Hill Education

Skills and Features

Charts, Graphs, and Diagrams

Maps

Primary Source Quotations

Chapter 1

Chapter 2

Chapter 3

John Smith. *Travels and Works of Captain John Smith.*

Getting Started

You have two social studies books that you will use together to explore and analyze important Social Studies issues.

The Inquiry Journal

is your reporter's notebook where you will ask questions, analyze sources, and record information.

The Research Companion

is where you'll read nonfiction and literature selections, examine primary source materials, and look for answers to your questions.

Every Chapter

Chapter opener pages help you see the big picture. Each chapter begins with an **Essential Question**. This **EQ** guides research and inquiry.

In the **Inquiry Journal,** you'll talk about the **EQ** and find out about the EQ Inquiry Project for the chapter.

In the **Research Companion**, you'll explore the **EQ** and use a time line and map to establish the lesson's time and place.

StasKhom/iStock/Getty Images

Explore Words

Find out what you know about the chapter's academic vocabulary.

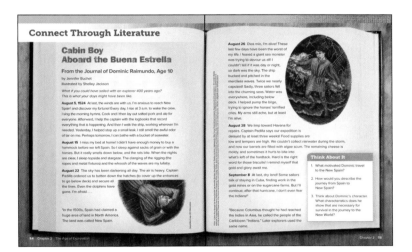

Connect Through Literature

Explore the chapter topic through fiction, informational text, and poetry.

People You Should Know

Learn about the lives of people who have made an impact in history.

Take Action

Present your Inquiry project to your class and assess your work with the project rubric. Then take time to reflect on your work.

Connections in Action

Think about the people, places, and events you read about in the chapter. Discuss with a partner how this gives you a deeper understanding of the EQ.

Every Lesson

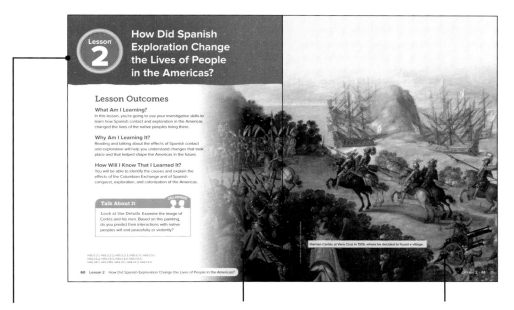

Lesson Question lets you think about how the lesson connects to the chapter EQ.

Lesson Outcomes help you to think about what you will be learning and how it applies to the EQ.

Images and text provide opportunities to explore the lesson topic.

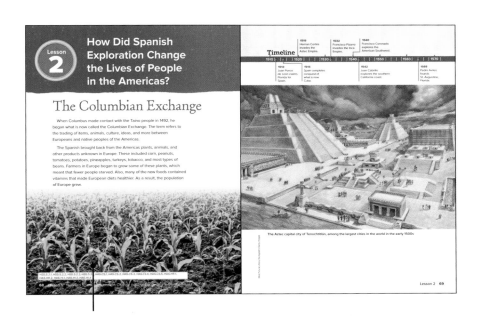

Lesson selections deepen your understanding of the lesson topic and its connection to the EQ.

Analyze and Inquire

The Inquiry Journal provides the tools you need to analyze a source. You'll use those tools to investigate the texts in the Research Companion and use the graphic organizer in the Inquiry Journal to organize your findings.

Inquiry tools assist with analysis and exploration.

Graphic Organizers help you organize information as you read.

Maps show where events happened.

Primary Sources let you read the words and study the artifacts of people from the past and present.

Stop and Check boxes provide opportunities for self-assessment, to consider different perspectives, and to make connections.

Report Your Findings

At the end of each lesson you have an opportunity in the Inquiry Journal to report your findings and connect back to the EQ. In the Research Companion, you'll reconsider the lesson focus question based on what you've learned.

Think about what you have learned.

Write about it using text evidence to support your ideas.

Connect to the EQ.

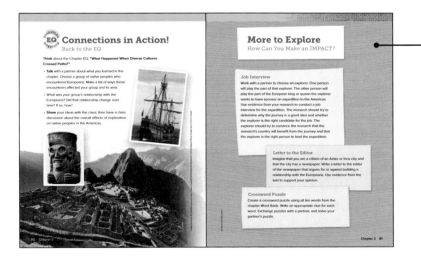

Think about what you read in the lesson. How does this give you a new understanding about the lesson focus question?

Be a Social Studies Detective

How do you learn about people, places, and events in the present or in the past and the impact they had on history? Become a Social Studies Detective!

Explore, investigate, report, and make an impact!

Investigate Primary Sources

Detectives ask questions and use clues to help them solve mysteries. You can do the same thing by examining primary sources.

What's a Primary Source?

A **primary source** is a record of an event by someone who was present at the event when it happened. Letters, diaries, newspaper articles, photographs, and drawings are all examples of primary sources. Birth certificates, bank records, and even clothes can be primary sources.

Did You Know?

A **secondary source** is information from someone who was not present at the event he or she is describing. Secondary sources are based on primary sources.

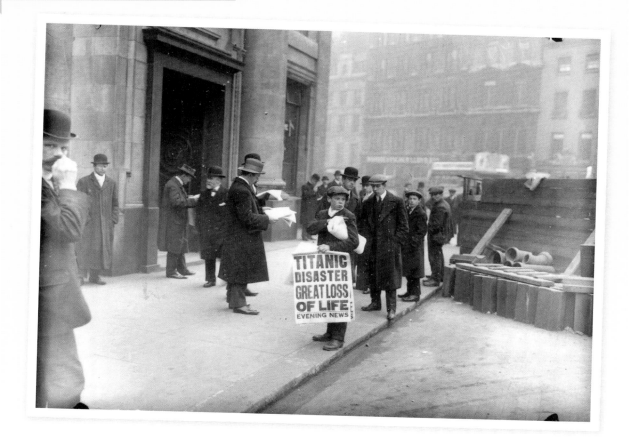

Social Studies Detective Strategies

Inspect

- Look closely at the source.
- Who or what is it?
- How would you describe it?

Find Evidence

- Where did the event take place?
- When did it happen?
- What are the most important details?

Make Connections

- Is this source like others you found?
- Are there other perspectives that you need to consider?
- What information supports your idea?

Social Studies Detectives examine primary sources to make connections. These connections help them learn about the past and understand the present. Use the Social Studies Detective Strategy to analyze the image below.

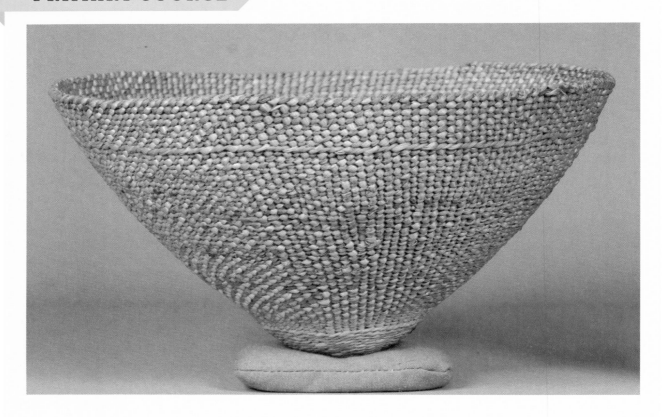

Social Studies Detective Strategies

1. Inspect
2. Find Evidence
3. Make Connections

Inspect the primary source below. Ask questions. Who wrote the diary? When did they write it? Why do you think they wrote it? Look for clues to answer your questions.

TEXT: Audubon, John W. Audubon's Western Journal: 1849-1850. Cleveland: The Arthur H. Clark Company, 1906.; PHOTO: McGraw-Hill Education

June 3d, Sunday. We left El Paso at eight this morning, and rode until ten, when we reached a deserted rancho, and with some trouble encamped near a river bed with waterholes along it. A beautiful lagoon with water holes a hundred yards long enabled us all to take refreshing baths, and I watched with pleasure the languid flight of the great blue heron, changing his position as he was approached. Two Mexicans, hunting cattle, came to us here, and Lieut. Browning bought a wild mule, for which he gave a few dollars and a broken down mule. (p.94)

September 2d. Two days out from Ures we came to some Pimos Indians washing gold from black ore, which they said produced well; we found some lumps of ore in the dust, all of irregular shapes. The value is only about one real (about ten cents) for each bushel of dirt. Each man made about two dollars a day.
We had fine grass and pond water here, and are off for Altar. (P.143)

from Audubon's Western Journal: 1849-1850

Explore Geography

Geographers are detectives who understand how our world is connected by studying the earth's surface and digging for clues about how people have shaped our planet. This section gives you the tools that you'll need as you explore geography..

Reading a Map

Maps are drawings of places on Earth. Most maps have standard features to help you read the map.

Map Title The map title tells you what information is on the map.

Inset Map An inset map is a small map included on a larger map. The inset map might show an area that is too large, too small, or too far away to be included on the main map.

Boundary Lines Boundary lines are political. The boundaries between states usually are drawn differently from the boundaries between nations.

Locator A locator map is a small map set into the main map. It shows the area of the map in a larger region.

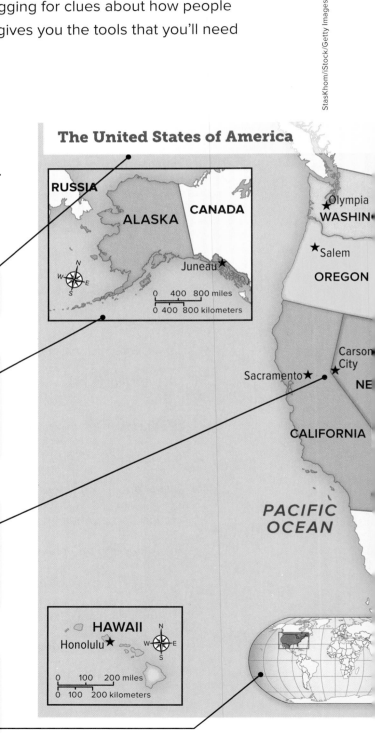

The United States of America

RUSSIA

CANADA

ALASKA

Juneau★

0   400   800 miles
0 400 800 kilometers

★Olympia
WASHIN

★Salem

OREGON

Carson
City★

Sacramento★

NE

CALIFORNIA

PACIFIC
OCEAN

HAWAII
Honolulu★

0   100   200 miles
0   100   200 kilometers

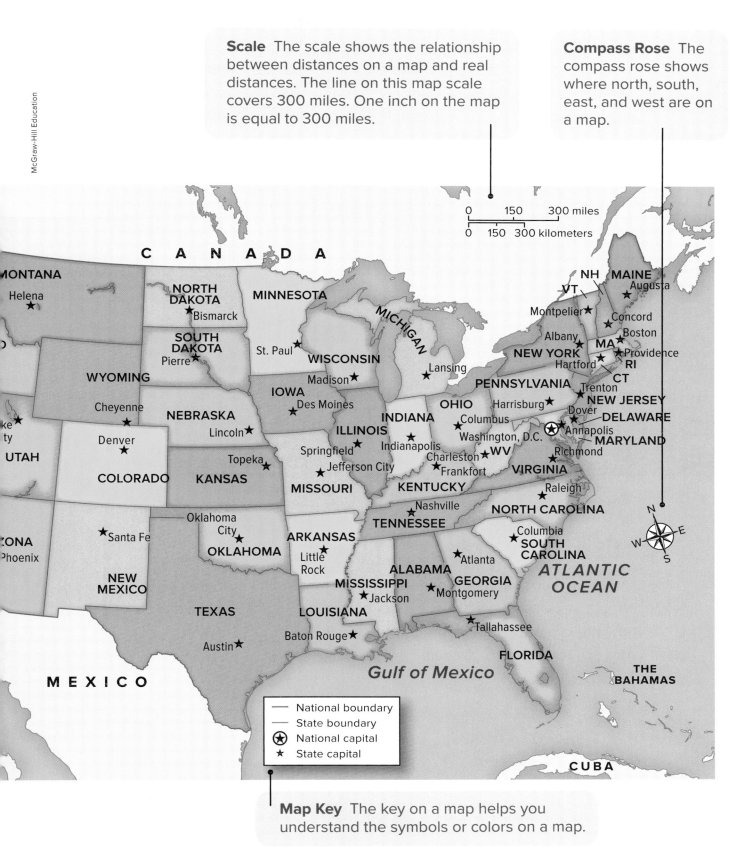

Scale The scale shows the relationship between distances on a map and real distances. The line on this map scale covers 300 miles. One inch on the map is equal to 300 miles.

Compass Rose The compass rose shows where north, south, east, and west are on a map.

0   150   300 miles

0   150   300 kilometers

Map Key The key on a map helps you understand the symbols or colors on a map.

— National boundary
— State boundary
⊛ National capital
★ State capital

Special Purpose Maps

Maps can show different kinds of information about an area such as how many people live there, where mountains and rivers stretch, and where the roads are. These kinds of maps are called special purpose maps. A historical map is an example of a special purpose map.

Lewis and Clark's route across the Louisiana Territory

Historical Maps

Historical maps capture a period in time. They show information about the places where past events occurred. The map above shows how the explorers Lewis and Clark found their way across North America to the Pacific Ocean.

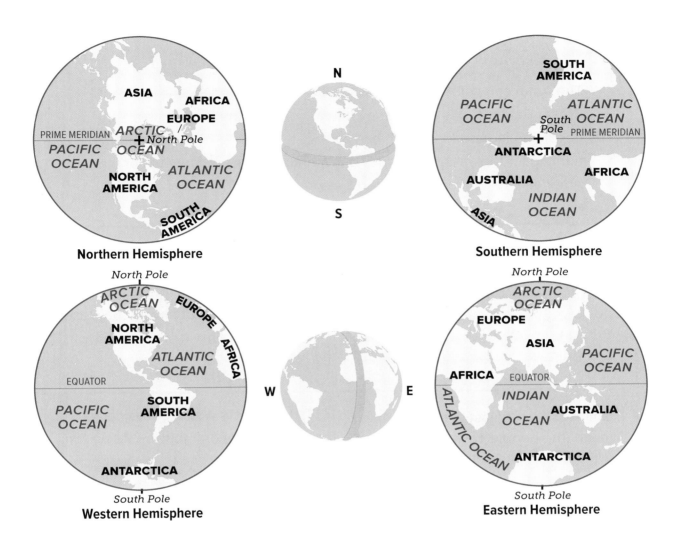

Northern Hemisphere

N

S

Southern Hemisphere

Western Hemisphere

W · E

Eastern Hemisphere

Looking At Earth

Another way to look at the earth is by using a globe. Geographers have divided the Earth into northern and southern hemispheres at the equator. The area north of the equator is called the Northern Hemisphere. The area south of the equator is called the Southern Hemisphere. The prime meridian runs from north to south around the Earth. The hemisphere east of the prime meridian is the Eastern Hemisphere. The hemisphere west of the prime meridian is the Western Hemisphere.

Explore Economics

The American colonists decided to fight for independence from Great Britain. To make this choice they had to consider the benefits of becoming independent and the costs, or things they would lose, in fighting for their freedom. Study a few of the costs and benefits of the American Revolution in the chart below.

Costs	Benefits
An independent new nation would not have the protection of Great Britain from other European powers and American Indians.	The colonists in an independent America would not have to pay taxes to Great Britain.
Going to war against Great Britain meant the people could be charged with treason or die in battle.	The colonists would get to decide how their new government would be run.
A war against Great Britain would be expensive and the colonists didn't have a lot of money to support the war effort.	The colonists would be able to trade goods and make deals with other countries.

Talk About It

If you were a colonist at the time of the American Revolution, would you have wanted to stay a part of Great Britain or fight to become an independent new nation? Use evidence to support your answer.

PRIMARY SOURCE

Currency from the period of the American Revolution

Explore Citizenship

You can learn to make an impact by being a good citizen. Some important words that define what it means to be a good citizen are listed on page 19a. They help us understand how to be better citizens in our home, neighborhood, school, community, country, and world.

Take Action!

You have learned to be a Social Studies detective by digging for clues and you practiced exploring and investigating geography, economics, and civics. Now it's time to explore the lessons in this book and make an impact!

President Lincoln at Antietam, Maryland, in 1862

Be a Good Citizen

COURAGE
Being brave in the face
of difficulty

FREEDOM
Making choices and holding beliefs
of one's own

HONESTY
Telling the truth

JUSTICE
Working toward fair
treatment for everyone

LEADERSHIP
Showing good behavior worth
following through example

LOYALTY
Showing support for people and
one's country

RESPECT
Treating others as you
would like to be treated

RESPONSIBILITY
Being worthy of trust

The Land and People Before Columbus

ESSENTIAL EQ QUESTION

Where and How Did American Indians Live Before the Arrival of Europeans?

In this chapter, you'll read about groups who lived in the Americas before the arrival of Christopher Columbus and other European explorers. You'll think about how native peoples' locations influenced their daily lives. You'll also learn more about their cultures and heritage.

Step into the Time Chronological Thinking

Look at the timeline. What was happening in other parts of the world while different civilizations were emerging in the Americas?

Americas

c. 12,000 B.C.
Early humans cross land bridge from Asia to North America.

c. 9000 B.C.
Clovis hunter-gatherers roam North America.

c. 1200 B.C.
Olmec civilization begins in Mexico.

c. 100 B.C.
Inuit people settle the Arctic.

c.120,000 B.C.

World Events

c. 120,000 B.C. to 80,000 B.C.
Modern humans evolve in Africa.

c. 7000 B.C.
Chinese build first Great Wall of China.

c. 2500 B.C.
Sailors navigate trade route between Greece and Egypt.

c. 27 B.C.
The Roman Empire begins.

A.D. 712
The Japanese people compile their first written history.

HSS.5.1.1, HSS.5.1.2, HSS.5.1.3, HAS.CS.1

Bering Strait — Beringian Land Bridge

INUIT CIVILIZATION

TLINGIT CIVILIZATION

PACIFIC OCEAN

ATLANTIC OCEAN

IROQUOIS CIVILIZATION

ANCESTRAL PUEBLO CIVILIZATION

0   300   600 miles
0   300   600 kilometers

OLMEC CIVILIZATION   MAYA CIVILIZATION

Migrations of Early Humans in North and Central America

Step into the Place

1. Where were some of the major civilizations of early American Indians?

2. What do you think led early humans to migrate and settle where they did?

Human settlement of the Americas began as long as 14,000 years ago when early humans crossed the Bering Land Bridge from Asia to modern-day Alaska. People migrated across the Western Hemisphere, creating civilizations as they went.

c. A.D. 900 Maya civilization declines in Central America and Mexico

c. A.D. 1150 Hopi civilization is at its height in desert Southwest.

c. late A.D. 1300s Navajo civilization begins in desert Southwest.

A.D. 1540 Spanish explorer Francisco Vásquez de Coronado begins battle with Zuni people

c. A.D. 1570 Iroquois Confederacy forms in Eastern Woodlands.

c. A.D. 1700 Tlingit people govern territory of Pacific Northwest

A.D. 1700

A.D. 1100–1300 Chinese, Arab, and European sailors use a magnetic compass.

A.D. 1492 King Ferdinand and Queen Isabella of Spain send Christopher Columbus to find a trade route to Asia.

A.D. 1519–1522 Magellan-Elcano expedition sails around Earth, proving Earth is round.

Connect Through Literature

The Legend of
Wishpoosh

retold by Elizabeth M. Tenney

Long ago when the world was very young, no people lived on earth. Only the Watetash—the animal people—roamed the land.

One of the Watetash was an enormous king-beaver who went by the name of Wishpoosh. Wishpoosh resided in Lake Keechelus[1] high in the snow-capped Cascade Mountains.

Now Wishpoosh was a very destructive beaver. He had a great appetite and ate absolutely everything that came his way. Soon he had eaten all the smaller creatures in the lovely mountain lake, as well as those that lived on the shore. Then he began devouring all the trees and the plants which surrounded the lake.

Wishpoosh was destroying so many creatures and so much vegetation that Speelyei, the coyote god of the mid-Columbia region, decided that he must do something to stop Wishpoosh.

Speelyei jumped into Lake Keechelus and struggled with Wishpoosh. They rolled and twisted and fought each other, causing the waters of the lake to boil. Wishpoosh became so violent that he tore out the banks of Lake Keechelus and the waters flooded down the canyon, sweeping everything before them. At the bottom of the canyon the waters stopped and held against the rocky ridges, forming another lake. This lake was larger than Lake Keechelus, and covered the Kittitas[2] Valley.

But the struggle between Wishpoosh and Speelyei was not over yet. Wishpoosh continued to thrash about madly, eating everything that he could find, growing larger and larger as he ate.

For a while, the rocky ridges restrained the flood, but Wishpoosh had become so large and so strong that at last even the ridges gave way and the loosened waters swept down to fill the great basins of Cowiche, Naches, and Ahtanum.

Yet even these basins, surrounded by their hills, could not hold the monster beaver. Before long they, too, gave way, and the waters flooded down in a torrent through the Yakima area. The waters cut a passage through barren hills and filled the level plains of what are now Simcoe and Toppenish.

For a long time this water was dammed by the Umatilla highlands, but Wishpoosh did not give up. As before, he continued to thrash about, eating everything he could find in the waters and everything he could find on the lands. Finally, again he broke the rocky hills that kept the waters in, and the water flooded to form the greatest lake of all between the Umatilla on the east and the Cascade Mountains on the west. The entire area was under water.

Yet even this huge lake could not hold the frenzied beaver. After a time, the mighty Cascades gave way before his onslaughts. The water then flowed to the sea, draining all the valleys behind.

But even that was not the end of Wishpoosh. Once in the ocean, Wishpoosh laid about himself with such fury that he devoured all the fish, even the whales! He threatened all creation.

Speelyei saw that he must bring an end to Wishpoosh or the world would be lost. Transforming himself into a floating branch, he drifted to Wishpoosh and was soon swallowed up.

Once inside the beaver, Speelyei turned back into himself, drew out his knife, and began to cut out all of the giant beaver's vital organs.

At last this was too much even for Wishpoosh. His life ceased. His huge carcass was cast up by the tide onto the beach at Clatsop near the mouth of the Great River.

Speelyei stood looking at the carcass. What should be done with it? The coyote god took his knife and cut off the beaver's head. From it, he fashioned a group of people—the Nez Perce—who were great in council and great in oratory. From the beaver's arms he made another people— the Cayuse—who were powerful with the bow and war-club. The beaver's legs became the Klickitats, a people who were swift runners. The belly of the beaver became the Chinooks whose lands offered much to eat. Finally there remained the hide and the insides. Speelyei picked these up and, turning toward the east, hurled them as far as he could. These became the Snake River Indians.

Thus were formed the various tribes of peoples who lived in the northwest corner of the land.

---

[1] Lake Keechelus (spelled "Kichelos" in the early literature) still exists as a mountain lake. It is situated near the summit of the Snoqualimie Pass, the main east-west highway (#90) which crosses the state of Washington, leading to Seattle. Lake Keechelus can be clearly seen from the highway which skirts its shores for several miles.

[2] Kittitas is a well-known valley in Central Washington which surrounds present-day Ellensburg. Kittitas was once the territory of the Kittitas tribe.

Think About It

1. How are Speelyei and Wishpoosh alike? How are they different?

2. Why did the two characters fight?

3. What conclusions about American Indian civilization can you draw from this story?

How Did the Characteristics of Early American Indian Groups Develop?

The First Hunter-Gatherers

The first humans to settle the Western Hemisphere were probably **hunter-gatherers** from Asia. These early humans lived by gathering wild plants and hunting animals. Many scientists today believe they reached North America by crossing a land bridge from Asia that formed when sea levels dropped during the last Ice Age.

For thousands of years this land bridge, which scientists call Beringia, linked what is now Siberia to Alaska. Herds of Ice Age animals crossed Beringia. The early humans hunted these animals, which included elephant-like wooly mammoths and mastodons.

An Ice Age mastodon was nearly as large as a modern elephant. It had short, powerful legs and long, sharp tusks. Its tough hide was covered with long, reddish brown hair. To hunt such a dangerous animal, early humans would have needed effective weapons and teamwork.

HSS.5.1, HSS.5.1.1, HSS.5.1.2, HSS.5.1.3, HAS.CS.4

8   Lesson 1   How Did the Characteristics of Early American Indian Groups Develop?

Time Line

c. 9000 B.C
Clovis people hunt Ice Age animals.

c. 1200 B.C.
Olmec civilization begins in Mexico.

c. A.D. 200
Hohokam settle in American Southwest.

c. A.D. 700
Mississippian people first occupy Cahokia.

c. A.D. 900
Maya civilization declines in Central America and Mexico.

| |8000| | |7000| | |6000| | |5000| | |4000| | |3000| | |2000| | |A.D. 1| | 900 |

Ice Age hunters followed woolly mammoths across a land bridge from Asia.

Archaeologists are people who study the tools and other artifacts of people who lived long ago. Using such evidence, they reach conclusions about how ancient people lived. Archaeologists have different views about exactly when early humans first reached North America. They have evidence that these people had migrated all the way to the southern tip of South America by about 10,500 B.C. The people's migrations must have taken place over a long time. So their arrival likely occurred centuries earlier.

Archaeologists also have different views about which route (or routes) these early American Indian groups might have used in their migrations throughout North and South America. Some scientists think they used an ice-free inland route. Others think early humans traveled by boat along the Pacific Coast.

Did You Know?

Beginning in the 1930s, archaeologists started to find evidence that early American Indians may have hunted large Ice Age animals. Mixed in with the bones of extinct animals, such as mammoths, scientists found slim, beautifully crafted stone spear points. The first site where these spear points were found was near present-day Clovis, New Mexico. So the early humans who made them became known as the Clovis people. Clovis sites date back to about 9000 B.C.

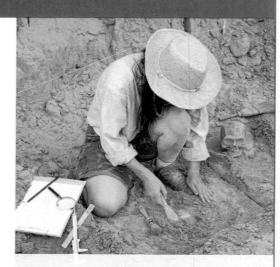

Archaeologists use special tools when uncovering artifacts.

✓ Stop and Check

Think Consider the routes that archaeologists believe early humans took when migrating into North America. What probably caused these people to select these routes?

Find Details As you read, add additional information to the graphic organizer on page 11 in your Inquiry Journal.

The Olmec

About 11,500 years ago, the last Ice Age ended. The climate of the Western Hemisphere slowly grew warmer and drier. Many of the Ice Age animals that the early American Indians had hunted became extinct. These hunter-gatherer cultures had to adapt to survive. Instead of gathering wild plants, they began to grow their own food. By about 4000 B.C., farmers in Mexico and Central America were raising three crops: maize (also called corn), beans, and squash.

One of the most important effects of farming is that a community can raise more food than it needs to feed itself. This food surplus allows some people in the community to focus on the arts and religion that help to create a civilization.

The first civilization to develop in the Western Hemisphere was started by the Olmec people. It developed in the hot rain forests of southern Mexico about 1200 B.C. The Olmec built temples, carved huge stone statues, played ball games, and created a calendar and a writing system. They spread their culture across Mexico and Central America through an effective trade network.

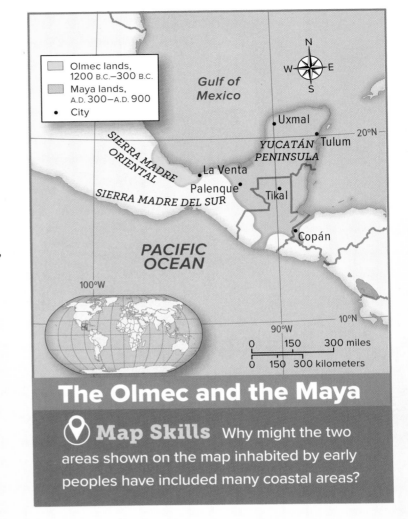

The Olmec and the Maya

Map Skills Why might the two areas shown on the map inhabited by early peoples have included many coastal areas?

 Stop and Check

Think Why is a food surplus so important to the growth of a civilization?

Called the "Pyramid of the Magician," this thousand-year-old structure rises more than 90 feet above the Maya city of Uxmal in Mexico.

The Maya

The Maya developed their culture in the same part of Mexico as the Olmec. They traded with their Olmec neighbors and were influenced by their culture. Between about A.D. 250 and 900, Maya culture reached its peak. Archaeologists call this the "Classic Period" of Maya civilization.

During the Classic Period, the Maya world grew to more than 40 cities, each with a population between 5,000 and 50,000. In cities such as Uxmal, Tikal, and Copan, the Maya built great palaces for their rulers and huge pyramid temples to honor their gods. These structures were covered with elaborate carvings and inscriptions in their system of picture writing. Scholars often refer to such inscriptions as **hieroglyphs**. The meaning of these inscriptions was unknown for centuries after Maya civilization collapsed. Thorough translations appeared in the mid-1900s.

Did You Know?

The Maya were fascinated with time. They created a 365-day calendar. The year was divided into 18 months of 20 days each. The remaining five days were not shown in any month and the Maya believed those days were unlucky. To show when historical events took place, they used a system of dating called the "Long Count." Translated to today's calendar, the Maya's Long Count suggests the world was created about 3114 B.C.

Mayan influence is seen in the design of this Aztec stone calendar.

Maya cities were ruled by kings who claimed that Maya gods had chosen them. These rulers directed huge building projects and commanded the army. To form alliances and strengthen trade, Maya rulers often married members of the royal families of other cities.

Maya civilization declined rapidly after A.D. 900. Archaeologists have looked for explanations in the environment. They think that as time passed, the population of the Maya cities outgrew their food supply. Rulers fought over farmland. People began to abandon the Maya cities in search of food. Drought may also have led to their decline. However, the Maya did not disappear. Today, more than six million descendants of the ancient Maya still live in Mexico, Belize, and Guatemala.

✓ Stop and Check

COLLABORATE

Talk How did cultural characteristics spread from one early American Indian group to another?

Early Desert Peoples

The early American Indian groups of the Southwest developed in an environment very different from the rain forests of Mexico and Central America. About A.D. 200, a group known as the Hohokam moved from a part of the Sonoran Desert in northern Mexico to present-day Arizona, between the Salt River and Gila River. At that time, the area received only about three inches of rain a year. Yet the settlers discovered ways to turn the desert into fields of corn, beans, squash, and cotton.

The Hohokam built a complex irrigation system to bring water to their fields. With simple tools such as sharpened sticks and stone blades, they dug shallow canals that stretched for hundreds of miles. Hohokam farmers used small gates to direct water from these canals into their fields. The Hohokam irrigation canals were built so well that some of them are still used today.

Hohokam farmers lived in small villages. They built their houses by digging a shallow pit and covering it with a wooden frame, roofed with plant material called thatch. Building underground helped to keep Hohokam houses cool during the day and warm at night. The Hohokam wove cotton into cloth for clothing. They made baskets and pottery for storage. Hohokam jewelry was crafted from turquoise mined in the desert and from shells. Shell jewelry was especially prized. Hohokam traders traveled long distances to trade cotton cloth and pottery for shells gathered by people on the Gulf of California and the Pacific Coast.

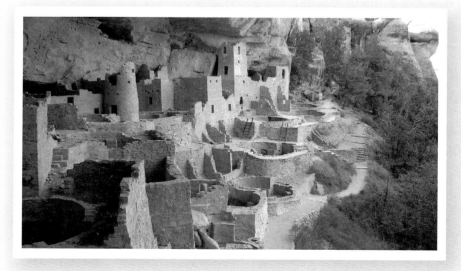

The Ancestral Pueblo people built the Cliff Palace at Mesa Verde, in what is now Colorado.

The Ancestral Pueblo were another of the American Indian groups to settle in the deserts of the Southwest. They are also known as the Anasazi. In about A.D. 700, the Ancestral Pueblo people settled in the "Four Corners" area where Utah, Colorado, Arizona, and New Mexico meet today. Like the Hohokam, the Ancestral Pueblo planted squash, corn, and beans. The high desert plateaus where they lived were not suited to the use of canals for irrigation, however. Instead, the Ancestral Pueblo developed a method called dry farming. They channeled rainwater and snowmelt into catch basins. Then this water was slowly released into narrow, pebbled-lined drains to the crops.

The Ancestral Pueblo are known as the first "cliff dwellers." They lived in huge apartment-like dwellings built along the steep sides of the cliffs. Living in cliff dwellings, such as Mesa Verde, made it easier for the Ancestral Pueblo to defend themselves against enemies. These dwellings were made of finely carved stone and logs that were plastered with adobe. Adobe is a mixture of mud and straw that dries into a hard clay. An adobe house stays cool during the heat of the day and warm during cold desert nights.

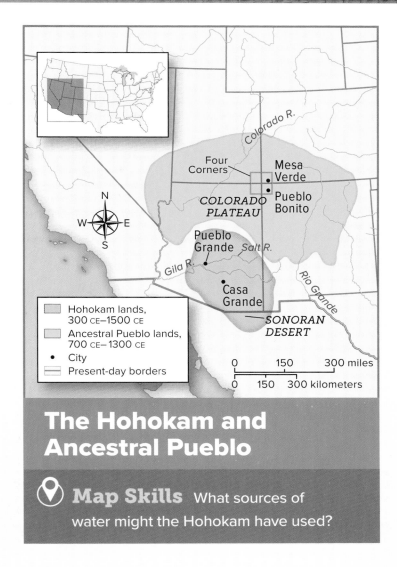

The Hohokam and Ancestral Pueblo

Map Skills What sources of water might the Hohokam have used?

✓ Stop and Check

COLLABORATE

Connect to Now Are there any features of the societies of the early desert peoples that modern American society should imitate? Why or why not? Discuss your opinion with a partner.

The Mound Builders

As Europeans began to settle the Ohio and Mississippi river valleys in the 1700s, they encountered a variety of earthen mounds. Some were cone-shaped hills. Others were earthen walls. A few even had the shapes of animals. The most amazing of these is the Great Serpent Mound in southern Ohio, which is more than 1,300 feet long. The people who built these mysterious structures and then left were once referred to simply as "Mound Builders." Archaeologists have identified several different Mound Builder cultures.

The earliest of these cultures is known as the Adena, after a site in Ohio where archaeologists first studied their mounds. The Adena culture lasted from about 500 B.C. to A.D. 100. These people lived in villages of round houses built from logs and roofed with bark. Originally hunter-gatherers, the Adena people later began to farm. Their crops included gourds and sunflowers.

The Adena used stone to craft both simple tools and complex objects such as smoking pipes used in rituals. They fashioned ornaments from copper, mica, and shells—materials that they obtained through trade with distant peoples. What is known about Adena culture comes from such objects, which the Adena people placed in the burial mounds they built for their dead.

Between about 200 B.C. and A.D. 500, another mound-building culture called the Hopewell occupied the same region as the Adena culture. The Hopewell people were also named for a site in southern Ohio where archaeologists first studied their culture. The Hopewell people shared many features of the Adena culture. Hopewell artists created objects from copper, mica, and obsidian, a volcanic glass. Like the Adena people, the Hopewell obtained these materials through a far-flung trade network.

The Adena people built the Great Serpent Mound.

Tony Linck/SuperStock

Then and Now

Archaeologists have been studying the Cahokia mounds since the late 1800s, but only a small part of the site has been excavated. Seventy of the original 120 mounds are preserved today in Illinois's Cahokia Mounds State Historic Site (established in 1979). Cahokia was named a World Heritage Site in 1982, meaning it deserves special protection.

An artist's depiction of Cahokia about A.D. 1100

One of the last major American Indian groups to develop before the arrival of Europeans was the Mississippian culture. Mississippian culture developed in the Mississippi River valley between A.D. 700 and 900.

Large-scale farming of corn, beans, squash, and other crops produced food surpluses. This encouraged the growth of large populations in Mississippian towns and cities. Priest-kings ruled Mississippian society. Each town or city controlled a group of outlying villages. High fences of sharpened logs defended these villages from attack. Warfare seems to have been frequent.

The greatest Mississippian city is the site known today as Cahokia. Built in what is now southern Illinois, Cahokia at its peak was home to more than 20,000 people. A plaza for holding ceremonies was the center of a Mississippian city. Around this plaza were groups of mounds on top of which might have been a temple or a chief's dwelling. Monk's Mound at Cahokia was 100 feet high and covered 14 acres. It was the largest pre-Columbian earthen structure in the Western Hemisphere.

COLLABORATE

✓ Stop and Check

Talk Which characteristics did the Adena, Hopewell, and Mississippian cultures share?

How Did the People of the Desert Southwest Meet Their Needs?

The Pueblo People

The Pueblo peoples of the American Southwest have inhabited the area for more than a thousand years. They mostly farmed crops such as corn and beans, and they built permanent homes out of stone and adobe clay. The Spanish word for these homes is *pueblo*, and that is how these people got their name.

Pueblo homes were modeled after the cliff dwellings of the Ancestral Pueblo. They are cube-like rooms stacked on top of each other. The largest rooms are at the bottom, while the smaller rooms are near the top. There are also fewer rooms near the top. So the entire house does not look like a big square or rectangle but more like a small, stepped pyramid. Wooden ladders outside of the rooms were usually used to get from one floor to another. Sometimes the bottom floor would have no doors or windows, and a person could get in only by climbing a ladder. This made the structure easy to defend because the ladder could be pulled up.

Pueblo buildings were usually home to several families and had connecting shared rooms. They also contained *kivas*, special below-ground rooms used for rituals and ceremonies.

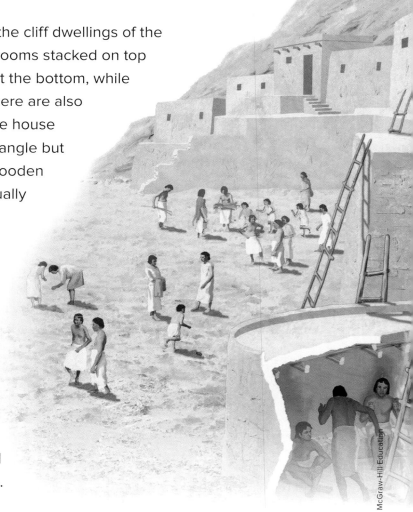

McGraw-Hill Education

HSS.5.1.1, HSS.5.1.2, HSS.5.1.3, HAS.CS.4

Time Line

1150
The Hopi build Oraibi, the oldest continuously occupied settlement in the United States.

1276–1299
The Great Drought causes cultural shift in Ancestral Pueblo peoples.

Late 1300s
The Navajo arrive in the Southwest.

1540
Spanish explorer Francisco Vásquez de Coronado interrupts a sacred Zuni ceremony and causes a battle.

150 | 1300 | 1540

A Southwest pueblo

There are many groups that make up the Pueblo people. Two of these are the Zuni and the Hopi.

The Zuni occupy their ancestral land in the Zuni River valley, though their territory is not as large as it was in the past. Attacks by Spanish treasure hunters and, later, settlers from the United States caused the Zuni to abandon some of their villages. They gathered into a single village to better protect themselves. This village was called Halona and is now called Zuni.

Another Pueblo group is the Hopi. The Hopi people are believed to be one of the oldest desert peoples. Their village of Oraibi is believed to be nearly nine hundred years old. They used dams and irrigation to grow crops such as corn, cotton, beans, and squash. They also took advantage of the sand dunes that formed against the sides of **mesas**. These dunes would trap moisture, and so the Hopi would plant crops in them.

Hopi men and women had different jobs. The men farmed and hunted. They also wove cloth from cotton. The women gathered food like nuts and berries. They also made baskets and pottery to store their food. The Hopi were among the first people to fire, or strengthen by heating, their pottery, using coal.

Kachina dolls

Chuck Place/Alamy Stock Photo

Important parts of Hopi culture include *kachinas*. According to Hopi beliefs, kachinas are spirits who live in sacred places for half of the year. During the other half, they live near the Hopi villages and bring with them rain and the growing season. The kachinas are represented by masked dancers who perform in the villages when the kachinas visit. There are hundreds of kachinas, so the dancers often give small carved kachina dolls to children to help them learn about the spirits.

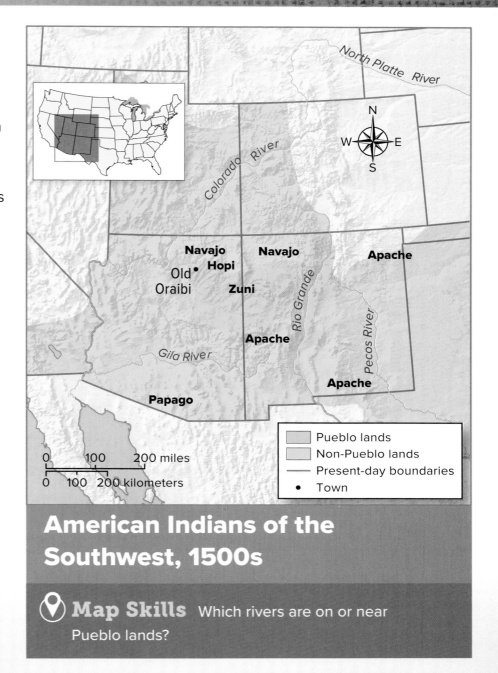

Pueblo lands
Non-Pueblo lands
Present-day boundaries
• Town

American Indians of the Southwest, 1500s

Map Skills Which rivers are on or near Pueblo lands?

✓ Stop and Check

COLLABORATE

Talk With a small group, list the advantages of the pueblo buildings. What makes them ideal for the Hopi and Zuni lifestyles?

Find Details As you read, add additional information to the graphic organizer on page 19 in your Inquiry Journal.

The Navajo

The Navajo were neighbors to the Pueblo and borrowed some of their ideas. They used irrigation to grow crops, made clothes with cotton, and were skilled in making jewelry and pottery. Despite these similarities, the Navajo were not related to the Pueblo. The Navajo were related to the Athabascans of Alaska and Canada. Scholars think the Navajo migrated from the northern tundra to the southwestern deserts in the late 1200s.

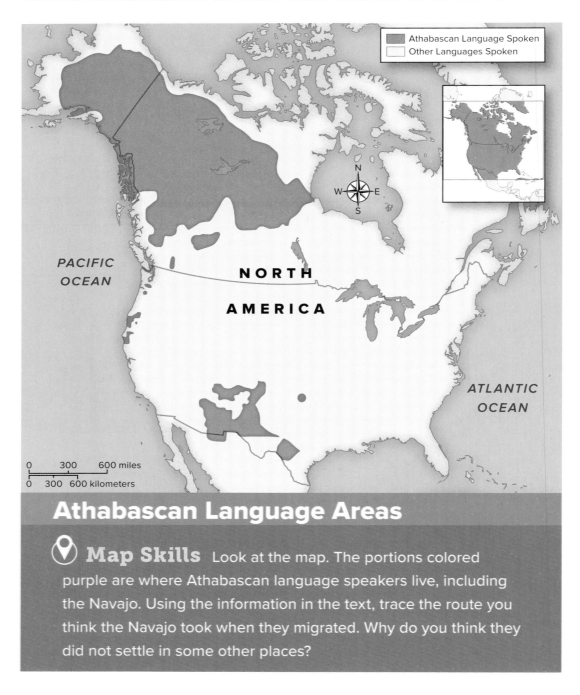

Athabascan Language Spoken
Other Languages Spoken

PACIFIC OCEAN

NORTH

AMERICA

ATLANTIC OCEAN

0   300   600 miles
0   300 600 kilometers

Athabascan Language Areas

⊙ **Map Skills** Look at the map. The portions colored purple are where Athabascan language speakers live, including the Navajo. Using the information in the text, trace the route you think the Navajo took when they migrated. Why do you think they did not settle in some other places?

The Navajo were originally hunter-gatherers but quickly adopted new techniques for surviving in the desert. In addition to learning farming from the Pueblo, the Navajo also learned from Spanish settlers when they arrived in the 1500s. They were interested in the animals the Spanish brought with them. The Navajo soon became skilled at herding sheep and cattle, as well as at riding horses. Their relationship with the Spanish was otherwise hostile. The culture of the Spanish clashed with several of the American Indian groups. The Navajo became close allies with the Pueblo and the Apache in fighting the Spanish.

The Navajo lived in *hogans*, large dome-shaped buildings. Hogans were made of logs or stone and covered in mud and dirt. They had one entrance, usually facing east and covered with a blanket. Hogans had no windows, only a hole in the roof so that smoke from the fire could escape.

A hogan

Traditionally, the Navajo believed in *hozho*, or "walking in beauty." This means maintaining balance with the earth. They believed that being out of harmony with the earth was the cause of illness and suffering. In order to restore harmony, they took part in long ceremonies involving singing and dancing. Many of these rituals are still practiced today.

✓ Stop and Check

Think What changes did the Navajo have to make when they moved from the North to the South?

Find Details As you read, add additional information to the graphic organizer on page 19 in your Inquiry Journal.

The Apache

The Apache language, like Navajo, is in the Athabascan family. Therefore, many historians believe the Apache also migrated from Canada. Apache **oral history**, on the other hand, claims it was the opposite. According to the oral history, the Athabascans to the north are descendants of the Apache in the south. Whatever their origins, the Apache are quite different from the Navajo and Pueblo peoples.

The Apache were not farmers, but hunter-gatherers. They hunted buffalo, deer, cougar, and other animals. The Apache were very skilled hunters and had tricks such as rubbing themselves with animal fat to hide their scent. They also gathered agave, cactus, nuts, and berries. Sometimes they would get food and supplies by trading with their Pueblo neighbors. Other times, they would conduct raids against Pueblo villages, earning them a reputation of being fierce and warlike. The name *Apache*, in fact, comes from the Zuni word for "enemy."

An Apache basket

InfoGraphic

How to Build a Wickiup

Step 1 The Apache made poles from green and flexible tree brances.

Step 2 Holes were dug in a circle for the poles.

Step 3 The poles were bent and tied with strips of animal skin to create a dome.

Although fearsome to enemies, the Apache were gentle and affectionate to their children and relatives. Like many tribes, the Apache trace their ancestors through their mothers, rather than their fathers. They traditionally lived in relatively small groups made up of their extended family. These groups were independent, and it was not until recent times that the Apache unified under a single government.

The Apache lived in *wickiups*. These houses were dome-shaped, like the Navajo hogans, but did not use earth or clay as building materials. Instead, they were covered in skins, reed mats, brush, or grass. Although the wikiups were not as strong as the pueblos or hogans, they could be easily taken apart and moved. This was helpful for the Apache, who moved from place to place.

Step 4 Smaller willow poles were tied around the sides and top.

Step 6 They finished the wikiup with a fire pit and smoke hole for a chimney.

Step 5 Animal skins or reed mats were used to cover the dome.

✓ Stop and Check

COLLABORATE

Write What made the Apache unique among Southwestern American Indians?

How Are the California and Pacific Northwest Peoples Shaped by Their Surroundings?

A Variety of Landscapes

American Indians settled in a number of vastly different natural environments in the American West. American Indians established settlements in the snowy Arctic regions of Alaska, the forested coasts of Oregon and Washington, and the arid deserts of southern California. Surviving in each of these climates required very specific skills, and, as a result, American Indians across the American West developed unique ways of life.

Ancestors of the Navajo and Apache people may have reached the Pacific Northwest about 5000 B.C. Eventually, some of the ancestors of these people migrated south, but others remained in the region. The Tlingit people belong to the same language family as the Navajo and Apache—meaning the groups share a common ancestor—but their surroundings have caused them to develop a very different way of life.

Hand-woven baskets were an important tool in Pomo life.

HSS.5.1.1, HSS.5.1.2, HSS.5.1.3, HAS.CS.5

Paul Marcus/Shutterstock.com

Time Line

c. 100 B.C.
Inuit settle the Arctic.

c. A.D. 1700
Tlingit people govern a large territory in the Pacific Northwest.

A.D. 1855
Chief Seattle and other Pacific Northwest Indian chiefs sign the Port Elliott Treaty, granting their land to the U.S. government.

100 B.C.   A.D. 1   1700   1800

A.D. 1
Miwok begin occupying lowlands of California.

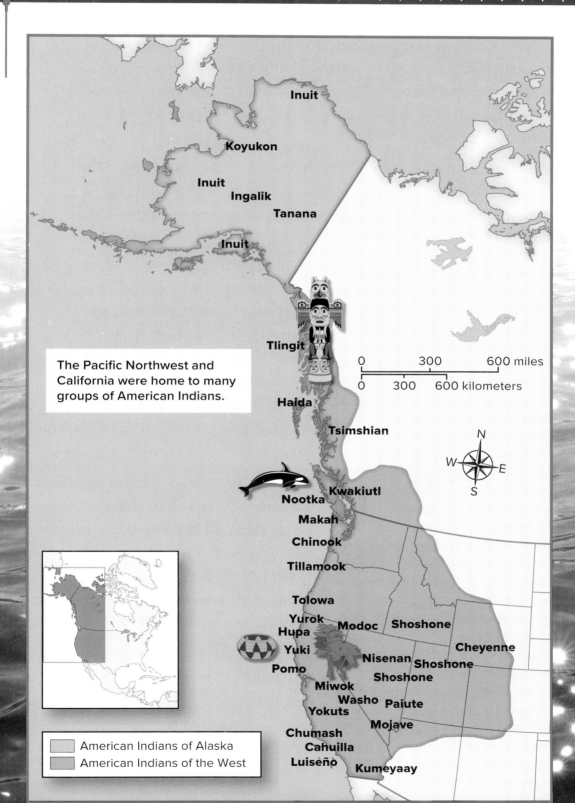

The Pacific Northwest and California were home to many groups of American Indians.

Inuit
Koyukon
Inuit
Ingalik
Tanana
Inuit
Tlingit
Haida
Tsimshian
Kwakiutl
Nootka
Makah
Chinook
Tillamook
Tolowa
Yurok
Hupa
Yuki
Pomo
Modoc
Shoshone
Nisenan
Shoshone
Cheyenne
Shoshone
Miwok
Washo
Yokuts
Paiute
Chumash
Mojave
Cahuilla
Luiseño
Kumeyaay

0   300   600 miles
0   300   600 kilometers

N
W   E
S

☐ American Indians of Alaska
☐ American Indians of the West

McGraw-Hill Education

American Indians of California

The American Indians of California can be divided into at least six distinct cultural regions—Northwestern, Northeastern, Central, Great Basin, Southern, and Colorado River. Groups in each area share cultural similarities. Some of the peoples living in the Central region, for instance, speak similar languages.

The location of each group directly affects their culture and way of life. The Cahuilla, for example, built irrigation systems to raise crops in the desert basins in the south, while the Yurok, living along the northern coast, fished for most of their food.

Tolowa
Yurok
Modoc
Hupa
Atsugewi
Yuki
Pomo
Nisenan
Coast Miwok
Washo
Miwok
Paiute
Yokuts
Shoshone
PACIFIC OCEAN
Salinan
Chumash
Mohave
Cahuilla
Quechan (Yuma)
Luiseño
Kumeyaay (Digueño)

Northwestern
Northeastern
Central
Great Basin
Southern
Colorado River
Present-day boundaries

0   50   100 miles
0   50   100 kilometers

American Indian Groups of California

◉ Map Skills Working with a partner, determine which of California's American Indian cultural areas was the largest and which was the smallest. Using the scale, measure the lengths of both the largest and smallest cultural areas from north to south.

The Pomo are part of the Central California cultural area. Before encountering Europeans, the Pomo thrived by making use of the plentiful natural resources available in their region. The Pomo collected acorns, fished with nets and traps, and hunted deer, birds, and other small game. Roundhouses made from wood, earth, and grass functioned as homes and gathering places.

Basket weaving played a large role in Pomo life and traditions. Pomo baskets, often decorated with feathers and shells, are well known around the world for quality among art collectors. Baskets served a purpose in a number of aspects of Pomo life, including cooking and childcare. Museums collect Pomo baskets as valuable works of art.

Farther to the south, in the Central Valley, pre-Columbian groups including the Miwok built their cultures around the region's resources. In the valley, Miwok hunters stalked deer, elk, and antelope. In the marshes, they set traps for otters and beavers.

Forests may have been the most pivotal source of the Miwok way of life. Oak trees provided the Miwok with their staple product, the acorn. Children would shake loose acorns from the oaks' upper branches, while women collected the fallen acorns in large baskets. The Miwok women ground the acorns into flour to make bread, biscuits, and soup.

Southern California's deserts do not have this same wealth of resources. There, groups such as the Cahuilla (kuh WEE uh), the Serrano, and the Chemehuevi (cheh mih HWEY vee) adapted to use the few plants that grow in the desert. The Cahuilla also developed irrigation systems to raise crops including corn, squash, beans, and melons. By digging ditches to feed into small lakes, the Cahuilla made use of the limited precipitation to sustain a vibrant culture.

PRIMARY SOURCE

How the World Grew... Miwok Legend

In the beginning the world was rock. Every year the rains came and fell on the rock and washed off a little; this made earth. By and by plants grew on the earth and their leaves fell and made more earth. Then pine trees grew and their needles and cones fell every year and with the other leaves and bark made more earth and covered more of the rock.

If you look closely at the ground in the woods you will see how the top is leaves and bark and pine needles and cones, and how a little below the top these are matted together, and a little deeper are rotting and breaking up into earth. This is the way the world grew—and it is growing still.

— translation of a Northern Miwok legend by C. Hart Merriam, published in 1910

✓ Stop and Check

Talk Why are the Miwok not known for building irrigation systems like the Cahuilla?

Find Details As you read, add additional information to your graphic organizer on page 27 in your Inquiry Journal.

Merriam, C. Hart, ed. The Dawn of the World. Cleveland: The Arthur H. Clark Company, 1910.

American Indians of the Pacific Northwest

Native peoples of this region reside in communities along the Pacific Coast from what is now British Columbia to northern California. The ocean supplies seafood and plants for the groups of American Indians living in the Pacific Northwest.

Long ago, wood from the area's forests allowed these people to construct homes, carve canoes and masks, and fashion household items including dishes and spoons. The Pacific Northwest peoples believed that all living things, including plants and animals, had rights that should be respected. They were careful to cut down only as many trees as they needed to continue their way of life.

Did You Know?

Chief Seattle (c. 1786–1866) was the leader of the Suquamish and Duwamish people who lived in what is now northwestern Washington state. Seattle wanted to work with European settlers to coexist with the groups of American Indians living in the area. In 1855, Seattle agreed to give over his people's land to the U.S. government and move to a reservation. When groups of American Indians tried to take back their land by force, Chief Seattle protected the Europeans. The settlers later named their new city after him.

Chief Seattle

Pacific Northwest groups such as the Tlingit carved **totem poles** as a way of chronicling their family histories. Totem poles are made from long logs that are carved and decorated to represent people or animals. Each totem pole is made up of a series of these symbols, called totems. The totems and their order often reflect the stories of the family.

These families often mark major life events, such as a wedding or a change of leader, with a ceremony known as a **potlatch**. At a potlatch, guests of the family receive gifts and enjoy feasting and music. The host is responsible for gift giving and sometimes can offer more than a hundred presents at a single potlatch. The host receives respect and standing among the community as a result of his or her generosity. Pacific Northwest peoples still hold potlatches today, and they are an important source of cultural identity for many people who live in the region.

The Makah people made their home on the shores of the Pacific Ocean and the Strait of Juan de Fuca. Though the Makah hunted many kinds of sea animals, including seals, porpoises, and sea otters, whale hunting held a special place in Makah life.

Makah canoes carrying as many as sixty hunters at a time would set out in search of whales. After a successful hunt, the Makah gave thanks for their triumph. Every part of a whale was used in different Makah activities.

A modern-day potlatch ceremony

✓ Stop and Check

Write Reread the text and make a list of all of the ways that American Indians of the Pacific Northwest used wood. Is there a material that is as important to Americans today as wood was to these groups of American Indians?

Then and Now: Totem Poles of the Pacific Northwest

A traditional totem pole

Edwin Verin/Shutterstock.com

Then

Historians can only speculate when the first totem poles were erected. Europeans recorded seeing them in the 1700s, when they first landed on the coast of the Pacific Northwest. Though immediately impressive in their size and detail, totem poles can be fully understood only with a deep knowledge of the culture that built them. The order of a pole's totems tells a story. The only way to read the pole is to first know the story. Each generation of Pacific Northwest people passed down the stories expressed in totem poles to the younger generation.

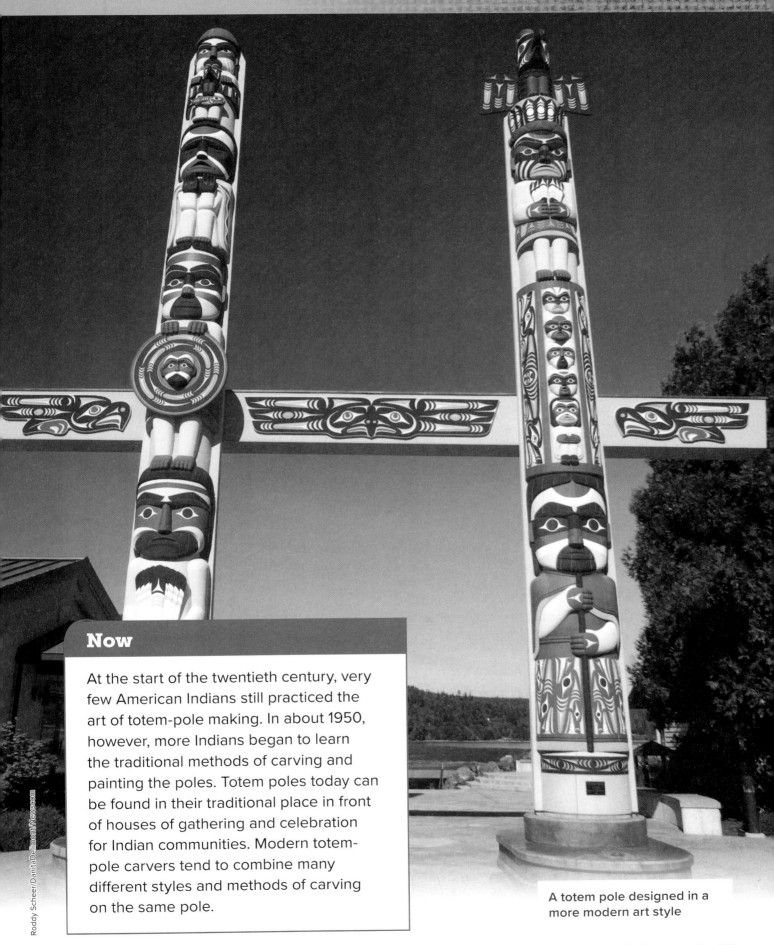

Now

At the start of the twentieth century, very few American Indians still practiced the art of totem-pole making. In about 1950, however, more Indians began to learn the traditional methods of carving and painting the poles. Totem poles today can be found in their traditional place in front of houses of gathering and celebration for Indian communities. Modern totem-pole carvers tend to combine many different styles and methods of carving on the same pole.

A totem pole designed in a more modern art style

How Did the Great Plains Influence the Traditions of the People Living There?

Grass and Sky for Miles

The Great Plains region covers a huge area of land that spreads from Canada south to Texas, and from the Rocky Mountains east to North Dakota, South Dakota, Nebraska, Kansas, and Oklahoma. It is mainly made up of hills and flat, grassy stretches of land called **prairies**. Except near rivers, it is difficult to grow crops in the Great Plains. Most native peoples who lived there could not depend on farming for food. Instead, they followed and hunted the huge herds of buffalo that roamed the prairies. (These animals were first called "buffalo" by early American settlers. The name stuck, but these large, cattle-like animals are actually bison.)

Plains people depended on the buffalo for more than just food. Buffalo hides were used to make clothes and shelter. Plains people made ropes, bowls, needles, thread, and tools from other parts of the buffalo. In fact, they had a use for every part of the buffalo.

HSS.5.1.1, HSS.5.1.2, HSS.5.1.3, HAS.HI.2

c. 1300
American Indians settle the Plains

1500s
Horses first come to North America.

1600s
The Lakota are pushed westward by competing tribes

1300 | | | | 1400 | | | | 1500 | | | | 1600 | | | | 1700

Buffalo were part of the spiritual practice of the Plains people. They prepared for each hunt with special ceremonies, and they believed they needed the support of the spirit for the hunt to be successful. Buffalo roamed from place to place, so many Plains people developed a lifestyle that allowed them to follow the herds.

Buffalo on the Great Plains

Marco Prati/Shutterstock.com

Peoples of the Plains

American Indians began settling the Great Plains as early as A.D. 1300. By the 1700s, groups included the Lakota, Dakota, and Nakota Sioux as well as the Pawnee, Cheyenne, Crow, Kiowa, and several others. Some people moved to the region because of drought, or a long period without rain, in the place where they used to live. Many people lived near rivers, which provided fertile land for them to farm. Others who followed the buffalo were nomads, or people who move from place to place with no fixed residence.

Plains Indians who traveled usually lived in cone-shaped homes called teepees. These structures consisted of buffalo hide spread across long poles. When the buffalo moved, women collapsed the teepees and set them back up in a new place. Those who lived near rivers set up more permanent homes called lodges made of logs, grasses, and dirt. But they also used teepees when they needed to travel to hunt.

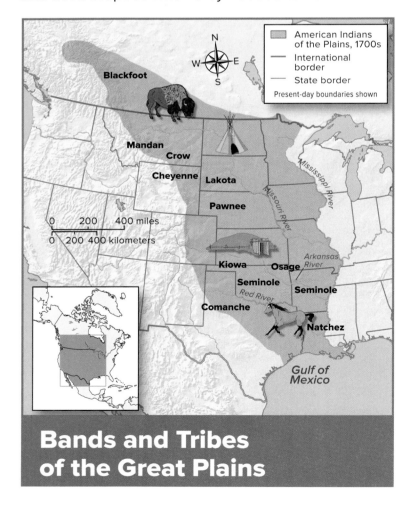

Bands and Tribes of the Great Plains

Did You Know?

Horses

You may have thought that people in the Great Plains region have been riding horses for thousands of years. Before the 1500s, however, nobody had ridden a horse in North America. Explorers from Spain brought horses to the Americas, and some of the horses escaped. After about one hundred years, the horses had traveled up to the Great Plains. There the Lakota caught and tamed them. After another hundred years, most American Indians on the Plains were using horses to help them hunt buffalo and move their camps.

The introduction of horses completely changed the way of life for the Plains people. Before they had horses, Plains people followed the buffalo on foot. They trained dogs to pull belongings on a special sled called a *hupak'in*. After the introduction of horses, a person's wealth was measured by the number of horses owned.

✓ Stop and Check

Talk How did the introduction of horses completely change the way of life for the Plains people?

Find Evidence As you read, add additional information to the graphic organizer on page 35 in your Inquiry Journal.

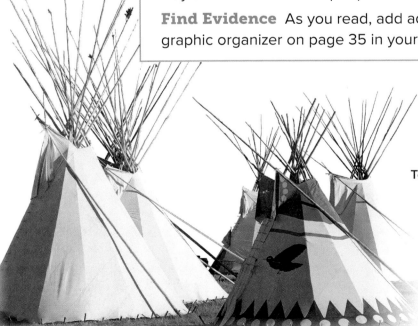

Teepees in Wyoming

Life on the Plains

What was life like if you were an American Indian on the Plains? Your daily activities greatly depended on whether you were a man or a woman.

Men

- Were responsible for boys' education.
- Could serve as keeper of the people's history and stories.
- Hunted buffalo and other game.
- Fought in wars.

Boys

- Played games to sharpen their wrestling, hunting, and shooting skills.
- Learned the value of courage in battle.

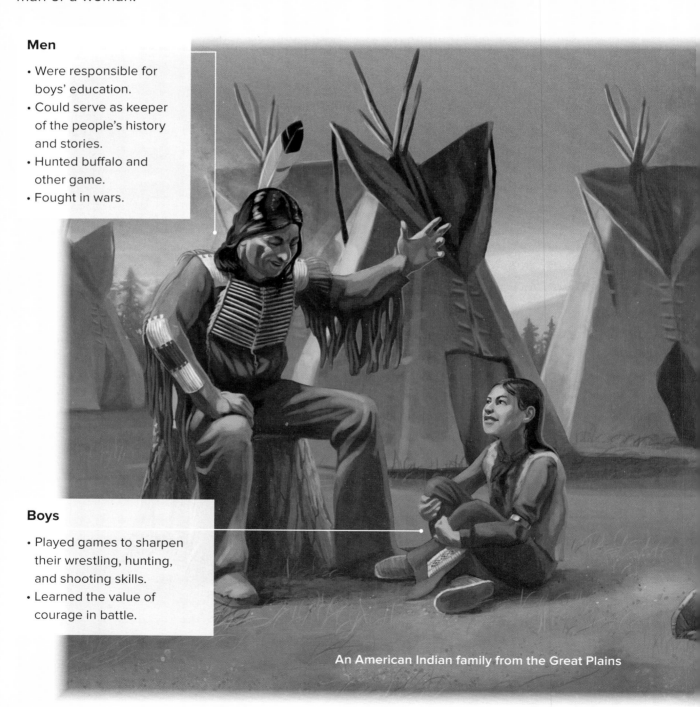

An American Indian family from the Great Plains

Boys and girls who grew up in native cultures on the Great Plains also had specific roles. For all children, education started early. Usually it consisted of listening to stories and learning songs.

What Do You Think? Was it fair for tasks to be divided between men and women among Plains people?

Women

- Were responsible for girls' education.
- Scraped animal hides to make teepees and clothes.
- Set up and took down teepees.
- Packed and unpacked belongings when it was time to move.
- Cooked meals.
- In some bands and tribes, grew corn, sunflowers, beans, and squash.

Girls

- Learned to cook.
- Sewed doll clothes and toy teepees.
- Learned to set up and take down a teepee.

✓ Stop and Check

Think How do your experiences compare with the experiences of the children of Plains people? Which are similar and which are different?

How Did the Eastern Woodlands Impact the Lives of Early People?

Terrain and Climate of the Eastern Woodlands

The Eastern Woodlands stretch from the Mississippi River to the Atlantic Ocean. In the past, most of this area was covered in thick forests. Since the Eastern Woodlands cover a large area, the early peoples of the region were often very different from one another.

The seasons often guided how the people of the Eastern Woodlands lived. During the winter, men hunted game such as deer, bear, rabbits, beavers, and wild turkeys. During spring, the soil was ideal for growing crops. In summer, men fished, carved canoes, and built homes while women gathered berries and wild plants. In autumn, the tribes gathered, dried, and stored the crops for the winter. After the **harvest**, they let the land rest for several years before replanting the crops. They used different land the next year.

The large area of the Eastern Woodlands can be divided into two regions: the Northeast and the Southeast. The Southeast was more thinly wooded and had a mild climate and a long growing season. These conditions were good for farming. The thicker forests of the Northeast made farming more challenging. There, many early peoples practiced a type of farming called **slash-and-burn**. They cut down and burned the trees in the forest, and ash from the burned vegetation helped make the soil fertile.

McGraw-Hill Education

HSS.5.1,1, HSS.5.1.2, HSS 5.1,3, HA.CS.4, HA.HI.2

c. A.D. 700
The Mississippian culture arises in the Southeast Woodlands.

c. 1570
The Iroquois Confederacy is formed.

c. 1722
Tuscarora join the Iroquois Confederacy.

700   1600   1700

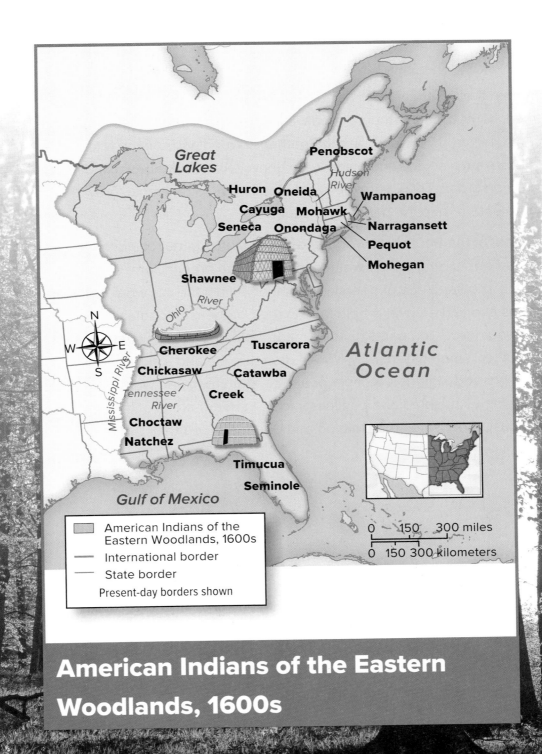

American Indians of the Eastern Woodlands, 1600s

Map labels: Great Lakes, Penobscot, Hudson River, Huron, Oneida, Wampanoag, Cayuga, Mohawk, Seneca, Onondaga, Narragansett, Pequot, Mohegan, Shawnee, Ohio River, Cherokee, Tuscarora, Atlantic Ocean, Chickasaw, Catawba, Mississippi River, Tennessee River, Creek, Choctaw, Natchez, Timucua, Seminole, Gulf of Mexico

Legend:
- American Indians of the Eastern Woodlands, 1600s
- International border
- State border
- Present-day borders shown

0   150   300 miles
0   150   300 kilometers

People of the Southeast Woodlands

Among the American Indian tribes that lived in the Southeast Woodlands were the Creek, Cherokee, Chickasaw, Catawba, Natchez, and Choctaw. Each tribe had its own unique customs and traditions.

In both the Southeast and the Northeast, people ate a variety of farmed, hunted, and gathered foods, including beans, corn, deer, nuts, and maple syrup. However, in the Southeast Woodlands, many wild resources such as rice and bison were unavailable. The tribes relied more heavily on crops. The Cherokee in the Southeast, for example, grew the "Three Sisters" of corn, beans, and squash.

People of the Southeast Woodlands wore clothing that could be adjusted depending on the weather. Men wore a breechcloth, which is a long rectangular piece of deerskin, cloth, or animal fur. It is worn between the legs and tucked over a belt. Men in the Southeast Woodlands also wore leggings, or leg pants, usually made from buckskin or some other soft leather. Women generally wore a deerskin top and a skirt to which they might add leggings, a cape, or a robe. Both men and women wore moccasins—soft-soled and heelless shoes. In hotter areas of the Southeast, men wore little clothing and often tattooed their bodies.

Moccasins—soft-soled, heelless shoes—made by American Indians of the Eastern Woodlands

Ways of life varied from tribe to tribe in the Southeast. The Cherokee, who lived mainly in what is now Tennessee and Georgia, constructed fairly large villages, with each having 20 to 60 houses and a large meeting building. Cherokee homes were usually made of wattle—twigs and branches woven together to make the house's frame—and daub, which is a sticky substance like mud or clay. The Cherokee covered the wattle frame with daub, which held it all together. This created the look of an upside-down basket. The Cherokee also placed fences around their villages for protection against enemies. Each Cherokee village had its own leaders and made its own decisions. However, during times of celebration or war, villages came together. One celebration, called the Green Corn Festival, honored the summer's first corn crop with dances and games.

Like the Cherokee, the Natchez built homes from wattle and daub. The Natchez lived in permanent villages in what today is Mississippi. They were successful farmers, but they also hunted, fished, and gathered food from plants. Like the Hopewell and Mississippian people before them, the Natchez built ceremonial mounds.

The Creek arranged their towns around a central town plaza, used for religious ceremonies and games. Surrounding the plaza were family homes built out of poles and covered with grass, mud, or thatch. Like the Cherokee, the Creek relied on the "Three Sisters" of corn, beans, and squash for food. In addition, they hunted small animals and gathered plants.

Stop and Check

Talk How did climate and terrain affect the diet and clothing of the Americans Indians in the Southeast Woodlands?

Find Details As you read, add additional information to the graphic organizer on page 43 in your Inquiry Journal.

The "Three Sisters" crops: corn, squash, and beans

People of the Northeast Woodlands

Like the Southeast Woodlands, the Northeast Woodlands area was populated by different tribes, each with their unique customs and traditions. The Mohawk, Narragansett, Seneca, Pequot, Iroquois, and Oneida tribes lived in the Northeast Woodlands.

Because of differences in climate and terrain, people in the Northeast ate food unavailable to people in the Southeast. Rivers in the Northeast, for example, had annual runs of fish, like salmon, that moved up rivers from the sea. In the North, people often had to rely more on fish than on crops because frost frequently destroyed crops. On the Atlantic coast and along major rivers, shellfish were plentiful and provided a major source of food for the people living there.

Because of the colder climate, the clothing worn by people in the Northeast differed from what people in the Southeast wore. While the basics—breechcloth and leggings for men and deerskin tops and skirts for women—remained the same, people in the Northeast wore heavier and warmer leggings and various furs. Northeast tribes also used snowshoes for walking in the snow. Snowshoes work by distributing a person's weight over a larger area so that the person does not sink in the snow.

Wampum, or stringed shell beads, was used for ceremonial purposes and for trade.

In the 1500s, the Iroquois lived mostly in what is now upstate New York. Historians call this group the Iroquois because they spoke languages in the Iroquoian language family. However, the Iroquois call themselves Haudenosaunee (hoe dee noh SHOH nee). In Iroquoian, this means "people of the longhouse."

For housing, the Iroquois depended on wigwams and longhouses. The Iroquois made wigwams by bending young trees to form the round shape of a dome. Then, over this basic shape, they wrapped pieces of tree bark to protect against bad weather. Over the bark layer they added thatch, or dried grass. A small hole at the top allowed smoke from the fire to escape.

Longhouses were long, rectangular homes. The Iroquois made their longhouses by building a frame from saplings, or young trees. They covered the frame with bark sewn together. Inside, they built a long hallway with rooms on both sides. Then they lined the walls with sleeping platforms, covered with deerskin. They also built in shelves for storing baskets, pots, and pelts (the skins of animals with the fur attached). Several families lived in the same longhouse.

Almost all Iroquois property was controlled by clans—groups of families who shared the same ancestor. Women were the leaders of their clans. Among the Iroquois, it was women who decided how the land would be used and who would use it. When a man married, he moved into his wife's longhouse and lived with her family. Children took their clan name from their mother. No important decision could be made without the approval of the clan mother. Although the leaders of each village were men, it was the clan mother who chose them.

✓ Stop and Check

COLLABORATE

Talk American Indian tribes found different ways to organize themselves and their members. Why was it important that the tribes organized themselves?

Government in the Woodlands

To help protect themselves, the Creek formed a confederacy. A confederacy is a group of people formed for a common purpose. The Creek Confederacy divided its towns into peace (white) towns and war (red) towns. Red towns declared war, planned military actions, and met with enemies. White towns passed laws and held conquered groups. However, during war, people in peace towns joined in the fighting.

Farther north, the Iroquois also had a system of government. When they were a small group, they cooperated on many matters. By about A.D. 1300, their numbers had grown, and their communities were crowded. Arguments arose and fighting broke out. The Iroquois believed that if one person was wronged, it hurt the whole clan. For this reason, wrongs had to be punished. The Iroquois also fought with other Eastern Woodlands peoples, often over hunting grounds. Warfare soon became a constant problem for the Iroquois.

According to Iroquois history, two Iroquois leaders, Deganawida and Hiawatha, saw that fighting was destroying their people. In the 1500s, these two leaders urged the Iroquois to join together to make peace. In about 1570, five separate Iroquois tribes joined together to form the Iroquois Confederacy, also known as the Iroquois League. The Confederacy is still active today.

PRIMARY SOURCE

Constitution of the Iroquois Nations

"If a nation, part of a nation, or more than one nation within the Five Nations should in any way endeavor to destroy the Great Peace by neglect or violating its laws and resolve to dissolve the Confederacy, such a nation or such nations shall be deemed guilty of treason and called enemies of the Confederacy and the Great Peace."

"They [the offending people] shall be warned once and if a second warning is necessary they shall be driven from the territory of the Confederacy. . . ."

TEXT: Constitution of the Iroquois Nations, art. 92. Prepared by Gerald Murphy. Distributed by the National Public Telecomputing Network and the Constitution Society. PHOTO: Ádám Aczél/EyeEm/Getty Images

The Iroquois Confederacy, 1600

Place Which group of Iroquois lived the farthest east?

Stop and Check

COLLABORATE

Talk What was the major reason the Iroquois formed a confederacy?

Find Details As you read, add additional information to the graphic organizer on page 43 of your Inquiry Journal.

Does the Iroquois Confederacy Resemble Our Government?

In order to keep the Great Peace, the Iroquois people developed the Great Law. This was a set of rules by which the Iroquois people lived. They also set up a way for each of the tribes in the Iroquois Confederacy to have a voice in making decisions. Representatives from all of the clans met at the Grand Council. These representatives were chosen by the clan mothers. The Grand Council made decisions through discussion and compromise, or settled a dispute by each side agreeing to give up part of what it wanted. The Grand Council continues to make decisions for the Iroquois today.

Some historians believe the Iroquois government influenced the plan of the American government. In fact, in 1988 the U.S. Senate passed a resolution acknowledging the influence of the Iroquois Confederacy on the U.S. Constitution. But just how much did the Iroquois Confederacy influence our government? How democratic was the Iroquois Confederacy?

PRIMARY SOURCE

In Their Words...   Concurrent Resolution 331

To acknowledge the contribution of the Iroquois Confederacy of Nations to the development of the United States Constitution and to reaffirm the continuing government-to-government relationship between Indian tribes and the United States established in the Constitution.

Whereas the original framers of the Constitution, including, most notably, George Washington and Benjamin Franklin, are known to have greatly admired the concepts of the Six Nations of the Iroquois Confederacy . . .

—U.S. Senate, October 21, 1988

TEXT: U.S. Congress. House. A Concurrent Resolution to Acknowledge the Contribution of the Iroquois Confederacy of Nations to the Development of the United States Constitution and to Reaffirm the Continuing Government-to-Government Relationship between Indian tribes and the United States Established in the Constitution. HR 331. 100th Cong., 2nd sess. (October 4, 1988); H.Rept 100-1031.

Build Citizenship
Justice

1. List ways the American government is like the Iroquois Confederacy.
2. List ways the American government is different from the Iroquois Confederacy.
3. Do you think the Iroquois Confederacy had more similarities or more differences with our government?

Think About It
Perspectives

1. Find a classmate that answered the question differently than you.
2. Take turns giving your perspective and supporting it with reasons and evidence.
3. Discuss with your classmate whether or not you think the Iroquois Confederacy was a democracy.

An 18th century French engraving of Deganawida meeting with the Iroquois Confederacy

Write About It

Think about how you described the Iroquois government. Write a paragraph answering the following questions. What makes a government a democracy? Is it the way leaders are chosen, or is it the way the government makes decisions?

Connections in Action!
Back to the EQ

Think about the Chapter EQ, **"Where and How Did American Indians Live Before the Arrival of Europeans?"**

- **Talk** with a partner about each group you learned about in the chapter. Which civilization did you find the most interesting, and why? Consider how that group's location affected its way of life. Create a graphic organizer that lists or compares and contrasts interesting facts about the groups you and your partner chose.

- What do you think will change about these American Indians' ways of life once Europeans arrive?

- **Share** your ideas with the class.

(bkgd)Stocktrek Images, Inc./Alamy; (t)Paul Marcus/Shutterstock.com; (tc)Frank van den Bergh/Getty Images; (bc)Photo Researchers, Inc/Alamy; (b)Image Source

More to Explore
How Can You Make an IMPACT?

Q and A

Work with a partner. Each of you will play the part of a member of an early American Indian tribe. Write three to five questions for your partner to answer about the culture and civilization of his or her chosen group. You will answer your partner's questions about the group you chose.

Travel Guide

Write a blog post for a travel website that will persuade early humans to migrate to a specific region of the Americas. Include information about the location's soil, rivers, or weather. Make suggestions about what kind of civilization the early humans could build in your chosen location. Draw a picture of the area to illustrate your blog post.

Picture It!

Choose three words from the Chapter Word Bank. Create an illustration or series of illustrations, such as a comic strip, that provides context for each word you chose. Share your images with the class, and tell how each one gives context to the vocabulary word.

Chapter 2

The Age of Exploration

ESSENTIAL EQ QUESTION

What Happened When Diverse Cultures Crossed Paths?

In this chapter, you'll read about how European exploration of the New World changed the Americas forever. You'll consider what the Europeans had to gain as well as how exploration affected the lives and cultures of native peoples.

Step into the Time Chronological Thinking

Look at the time line. What was happening in other parts of the world while Europeans were exploring the Americas?

Americas

Late 1300s
The Navajo arrive in what is now the southwestern United States.

1492
Christopher Columbus reaches the New World.

1497
John Cabot explores the eastern coast of Canada.

1250	1300	1350	1400	1450	1500

World Events

1295
Marco Polo returns from China.

1347
Plague called the "Black Death" begins, eventually killing approximately one-third of the European population.

c. 1425
Prince Henry of Portugal begins sponsoring explorations of the west coast of Africa.

1453
Ottoman Turks capture Constantinople.

1478
Spanish Inquisition begins.

1488
Portugal's Bartolomeu Dias sails around Africa to the Indian Ocean.

HSS.5.2.1, HSS.5.2.2, HSS.5.2.3, HAS.CS.1

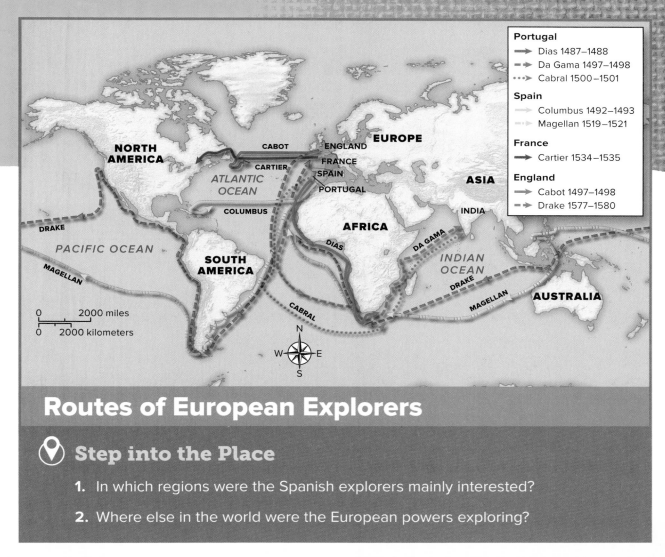

Routes of European Explorers

Portugal
→ Dias 1487–1488
⇢ Da Gama 1497–1498
••▸ Cabral 1500–1501

Spain
→ Columbus 1492–1493
⇢ Magellan 1519–1521

France
→ Cartier 1534–1535

England
→ Cabot 1497–1498
⇢ Drake 1577–1580

Step into the Place

1. In which regions were the Spanish explorers mainly interested?

2. Where else in the world were the European powers exploring?

Over the course of about 100 years, the major European powers of Spain, Portugal, France, England, and the Netherlands participated in a mad dash to explore and claim land in the New World. Reports of gold and other resources that could enrich their nations tempted these Europeans to spend money and take risks to sponsor several voyages. Some were successful and others were not. While the voyages led to different places in the Americas, they all led to a similar result for the peoples who already lived there: sweeping change.

1513 Juan Ponce de León claims Florida for Spain.

1519 Hernan Cortés invades the Aztec Empire.

1532 Francisco Pizarro invades the Inca Empire.

1534 Jacques Cartier claims land along the St. Lawrence River for France.

1609 Henry Hudson sets sail from the Netherlands to explore North America.

1498 Portugal's Vasco da Gama reaches India by sea.

1522 Spanish Magellan-Elcano expedition completes voyage around the world.

1543 Nicolas Copernicus argues that the Earth revolves around the Sun, challenging most people's beliefs.

1500   1550   1600   1650

Connect Through Literature

Cabin Boy Aboard the Buena Estrella

From the Journal of Dominic Raimundo, Age 10

by Jennifer Buchet
illustrated by Shelley Jackson

What if you could have sailed with an explorer 400 years ago?
This is what your days might have been like.

August 5, 1524 At last, the winds are with us. I'm anxious to reach New Spain[1] and discover my fortune! Every day, I rise at 3 a.m. to wake the crew. I sing the morning hymns. Cook and I then lay out salted pork and ale for everyone. Afterward, I help the captain with the logbooks that record everything that is happening. And then I walk the ship, working wherever I'm needed. Yesterday, I helped stop up a small leak. I still smell the awful odor of tar on me. Perhaps tomorrow, I can bathe with a bucket of seawater.

August 15 I miss my bed at home! I didn't have enough money to buy a hammock before we left Spain. So I sleep against sacks of grain or with the horses. But it really smells down below, and the rats bite. When the nights are clear, I sleep topside and stargaze. The clanging of the rigging (the ropes and metal fixtures) and the whoosh of the waves are my lullaby.

August 22 The sky has been darkening all day. The air is heavy. Captain Padilla ordered us to batten down the hatches (to cover up the entrances to go below deck) and secure all the lines. Even the dolphins have gone. I'm afraid . . .

[1]In the 1500s, Spain had claimed a huge area of land in North America. The land was called New Spain.

August 26 Dios mío, I'm alive! These last few days have been the worst of my life. I feared a giant sea monster was trying to devour us all! I couldn't tell if it was day or night, so dark was the sky. The ship bucked and pitched in the merciless waves. Twice we nearly capsized! Sadly, three sailors fell into the churning seas. Water was everywhere, including below deck. I helped pump the bilge, trying to ignore the horses' terrified cries. My arms still ache, but at least I'm alive.

August 28 We limp toward Havana for repairs. Captain Padilla says our expedition is delayed by at least three weeks! Food supplies are low and tempers are high. We couldn't collect rainwater during the storm, and now our barrels are filled with algae scum. The remaining cheese is moldy, and sometimes it hurts to bite into what's left of the hardtack. Hard is the right word for those biscuits! I remind myself that gold and glory await me.

September 8 At last, dry land! Some sailors talk of staying in Cuba, finding work in the gold mines or on the sugarcane farms. But I'll continue; after that hurricane, I don't even fear the Indians![2]

[2]Because Columbus thought he had reached the Indies in Asia, he called the people of the Caribbean "Indians." Later explorers used the same name.

Think About It

1. What motivated Dominic to travel to the New Spain?

2. How would you describe the journey from Spain to New Spain?

3. Think about Dominic's character. What characteristics does he show that are necessary for survival in the journey to the New World?

People You Should Know

Moctezuma II

Marco Polo

At the time of the arrival of Spanish conquistador Hernan Cortés, Moctezuma II controlled the Aztec empire. Moctezuma, however, often demanded sacrifices from tribes that were his subjects. Years of these demands had led many people to dislike him. When Cortés kidnapped Moctezuma, Cortés assumed the Aztecs would not fight for fear of endangering their ruler. The people were only too glad to be rid of Moctezuma, however, and the fight that followed resulted in Moctezuma's death.

The Italian merchant Marco Polo was one of the world's first travel writers. He, his father, and his uncle traveled from Europe across the Middle East, India, China, Vietnam, and back again. Polo told of his 24 years of adventures in a classic piece of literature called *Il Milione*, or *The Million*. This title probably comes from Polo's nickname, which referred to his tendency to talk about the millions of things he had seen.

Queen Isabella I of Spain

Atahualpa

Born a princess of Castile, Isabella united all of Spain when she married Ferdinand I of Aragon. Together, they conquered Grenada and increased the size of their empire. It was as she was encamped with her army at Grenada that an Italian explorer named Christopher Columbus approached her. He asked for her support for an expedition to find a western route to Asia. She agreed to give him some money, seeing an opportunity to enrich her country.

After the death of his father, Inca emperor Huayna Capac, Atahualpa waged a war with his half-brother for the Inca throne. Only a few months after his victory, however, Atahualpa's reign was cut short. Spanish conquistador Francisco Pizarro entered the Inca city of Cuzco in November of 1532. Pizarro invited Atahualpa to a feast. Using the example set by Hernan Cortés, Pizarro captured Atahualpa and killed his soldiers. The Inca emperor promised the Spaniard mountains of gold and silver in return for his release. Once the riches had been delivered, however, Pizarro killed Atahualpa anyway and ended the Inca empire.

Lesson 1

Why Did the Spanish Explore the Americas?

A Time of Change in Europe

During the Middle Ages—the period between ancient and modern times—most Europeans rarely traveled. However, toward the end of the period they began making pilgrimages, or religious journeys, to Christian holy sites. Some went as far away as areas in the Middle East considered the "Holy Land" by Jews, Christians, and Muslims. The contact with new regions made Europeans desire goods from foreign lands.

Soon, a new class of Europeans developed, **merchants** who made their living by buying and selling goods. They prospered especially in Italian port cities like Venice. They traded for the gems, silks, and spices of China and the East Indies, the islands off Southeast Asia. Members of one Venetian family, the Polos, actually traveled to China themselves and met with the great ruler Kublai Khan. On a second journey, they took 17-year-old Marco Polo. He returned to Italy years later and told of the wonders he had seen. His impressions were recorded in a book now called *The Travels of Marco Polo*, which further stirred people's imaginations. Another person who encouraged Europeans to travel to new lands was Prince Henry of Portugal, whose sailors explored the west coast of Africa in the early 1400s.

HSS.5.2.1, HSS.5.2.2, HSS.5.2.3, HAS.CS.1, HAS.CS.2, HAS.CS.4, HAS.CS.5, HAS.HR.1, HAS.HR.2, HAS.HR.3, HAS.HI.1, HAS.HI.3.

1295
Marco Polo returns from China.

c. 1425
Prince Henry of Portugal begins sponsoring explorations of the west coast of Africa.

1453
Ottoman Turks capture Constantinople.

1492
Christopher Columbus reaches the New World.

1522
Spanish Magellan-Elcano expedition completes voyage around the world.

|1200| |1300| |1400| |1500| |1600| |1700|

1488
Portugal's Bartolomeu Dias sails around Africa to the Indian Ocean.

1498
Portugal's Vasco da Gama reaches India by sea.

This historical map, circa 1700, shows the east and west hemispheres of the earth.

Trade with Asia usually moved along a route called the Silk Road. It was named for a product much in demand—Chinese silk. Sometimes, goods from China came by sea, because the Chinese had made many advances in sailing. Goods from the East Indies also came partly by sea. But whether entirely or only partly over land, the trade from Asia had to pass through the Middle East to reach the Mediterranean Sea and Italy.

In 1453, the Ottoman Turks captured Constantinople (now Istanbul, Turkey). They cut off most European trade through the Middle East. European leaders began to sponsor, or pay for, voyages of exploration. They hoped to make their countries rich by finding new trade routes that did not go through the Middle East. Important advances in **navigation**, or the science of guiding a boat, made this possible.

During the Age of Exploration, Europe was bursting with religious conflict and change. Spain wished to become an even more powerful country after recapturing land it had lost to invading peoples from North Africa. Spaniards called this violent recapturing of territory the *Reconquista.* The Protestant Reformation caused many people who were upset with the Roman Catholic Church to break away and form new churches. Some people wished to stay and improve the Catholic Church—an effort called the Counter-Reformation. Competing religions, ideas, and countries would become key drivers of the Age of Exploration.

Merchants trading in Venice, Italy

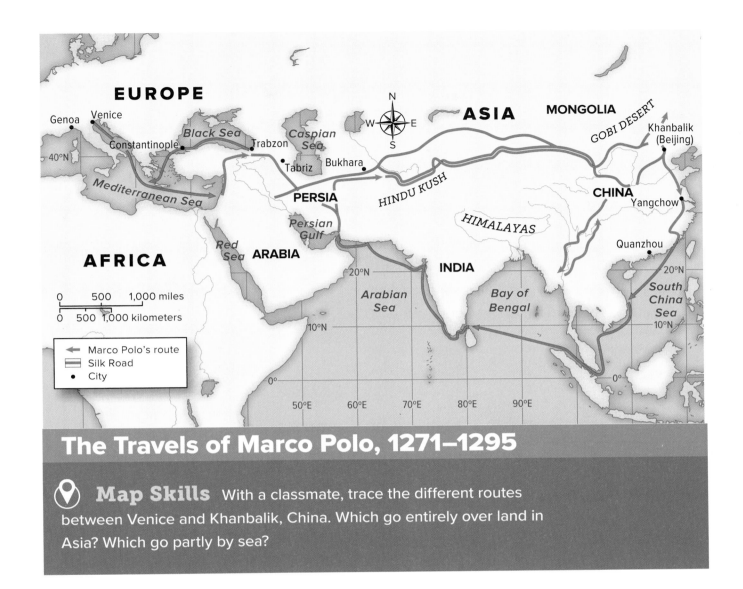

The Travels of Marco Polo, 1271–1295

 Map Skills With a classmate, trace the different routes between Venice and Khanbalik, China. Which go entirely over land in Asia? Which go partly by sea?

✓ Stop and Check

COLLABORATE

Talk How did Marco Polo and Prince Henry of Portugal each help encourage the growth of trade?

Find Details As you read, add additional information to the graphic organizer on page 57 in your Inquiry Journal.

Technological Advances

The Spanish explored the Americas in a time of adventure and discovery. A number of technological advances helped make their adventures and Portugal's explorations possible.

The Astrolabe

An astrolabe measures the position of the stars in the sky. It helps sailors determine a ship's latitude, or how far north or south of the Equator they are. Europeans learned of the astrolabe from Arab traders in the 1100s.

The Compass

A compass has a magnetic arrow that points north so that people can figure out in which direction they are going. The compass was invented in China and introduced to Europeans in the 1200s, probably by Arab sailors.

The Stern Rudder

Chinese sailors used an oar that hung off the stern, or back of the boat, to help control its direction. This evolved into the stern-mounted rudder, which directed the flow of water passing over it to help steer a ship. By the 1400s, European shipbuilders had adopted and improved the stern-mounted rudder.

The Printing Press

Around 1450, German inventor Johannes Gutenberg built Europe's first printing press that used movable type to print the text. Printed materials could be mass-produced far more easily and cheaply than handwritten documents. They helped spread news about explorers' discoveries and encouraged others to take to the seas.

The Carrack

The carrack was a three- or four-masted sailing ship developed in the Italian city of Genoa in the late 1400s. It was very strong and useful on long voyages. The *Santa Maria*, the ship on which Columbus sailed to the New World, was a carrack.

Sextant and Chronometer

In 1759, John Bird invented the sextant. This tool uses two mirrors and a movable arm to measure the angles of stars in the sky. Also invented in the middle of the 18th century, the chronometer is a device that helps keep accurate time at sea. These two devices finally allowed sailors to determine longitude, or the distance east or west of the Prime Meridian. Measuring longitude as well as latitude made navigation and mapmaking more accurate.

✓ Stop and Check

Talk Based on what you've just read, how important do you think technology was in encouraging the explorers of the day? Discuss your opinion with a partner.

A Sea Route to the Indies

By the late 1400s, Europeans knew that China and the islands off Southeast Asia held great riches. Explorers from Portugal, such as Bartolomeu Dias and Vasco da Gama, were trying to reach these lands. They wanted to sail around the southern tip of Africa and then across the Indian Ocean. Christopher Columbus, a sailor from Genoa, Italy, had a different idea. He believed that he could reach the East Indies more quickly by sailing west across the Atlantic Ocean, known then as the Ocean Sea. He did not know the North and South American continents would get in the way. He persuaded King Ferdinand and Queen Isabella of Spain, Portugal's neighbor and rival, to pay for his voyage. In return, he would **claim** lands and open valuable trade for Spain.

On August 3, 1492, Columbus sailed from Spain with three ships—the *Niña,* the *Pinta*, and the *Santa Maria*. For weeks, the ships traveled across unknown waters. Finally, on October 12, a member of the crew, called the lookout, spotted land. Columbus would call the island he had reached San Salvador. Today, we know it as part of the Bahama Islands. A native people called the Taíno warmly greeted his crew. The two groups exchanged gifts.

PRIMARY SOURCE

In Their Words... Christopher Columbus

"... to some of them I gave red caps, and glass beads which they put on their chests, and many other things of small value, in which they took much pleasure and became so much our friends that it was a marvel. Later they came swimming to the ships' launches where we were and brought us parrots and cotton thread in balls and javelins and many other things, and they traded them to us for other things which we gave them, such as small glass beads and bells. In sum, they took everything and gave of what they had very willingly."

—from the journal of Christopher Columbus, October 12, 1492

TEXT: Olson, Julius E., and Edward Gaylord Bourne, eds. The Northmen, Columbus and Cabot, 985-1503. New York: Charles Scribner's Sons, 1906.; PHOTO: GL Archive/Alamy

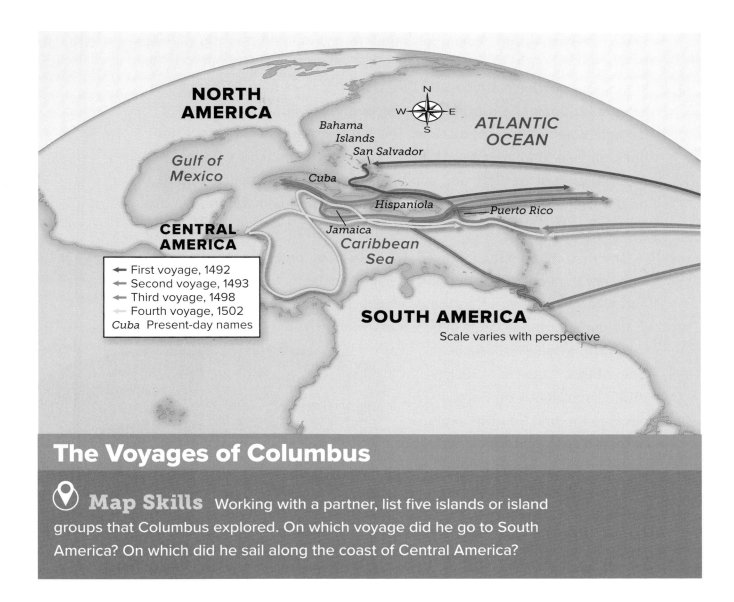

The Voyages of Columbus

Map Skills Working with a partner, list five islands or island groups that Columbus explored. On which voyage did he go to South America? On which did he sail along the coast of Central America?

Did You Know?

Because he thought he had reached the East Indies, Columbus called the people he encountered *Indios*, Spanish for *Indians*. The name stuck, even though it was an error. The people Columbus actually met, the Taíno, did not survive long after the coming of the Spanish, mainly because of the diseases the Spanish brought. However, some of their culture is still evident in certain English and Spanish words such as *barbecue* and *hurricane*.

On his first voyage, Columbus sailed to several neighboring islands in addition to the Bahamas. He still believed he had landed in the East Indies. But nowhere did he find the "riches of the Indies." Claiming the islands for Spain, he reported his discoveries to Ferdinand and Isabella when he returned home. The king and queen soon sent him back on a second voyage to extend Spanish claims. This time he brought enough settlers and supplies to establish a Spanish **colony** on the island he named Hispaniola. In all, Columbus made four voyages to the area.

Other explorers soon followed. By now, they knew that the islands were not the East Indies but part of a mass of lands between Europe and Asia—a New World, as they called it. The name *Americas* began to be used for these lands in honor of Amerigo Vespucci, who sailed one of Columbus's routes in 1499. In 1513, Vasco Núñez de Balboa became the first Spanish explorer to record seeing the great waters to the west of these lands. Another explorer, Ferdinand Magellan, named those waters the Pacific Ocean. Magellan died as he attempted to sail around the world. His voyage was completed in 1522 by his crew under the command of Juan Sebastián Elcano. The voyage took three years.

A Taíno artifact

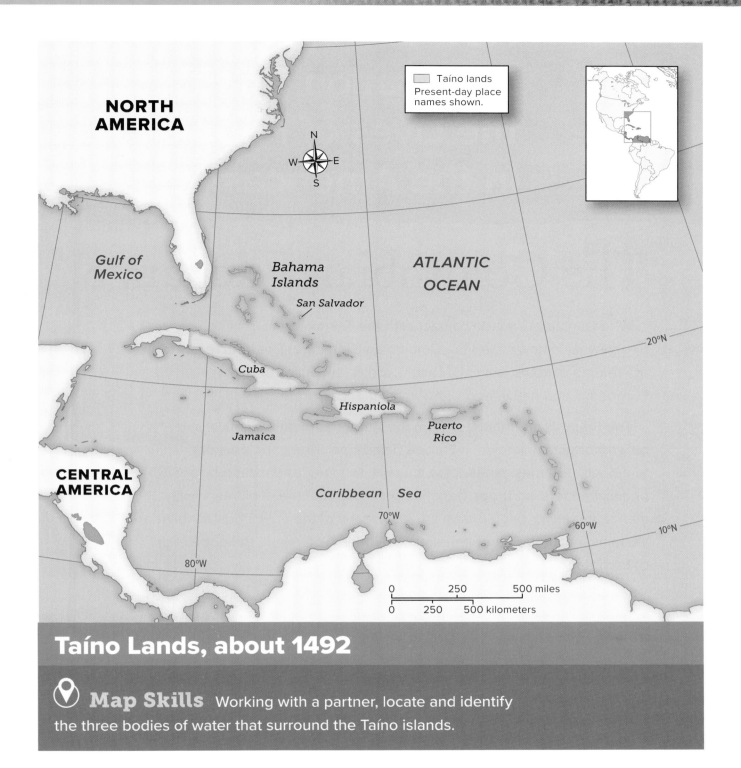

NORTH AMERICA

Taíno lands
Present-day place names shown.

Gulf of Mexico

Bahama Islands

San Salvador

ATLANTIC OCEAN

20°N

Cuba

Hispaniola

Jamaica

Puerto Rico

CENTRAL AMERICA

Caribbean Sea

70°W

60°W

10°N

80°W

| 0 | 250 | 500 miles |
| 0 | 250 | 500 kilometers |

Taíno Lands, about 1492

◉ **Map Skills** Working with a partner, locate and identify the three bodies of water that surround the Taíno islands.

COLLABORATE

✓ Stop and Check

Think What did the Magellan-Elcano voyage prove that Columbus was right about? How did it prove that he was wrong about some things?

How Did Spanish Exploration Change the Lives of People in the Americas?

The Columbian Exchange

When Columbus made contact with the Taíno people in 1492, he began what is now called the Columbian Exchange. The term refers to the trading of items, animals, culture, ideas, and more between Europeans and native peoples of the Americas.

The Spanish brought back from the Americas plants, animals, and other products unknown in Europe. These included corn, peanuts, tomatoes, potatoes, pineapples, turkeys, tobacco, and most types of beans. Farmers in Europe began to grow some of these plants, which meant that fewer people starved. Also, many of the new foods contained vitamins that made European diets healthier. As a result, the population of Europe grew.

HSS.5.2.1, HSS.5.2.2, HSS.5.2.3, HSS.5.3.1, HAS.CS.1, HAS.CS.2, HAS.CS.3, HAS.CS.4, HAS.CS.5, HAS.HR.1, HAS.HR.2, HAS.HI.1, HAS.HI.3, HAS.HI.4

68 Lesson 1 How Did Spanish Exploration Change the Lives of People in the Americas?

Timeline

1519
Hernan Cortés invades the Aztec Empire.

1532
Francisco Pizarro invades the Inca Empire.

1540
Francisco Coronado begins to explore the American Southwest.

| 1510 | | | 1520 | | | | 1530 | | | | 1540 | | | 1550 | | | | 1560 | | | 1570 | |

1513
Juan Ponce de León claims Florida for Spain.

1515
Spain completes conquest of what is now Cuba.

1542
Juan Cabrillo explores the southern California coast.

1565
Pedro Avilés founds St. Augustine, Florida.

The Aztec capital city of Tenochtitlán, among the largest cities in the world in the early 1500s

DEA Picture Library/De Agostini/Getty Images

The Spanish also brought new products to the Americas. These included wheat, sugar, oranges, peaches, bananas, cattle, goats, sheep, pigs, and horses. Many of these items changed the way of life for native peoples of the Americas. Horses, for example, changed the way in which American Indians hunted buffalo on the Great Plains.

The Columbian Exchange did not involve just Europe and the Americas. It transformed the whole planet. Some of the plants Europeans brought to the Americas originally came from Asia and Africa. Many American plants traveled around the world as well. Chili peppers, for instance, were brought to Asia by European sailors and became popular ingredients in many Asian dishes.

Not all things traded in the Columbian Exchange were useful. The Europeans also brought diseases such as smallpox and measles to the Americas. Because these diseases were new to the natives, they had not developed any **resistance** to them. As a result, they died in very large numbers.

The Spanish also forced many natives to work as enslaved persons and even shipped some back to Spain on voyages during which many died. By 1550, few Taíno survived. African slaves were brought to the islands to replace them. This forced relocation of peoples was also part of the Columbian Exchange.

✓ Stop and Check

COLLABORATE

Talk What positive effects did the Columbian Exchange have on people native to the Americas? What negative effects did the Columbian Exchange have on them and on others?

Find Details As you read, add additional information to the graphic organizer on page 65 in your Inquiry Journal.

Spanish Exploration and Conquest in the Americas

By 1515, Spain had spread its control to several islands in the Caribbean Sea. Spain's **conquests** gave them land to settle and people to enslave, but they did not bring the riches the Spanish sought. Sometimes they saw bits of gold in the hands of the island natives. The Spanish wondered, *Where did this gold come from?*

Juan Ponce de León was a Spanish explorer who came to the Americas on Columbus's second voyage. Later he was governor of the island that would come to be known as Puerto Rico. In 1513, Ponce de León became the first Spanish explorer to land in what is now part of the United States. He called the area *La Florida* (Spanish for "full of flowers") and claimed it for Spain. He was looking for gold, although legend says that he was also seeking a Fountain of Youth—a place where magical waters could restore one's youth. But Ponce de León found no gold in Florida, and no Fountain of Youth, either. When he returned there in 1521 to establish a Spanish **settlement**, he was wounded in fighting with the Calusa people of the area. He returned to Cuba and died there of his wounds.

Ponce de León became the first Spanish explorer to claim land in what is now the United States.

Hernan Cortés, another Spanish explorer, was more successful in his search for riches. In fact, he is called a *conquistador*, Spanish for "conqueror." Like Ponce de León, Cortés was very interested in finding gold. Having heard stories from the native people, he decided there must be a great empire rich in gold to the west of the Caribbean islands. He was right.

An empire is a large area in which different groups are controlled by one ruler. Since the 1430s, the Aztec Empire had ruled over several native groups in what is now central Mexico. The Aztecs built a magnificent capital, Tenochtitlán, where more than 300,000 people lived. In 1502, Moctezuma II became the emperor, or ruler of the empire. However, many native peoples under his rule had started to rebel against the Aztecs.

In 1519, Hernan Cortés left Cuba seeking the great riches he had heard about. After landing in what is today the coastal city of Veracruz, Mexico, he and his soldiers moved inland. When he arrived at Tenochtitlán, Moctezuma met with him. He offered Cortés gifts of gold and precious jewels. These were not enough for Cortés, however. He took Moctezuma prisoner, causing a riot in which the emperor was killed.

Statue of an Aztec eagle knight warrior found at the main temple in Tenochtitlán

Did You Know?

Tenochtitlán was built on watery, swampy land. The Aztecs developed floating gardens called *chinampas*. They stuck rows of thick posts into the swamp. Then, they filled spaces between the posts with mud.

The Aztecs then drove Cortés and his troops from the city. They battled on the plains of Otumba, where Cortés and his troops killed the Aztec commander. The Spanish then retreated to a friendlier area.

A few months later, Cortés returned with a larger force to fight the Aztecs. Along the way, his army was joined by a number of native fighters unhappy with Aztec rule.

This help from native allies was just one reason the Spanish were able to defeat the Aztecs. The Spanish soldiers also had two things that the Aztecs did not: fine swords and horses. These gave the Spanish a clear fighting advantage. In fact, even when outnumbered, forces with swords and lances fighting on horseback usually won the day.

After 75 days of battle, Cortés and his army destroyed the Aztec capital. On its ruins, the Spanish built Mexico City. It would be the capital of a colony the Spanish called *Nueva España*, or New Spain.

Spanish and Aztec warriors fighting at the Battle of Otumba

Prisma Archivo/Alamy

In 1531, Francisco Pizarro, another Spanish conquistador, sailed to the west coast of South America with a small army. Like Cortés, he was following rumors he had heard of an empire rich in treasures. From the coast, he traveled with his troops to the mighty Inca Empire high in the Andes Mountains.

The Incas ruled an empire of 12 million people. Because they lived in thick stone cities high in the mountains, they did not fear the Spanish attack. The Spanish, however, had new weapons the Incas had never seen. Gunpowder had come to Europe from China centuries before. The troops Pizarro brought with him were armed with a type of gun called the *harquebus*. Incan weapons were no match for this.

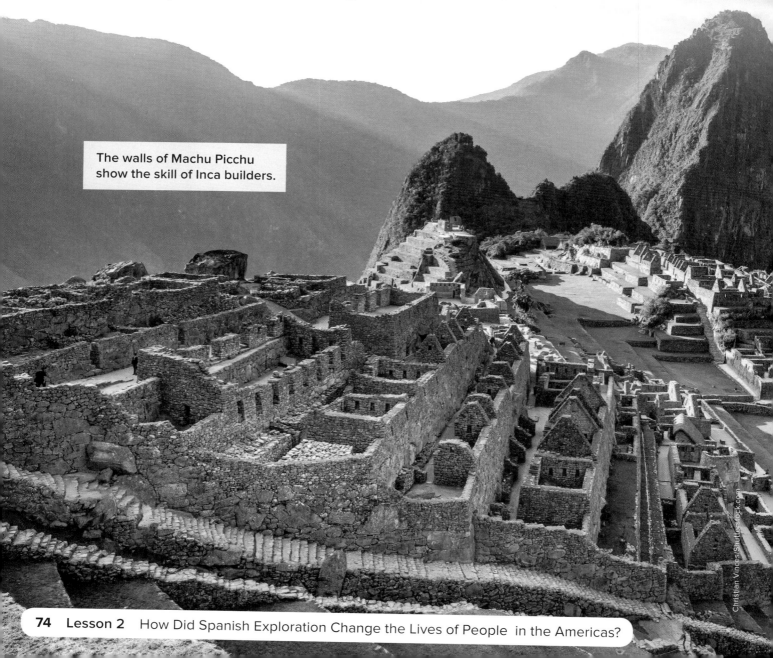

The walls of Machu Picchu show the skill of Inca builders.

Christian Vinces/Shutterstock.com

Pizarro's army captured Atahualpa, the Inca emperor, and killed 1,500 of his followers. When Atahualpa offered a roomful of gold in return for his freedom, Pizarro agreed. From all over the empire, valuable gold objects poured in. Yet, after the treasure was delivered, Pizarro had Atahualpa killed anyway. In 1533, the Spanish completed their conquest of the Inca Empire by capturing its capital of Cuzco.

The Aztec and Inca Empires

 Map Skills Using the information in the text and the labels on the map, identify the Aztec Empire and Inca Empire on the map. How many Aztec Empires could fit inside the territory of the Inca Empire?

✓ Stop and Check

Talk What seems to have been the strongest motive, or reason, for Spanish exploration and conquest? What advantages did the Spanish have to help them conquer the Aztecs and Incas?

New Spain Expands

By 1525, the Spanish territory of New Spain included most of present-day Mexico and Central America. Despite its size, Spanish explorers and conquistadors continued looking for rich new lands for Spain to control.

In 1528, Alvar Nuñez Cabeza de Vaca was exploring the coast along the Gulf of Mexico. He was shipwrecked by a hurricane and landed in what is now Texas. There he and his crew lived among American Indians for four years. Eventually they left on foot. They walked through parts of what are now New Mexico and Arizona to return to Mexico. His experiences made him sympathetic to native peoples, and he urged the king of Spain to treat them better.

Hunting for riches, Hernando de Soto began an expedition in 1538 through what is now the southeastern United States. De Soto found no riches. But he and his group did become the first Europeans to see the Mississippi River. Then, in 1542, De Soto became ill and died not far from the river.

In 1540, Francisco Vásquez de Coronado, having heard tales of Seven Cities of Gold, went searching to find them. He discovered no such cities. He and his group did, however, become the first Europeans to see the Grand Canyon. They also claimed for Spain large areas of what is now the American Southwest.

Nuñez Cabeza de Vaca, Alvar. The Journey of Alvar Nunez Cabeza de Vaca and his Companions from Florida to the Pacific, 1528-1536. Edited by AD. F. Bandelier. Translated by Fanny Bandelier. New York: A.S. Barnes & Company, 1905.

PRIMARY SOURCE

In Their Words... Alvar Nuñez Cabeza de Vaca

At sunset we came in sight of the lodges, and [the length of] two crossbow shots before reaching them met four Indians waiting for us, and they received us well. We told them in the language of the Mariames that we had come to see them. They appeared to be pleased with our company and took us to their homes.

—from the journal of Alvar Nuñez Cabeza de Vaca

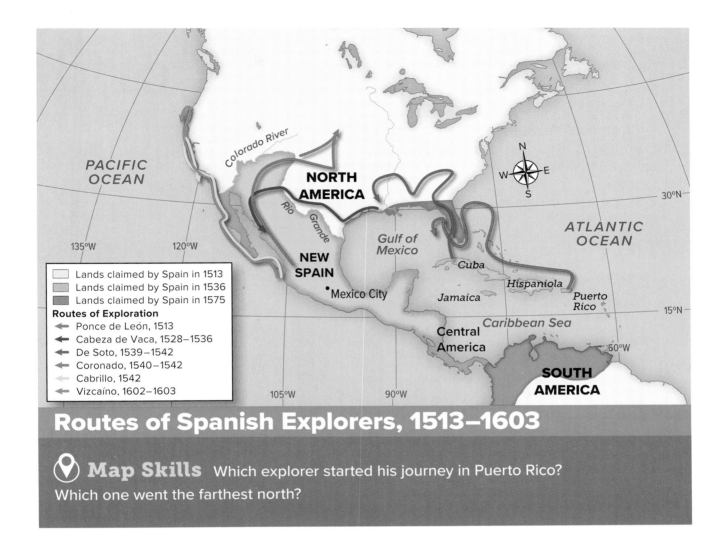

Routes of Spanish Explorers, 1513–1603

PACIFIC OCEAN

Colorado River

NORTH AMERICA

Rio Grande

NEW SPAIN

•Mexico City

Gulf of Mexico

Cuba

Jamaica

Hispaniola

Puerto Rico

Caribbean Sea

Central America

ATLANTIC OCEAN

SOUTH AMERICA

135°W   120°W   105°W   90°W   60°W

30°N   15°N

Lands claimed by Spain in 1513
Lands claimed by Spain in 1536
Lands claimed by Spain in 1575
Routes of Exploration
Ponce de León, 1513
Cabeza de Vaca, 1528–1536
De Soto, 1539–1542
Coronado, 1540–1542
Cabrillo, 1542
Vizcaíno, 1602–1603

Map Skills Which explorer started his journey in Puerto Rico? Which one went the farthest north?

Spanish claims on what is now California began with Juan Rodríguez Cabrillo, who explored the coast around present-day San Diego in 1542. Sixty years later, Sebastián Vizcaíno sailed up the California coast, giving many places the Spanish names we still use today. Spain also continued to pursue its claims in what is now Florida. After several failed attempts at a settlement there, Pedro Menéndez de Avilés in 1565 built a fort in an area on the east coast that he named St. Augustine.

Stop and Check

COLLABORATE

Talk Which sections of what is now the United States did the Spanish explore? How often did they find what they were looking for? Give examples to explain your answer.

St. Augustine, Florida

St. Augustine, Florida, is the oldest permanent European settlement in the United States. After coming ashore in August of 1565, Spanish admiral Pedro Menéndez de Avilés turned the site into a fort and named it St. Augustine. It remained a Spanish city for more than 200 years. Today, you can see the Spanish influence in the city's historic district.

St. Augustine

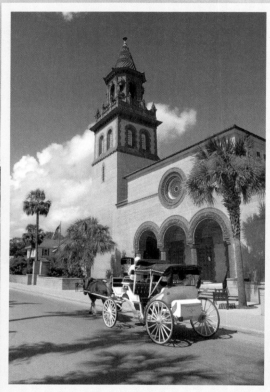

Grace United Methodist Church

Castillo de San Marcos
This fort was built by the Spanish between 1672 and 1695 to protect the city from naval attacks by the British and the French. It was constructed from blocks of coquina, a combination of limestone and seashells. When you tour the two levels of the fort, you can see how carefully it was built. It was never captured by military force.

A map of Old St. Augustine, Florida

✓ Stop and Check

Write Compose a speech for a tour guide in St. Augustine. Your speech should describe the sights of the old city.

What Do You Think? Do you think you would like to visit St. Augustine? Why or why not?

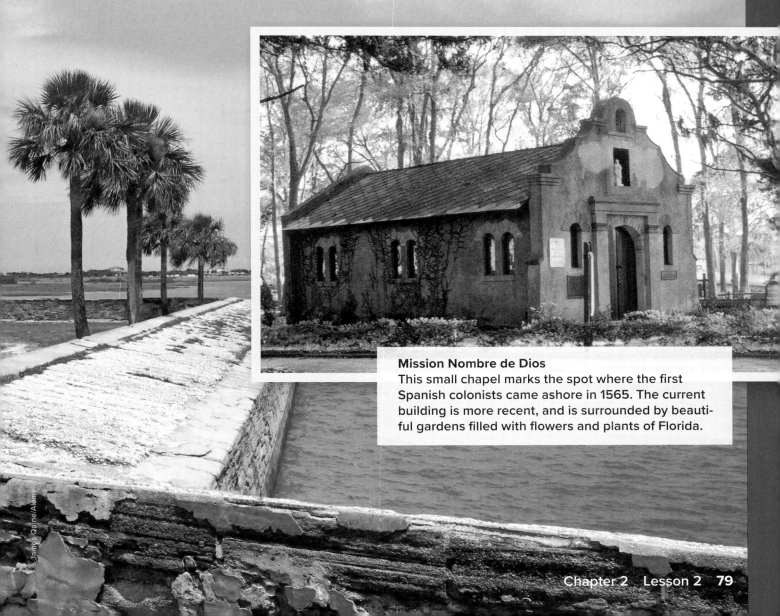

Mission Nombre de Dios
This small chapel marks the spot where the first Spanish colonists came ashore in 1565. The current building is more recent, and is surrounded by beautiful gardens filled with flowers and plants of Florida.

James Quine/Alamy

How Did European Exploration Affect the Americas?

The Search for a Northwest Passage

Spain was not the only European country that sailed west to look for a shorter route to Asia. England, France, the Netherlands, Portugal, and Sweden also sent explorers across the Atlantic Ocean. While Spain focused on exploring South America and the southern part of North America, the other nations explored the east coast of North America. They were trying to find a route to Asia through North America by using waterways, such as bays and straits. This supposed route was called the Northwest Passage.

In 1497, just five years after Columbus's first voyage, John Cabot set sail on a voyage across the Atlantic. Cabot, an Italian, had received permission from the English king to sail west to explore unknown lands. Cabot took along goods from merchants in the port of Bristol. He hoped to trade for Asian goods.

HSS.5.2.3, HSS.5.2.4, HAS.HI.2

80 Lesson 3 How Did European Exploration Affect the Americas?

1497
John Cabot explores the eastern coast of what is now Canada while searching for the Northwest Passage.

1524
Giovanni da Verrazzano reaches an area now known as New York Harbor.

1534
Jacques Cartier claims land along the St. Lawrence River for France.

1584
Queen Elizabeth I of England grants a charter allowing Sir Walter Raleigh to send a group of colonists to Roanoke Island.

400   1450   1500   1550   1600   1650

1608
Samuel de Champlain establishes the colony of Quebec for France.

1623
The Dutch West India Company establishes the colony of New Netherland.

1638
The Swedish South Company forms a colony along the Delaware River.

Henry Hudson's ship, the Half Moon

Cabot reached the North American coast somewhere in the region of what is now Newfoundland, an area in Canada. He could not find any people to trade with. What he did find were huge quantities of fish in the coastal waters. The English merchants were interested in this discovery. Dried fish was an important source of food at the time.

An oil painting of John and Sebastian Cabot

Unfortunately, Cabot disappeared during his next voyage, probably the victim of a huge storm. Following Cabot's lead, Portugal sent sailors to the Newfoundland area. It established a small colony there as a base for fishing ships.

Another Italian, Giovanni da Verrazzano, obtained the support of the king of France. Verrazzano traveled up the Atlantic Coast. He explored areas including what are now New York Harbor and the mouth of the Hudson River. He had friendly encounters with American Indians on this voyage.

Verrazzano's next voyage was to Brazil, where he found a type of wood that is valuable in creating dyes for textiles. Verrazzano's voyages were overlooked in Europe, however. They occurred during the same decade that Spain conquered the Aztec Empire and brought large amounts of gold home to Europe.

Giovanni da Verrazzano

The Hudson River, named for the English explorer Henry Hudson.

Henry Hudson's voyages to the area that is now New York occurred in the early 1600s. Hudson was from England, but he worked for both England and the Netherlands. The Dutch East India Company hired Hudson in 1608 to try to find a shorter route to Asia. This company had been set up to increase Dutch trade with what is now Indonesia.

In 1609, Hudson's ships reached the same area near New York that Verrazzano had visited. Hudson sailed far up a river that was later named after him, the Hudson River. He concluded that it did not lead to a Northwest Passage because it became shallow as he moved north; also, it contained fresh water, not saltwater.

Hudson returned to Europe and then began exploring for England in 1610. This time his effort to find the Northwest Passage ended in disaster. He sailed into a bay in northern Canada now called Hudson Bay. He became stuck in the ice and spent the winter there. He and his crew had to eat spoiled food. When spring came and the ice melted, the crew took over the ship and put Hudson and his son in a rowboat with a few other crew members. They were never heard from again. The crew was arrested when it returned to England.

During his second voyage to North America, Henry Hudson, his son, and others were abandoned in a rowboat after most of his crew rebelled.

Stop and Check

COLLABORATE

Talk Why did European explorers want to find a Northwest Passage?

Find Details As you read, add additional information to the graphic organizer on page 73 in your Inquiry Journal.

What Do You Think? In your opinion, why were the explorers unable to find a Northwest Passage?

New Netherland

In 1621, a group of Dutch merchants formed the Dutch West India Company. This company established the colony of New Netherland in 1623. This colony was the earliest European settlement in what is now New York state. The Dutch West India Company established the colony in that location because Henry Hudson had claimed the land for the Netherlands in 1609.

The first settlements in New Netherland were established along the Hudson River. The Dutch colonists benefited from the rich resources in the area, particularly fur obtained by trading with native peoples. In 1626, Peter Minuit became the colony's governor. Some Dutch settlers established a profitable trading post on the southern tip of Manhattan Island. Minuit negotiated with native peoples there to recognize and accept the Dutch settlement, called New Amsterdam.

Minuit offered the native peoples weapons, tools, and other supplies as part of the agreement. These goods were worth about 60 guilders, or about 700 dollars in today's money. But the native peoples did not believe that they were selling Manhattan. Because of communication difficulties, they thought they were agreeing only to share the land.

New Netherland was one of the most **diverse** European colonies in North America. People of different religious and ethnic backgrounds were allowed to settle there. However, New Netherland was also one of the first colonies to bring African slaves to North America. Fighting occurred between the colonists and native peoples in the early 1640s. The governor of New Netherland, Willem Kieft, was unhappy that native peoples were moving into the northern part of New Netherland.

Dutch West India House was built in the Netherlands in 1623.

Ger Bosma/Alamy

These peoples were trying to escape attacks by other Northeast Woodlands tribes that were seeking to expand their territories. Against the advice of other colonial leaders, Kieft sent Dutch soldiers to attack native villages. The result was a series of attacks by both sides that left hundreds dead. Many Dutch settlers returned to Europe because of the violence.

In 1647, Peter Stuyvesant became the leader of New Netherland. He had a conflict with a Swedish colony along the Delaware River. He believed the colony was on Dutch territory. He had a fort built in the area. When the Swedes took over the fort, Stuyvesant sent a force to take over the Swedish colony, which had log cabins that were later widely copied.

As English colonies in North America grew, some English leaders became interested in New Netherland. England and the Netherlands fought wars in Europe in the 1600s. In 1664, the brother of the King of England sent four **warships** to New Amsterdam harbor. His troops demanded that Stuyvesant surrender the entire Dutch colony. Stuyvesant wanted to fight, but his colonists instead surrendered. Most stayed in North America, living under British rule.

Then and Now

The Northwest Passage

Although there is a Northwest Passage from the Atlantic Ocean to the Pacific Ocean, it was nearly impossible to pass through during the age of European exploration. This is because the passage lies far to the north and was usually covered by Arctic ice. The illustration at the upper right shows a Dutch explorer stuck in this ice in the 1500s.

But with the gradual melting of the Arctic ice cap in recent years, the Northwest Passage is now nearly ice-free during the summer. Ships are able to travel through the passage in warmer months. The photograph at the lower right shows the Northwest Passage in August 2016.

✓ Stop and Check

Think Why did Dutch settlers choose to settle in what is now New York state?

The Founding of New France

After Giovanni da Verrazzano failed to find the Northwest Passage for France, the king of France sent Jacques Cartier in 1534 to continue the search. Cartier explored what is now Canada, sailing up the St. Lawrence River. The French adapted the name *Canada* from the Huron group of native peoples. In the Huron language, *kanata* means "village."

This map shows France's first fort in Quebec, Canada.

TEXT: Jacques Cartier. 1534. Quoted in H.P. Biggar, trans., A Collection of Documents Relating to Jacques Cartier and the Sieur de Roberval (Public Archives of Canada, 1924), 26.; PHOTO: (t)Library of Congress Geography and Map Division [G3454.Q452 1670 .A9 Vault]; (b)The Miriam and Ira D. Wallach Division of Art, Prints and Photographs: Print Collection, Emmet Collection of Manuscripts Etc. Relating to American History,The New York Public Library

PRIMARY SOURCE

In Their Words... Jacques Cartier

July 24 – We had a cross made thirty feet high, which was put together in the presence of a number of savages on the point at the entrance to this harbor, [and on it] was written LONG LIVE THE KING OF FRANCE. When we had returned to our ships, the chief, dressed in an old black bearskin, arrived in a canoe with three of his sons and his brother … And pointing to the cross he made us a long harangue, making the sign of the cross with two of his fingers, and then he pointed to the land all around about, as if he wished to say that all this region belonged to him, and that we ought not to have set up the cross without his permission.

—from the journal of Jacques Cartier, 1534

The French Explore New France, 1617–1673

Map Skills The map shows the routes of French explorers. Which river did Nicollet use to search for the Northwest Passage?

The next important French explorer in Canada was Samuel de Champlain. King Henry VI of France appointed him governor of French settlements in North America, called New France. Champlain made four voyages to North America. On one voyage, he established a colony in what is now Quebec City. Champlain was on friendly terms with native peoples. This allowed the French to expand their fur trade.

On another voyage, Champlain brought along a young explorer named Étienne Brûlé. In 1615, he sent Brûlé to continue the search for a passage to Asia. Brûlé was unable to find it, but he did explore what are now Lake Ontario, Lake Erie, and Lake Superior. In 1634, a French explorer named Jean Nicollet explored what is now Lake Michigan.

Although some French people moved to Canada, growth was slow. French rulers were disappointed that Cartier could find neither gold nor a Northwest Passage. The focus of New France's economy continued to be the fur trade, and only a few large settlements thrived.

 Stop and Check

Think In your opinion, why did French rulers not make a greater effort to expand the size of the colonies in New France?

The Lost English Colony

After the voyages of John Cabot and Henry Hudson, England did little to explore North America until the 1580s. Then, an English noble named Sir Walter Raleigh asked Queen Elizabeth I for permission to establish a colony in North America. Raleigh wanted to create settlements that would serve as bases to explore for treasure and to attack the ships of Spain, an enemy of England.

The English queen granted Raleigh a **charter**, a document that allowed him to found a colony. In 1585, Raleigh sent a group of men to North America to start the colony. They chose an island called Roanoke in what is now North Carolina. The colonists were not skilled at farming, and so they tried to get goods by trading with native peoples. The native peoples lost interest in trading, and the colonists decided they had to steal food from them. This led to fighting. After a difficult winter, the colonists returned to England in 1586.

Sir Walter Raleigh

John White arrives in Roanoke to find the colony abandoned.

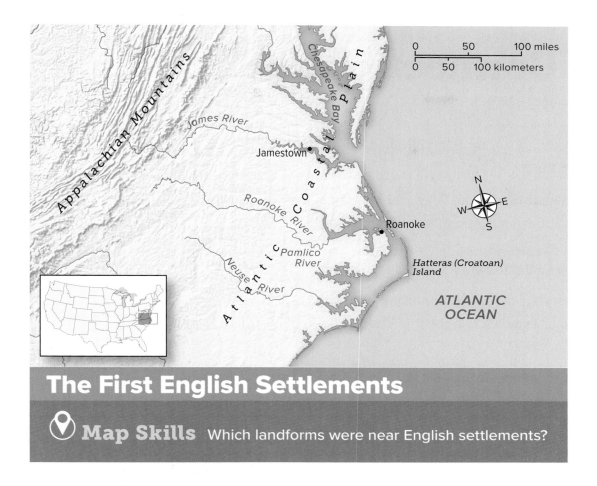

The First English Settlements

⊙ **Map Skills** Which landforms were near English settlements?

In 1587, another group of colonists led by John White returned to Roanoke. This time the group included women and children. The colony again had difficulty finding enough food. White sailed back to England to get supplies. But while he was there, war broke out between England and Spain. England needed all of its ships for the war. By the time White returned to the colony three years later, it had been abandoned. The only clue was the word *Croatoan* carved on a tree. The Croatoan were a native people in the area. What happened to the English settlers has never been determined.

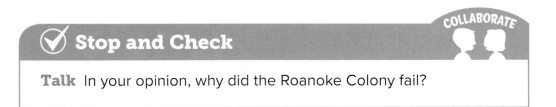

✓ Stop and Check

COLLABORATE

Talk In your opinion, why did the Roanoke Colony fail?

What Do You Think? What do you think happened to the people in the "lost colony"?

EQ Connections in Action!
Back to the EQ

Think about the Chapter EQ, **"What Happened When Diverse Cultures Crossed Paths?"**

- **Talk** with a partner about what you learned in the chapter. Choose a group of native peoples who encountered Europeans. Make a list of ways these encounters affected your group and its area.

- What was your group's relationship with the Europeans? Did that relationship change over time? If so, how?

- **Share** your ideas with the class; then have a class discussion about the overall effects of exploration on native peoples in the Americas.

(bkgd)Christian Vinces/Shutterstock.com; (l)akg-images/CDA/Guillemot/Newscom; (r)Clive Mason/Getty Images Sport/Getty Images

More to Explore
How Can You Make an IMPACT?

Job Interview

Work with a partner to choose an explorer. One person will play the part of that explorer. The other person will play the part of the European king or queen the explorer wants to have sponsor an expedition to the Americas. Use evidence from your research to conduct a job interview for the expedition. The monarch should try to determine why the journey is a good idea and whether the explorer is the right candidate for the job. The explorer should try to convince the monarch that the monarch's country will benefit from the journey and that the explorer is the right person to lead the expedition.

Letter to the Editor

Imagine that you are a citizen of an Aztec or Inca city and that the city has a newspaper. Write a letter to the editor of the newspaper that argues for or against building a relationship with the Europeans. Use evidence from the text to support your opinion.

Crossword Puzzle

Create a crossword puzzle using all ten words from the chapter Word Bank. Write an appropriate clue for each word. Exchange puzzles with a partner, and solve your partner's puzzle.

A Changing Continent

How Did European Settlements Impact North America?

In this chapter, you'll read about how European settlements developed across the East Coast of North America. You'll learn how those settlements affected the lives of American Indians who lived in those areas.

Step into the Time Chronological Thinking

Look at the time line. What was happening in other parts of the world while Europeans were settling North America?

Americas

1607
Jamestown colony is established in Virginia.

1608
Samuel de Champlain founds Quebec City in Canada.

1620
Pilgrims arrive in Massachusetts on the *Mayflower*.

1622
First Powhatan War begins.

1624
Dutch traders found New Netherland.

| 1600 | 1610 | 1620 | 1630 | 1640 |

World Events

1602
Dutch East India Company is established to protect Dutch trade on the Indian Ocean.

1603
Queen Elizabeth I of England dies after ruling for 44 years, succeeded by King James I.

1603
Edo period begins in Japan, leading to growth in the economy, arts, and culture, but isolation from other nations.

1632
Work begins on Taj Mahal in India.

HSS.5.4.1, HSS.5.4.2, HSS.5.4.3, HAS.CS.1

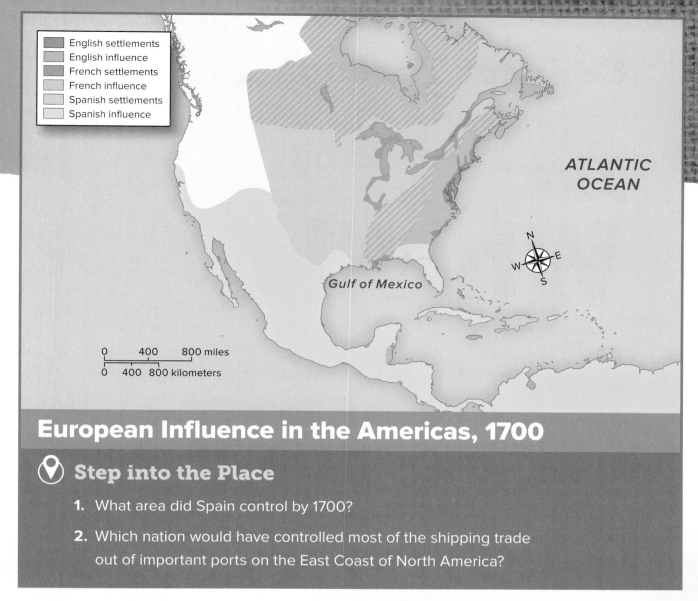

Legend:
- English settlements
- English influence
- French settlements
- French influence
- Spanish settlements
- Spanish influence

ATLANTIC OCEAN

Gulf of Mexico

N
W E
S

0   400   800 miles
0   400   800 kilometers

European Influence in the Americas, 1700

Step into the Place

1. What area did Spain control by 1700?

2. Which nation would have controlled most of the shipping trade out of important ports on the East Coast of North America?

Between 1600 and 1700, three major powers fought for control of territory in North America. England, Spain, and France created settlements across the East Coast. Most coastal territory ultimately belonged to England, but Spain kept control of the area that is now Florida. France gained control of much of the interior areas of what is now the United States and Canada.

1634 Lord Baltimore founds Maryland.

1636–1637 Pequot War

1675–1676 King Philip's War

1692 Salem Witch Trials

1712 Carolina colony splits into north and south.

1718 Jean-Baptiste Le Moyne de Bienville founds New Orleans.

1640   1650   1660   1670   1680   1690   1700   1710   1720

1682 Peter the Great becomes ruler of Russia, resulting in a more European culture.

1688 Glorious Revolution results in English monarchs becoming subject to a constitution.

McGraw-Hill Education

Connect Through Literature

The Whistle

by Benjamin Franklin

When I was a child of seven years old, my friends, on a holiday, filled my pocket with coppers. I went directly to a shop where they sold toys for children; and being charmed with the sound of a *whistle*, that I met by the way in the hands of another boy, I voluntarily offered and gave all my money for one. I then came home, and went whistling all over the house, much pleased with my *whistle*, but disturbing all the family. My brothers, and sisters, and cousins, understanding the bargain I had made, told me I had given four times as much for it as it was worth; put me in mind what good things I might have bought with the rest of the money; and laughed at me so much for my folly, that I cried with vexation; and the reflection gave me more chagrin than the *whistle* gave me pleasure.

This, however, was afterwards of use to me, the impression continuing on my mind; so that often, when I was tempted to buy some unnecessary thing, I said to myself, *Don't give too much for the whistle*; and I saved my money.

As I grew up, came into the world, and observed the actions of men, I thought I met with many, very many, *who gave too much for the whistle*.

When I saw one too ambitious of court favor, sacrificing his time in attendance on levees, his repose, his liberty, his virtue, and perhaps his friends, to attain it, I have said to myself, *This man gives too much for his whistle*.

When I saw another fond of popularity, constantly employing himself in political bustles, neglecting his own affairs, and ruining them by that neglect, *He pays, indeed*, said I, *too much for his whistle*.

If I knew a miser, who gave up every kind of comfortable living, all the pleasure of doing good to others, all the esteem of his fellow-citizens, and the joys of benevolent friendship, for the sake of accumulating wealth, *Poor man*, said I, *you pay too much for your whistle*.

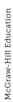

When I met with a man of pleasure, sacrificing every laudable improvement of the mind, or of his fortune, to mere corporeal sensations, and ruining his health in their pursuit, *Mistaken man, said I, you are providing pain for yourself, instead of pleasure; you give too much for your whistle.*

If I see one fond of appearance, or fine clothes, fine houses, fine furniture, fine equipages, all above his fortune, for which he contracts debts, and ends his career in a prison, *Alas!* say I, *he has paid dear, very dear, for his whistle.*

When I see a beautiful sweet-tempered girl married to an ill-natured brute of a husband, *What a pity,* say I, *that she should pay so much for a whistle!*

In short, I conceive that great part of the miseries of mankind are brought upon them by the false estimates they have made of the value of things, and by their *giving too much for their whistles.*

Yet I ought to have charity for these unhappy people, when I consider that, with all this wisdom of which I am boasting, there are certain things in the world so tempting, for example, the apples of King John, which happily are not to be bought; for if they were put to sale by auction, I might very easily be led to ruin myself in the purchase, and find that I had once more given too much for the *whistle.*

Think About It

1. Based on the text on page 94, what does the word *levee* mean?

2. What does Ben Franklin mean when he says that someone pays too much for a whistle?

3. What are some situations today that you think cause people to "give too much for their whistle"?

TEXT: Franklin, Benjamin. *The Whistle.* Boston: Brad Stephens & Company, 1921.; PHOTO: McGraw-Hill Education

People You Should Know

Olaudah Equiano

Kidnapped from his home in Nigeria at the age of 11 in 1756, Olaudah Equiano was sold into slavery. He was eventually purchased by a sea captain, and he sailed the world before purchasing his own freedom. After he settled in England, he wrote the story of his life: *The Interesting Narrative of the Life of Olaudah Equiano.* The book helped to persuade many people of the evils of the slave trade.

Anne Hutchinson

The well-educated daughter of an Anglican church leader in London, Anne Hutchinson was vocal about her religious beliefs. After emigrating to Boston at the age of 43, she spoke out against the Puritans' strict rules about how people should worship. Many people in the Massachusetts Bay Colony agreed with her and attended the discussions she hosted. Governor John Winthrop disagreed with her, however, and she was ultimately banished from the colony. She started her own settlement in what is now Rhode Island in 1638.

North Wind Picture Archives/Alamy

John Winthrop

Benjamin Franklin

(t)McGraw-Hill Education, (bl)Stock Montage/Archive Photos/Getty Images; (br)Courtesy National Gallery of Art, Washington

As the governor of the Massachusetts Bay Colony for parts of the 1630s and 1640s, John Winthrop believed the new Puritan settlement should be a "city on a hill," a model of perfect morals and social behavior. He wanted everyone to sign a covenant, or sacred agreement, with the Puritan faith. He also worked to make sure that anyone who disagreed with his strict rules was removed from the colony.

Most people know about Benjamin Franklin as one of the authors the Declaration of Independence and as a scientist and ambassador. But his career began at the age of 16 in 1722 when he started writing essays in his brother's newspaper. He convinced his brother and the readers of the paper that his essays were written by a middle-aged woman named Silence Dogood. Later, Franklin earned fame and fortune as a newspaper printer in his own right.

How Did Early English Settlers Cooperate and Clash with American Indians?

England's First Permanent Colony in North America

After the failure of the Roanoke colony, England did not attempt another colony until Queen Elizabeth's successor, King James I, came to power. In 1606, he granted a group of merchants called the Virginia Company a charter to establish another colony. In December 1606, the Virginia Company sent 144 men and boys to establish the colony of Jamestown near the mouth of Chesapeake Bay in what is now the state of Virginia. It was England's first permanent North American colony.

Jamestown nearly failed from the start. The location was poorly chosen. The settlers wanted a place that they could easily defend. They also wanted a place with water deep enough to allow ships to anchor near the shore. What they did not consider, however, was that the land was swampy and the water from that part of the James River was salty and dangerous to drink.

HSS.5.3.1, HSS.5.3.2, HSS.5.4.1, HSS.5.4.2, HSS.5.4.6, HAS.HR.3

Time Line

1612
John Rolfe introduces tobacco to the colony.

1614
Pocahontas marries John Rolfe.

1619
The House of Burgesses meets for the first time; African slaves are brought to Jamestown.

1622
The Second Powhatan War begins.

00 | | |1605| | | | |1610| | | | |1615| | | | |1620| | | | |1625| | | | |1630| | | | |1635| | |

1607
Jamestown is established.

North Wind Picture Archives/Alamy

Settlers building Jamestown

Many of the colonists were not prepared for the challenges of Jamestown. Many came from the upper class and were interested in finding treasure. They had little experience or desire to do hard outdoor work, such as building or farming. They did not plan to stay permanently but wanted to find gold and return to England. Their participation did little to help. Also, the seven men on the council selected to lead the colony were distrustful of one another and did not cooperate well.

The poor conditions at Jamestown led to starvation and disease. After two-thirds of the colony had died, Captain John Smith took over as leader. He understood the importance of hard work, especially in a survival situation. He required every person to work four to six hours every day. According to some sources, he told the colonists, "Those who don't work, don't eat." His firm leadership saved the colony, but its troubles weren't over yet.

The Virginia Company continued to support the colony. It would send supply ships with food, tools, goods for trading, and additional settlers. These ships did not come often, however. The "First Supply" arrived in January 1608. It carried about 100 new settlers. The "Second Supply" did not come until October of that year. It carried 70 new settlers, including the first two women of the colony, Martha Forest and her maid, Anne Burras. It was also an all-male colony. Even after women began to arrive, the gender ratio remained skewed throughout most of the seventeenth century. This social structure posed significant challenges for a society that saw family as a main center of social order, economy, and survival.

Jamestown men wore chest plates in battle.

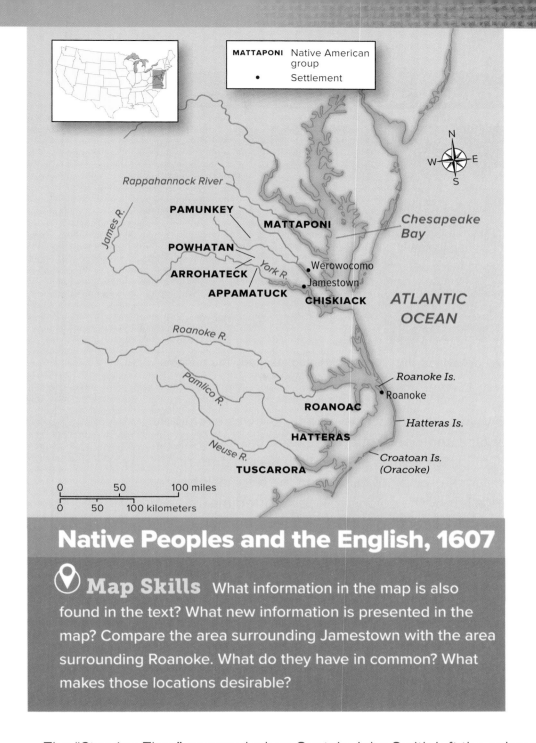

MATTAPONI Native American group
• Settlement

Rappahannock River

PAMUNKEY

MATTAPONI

Chesapeake Bay

James R.

POWHATAN

York R.

ARROHATECK

•Werowocomo

APPAMATUCK

•Jamestown

CHISKIACK

ATLANTIC OCEAN

Roanoke R.

Pamlico R.

Roanoke Is.

•Roanoke

ROANOAC

Hatteras Is.

HATTERAS

Neuse R.

Croatoan Is. (Oracoke)

TUSCARORA

0   50   100 miles
0   50   100 kilometers

Native Peoples and the English, 1607

Map Skills What information in the map is also found in the text? What new information is presented in the map? Compare the area surrounding Jamestown with the area surrounding Roanoke. What do they have in common? What makes those locations desirable?

The "Starving Time" occurred when Captain John Smith left the colony in 1609 and it nearly collapsed. Tensions with the Powhatan Indians and lack of leadership caused the majority of the colonists to die of starvation and disease. When the group of settlers who had been shipwrecked in Bermuda reached Jamestown in May 1610, they found the colony in such poor condition that they considered abandoning it. They received news that more ships bringing supplies and people would be arriving, so they stayed and rebuilt the colony with the survivors. Among the shipwrecked settlers was John Rolfe, who would end up helping to save the colony.

Then and Now

Jamestown may have looked like this at its peak.

Archaeologists study the remains of old Jamestown.

As the Jamestown colony grew, the original fort was eventually abandoned. Over time, the wood rotted away and the foundations became buried in mud. For a while, the location was forgotten. An archaeologist, William Kelso, eventually found the original location by studying writings left by the colonists. Kelso started the Jamestown Rediscovery Project in 1994. He and others began to uncover, study, and preserve the original fort. Visitors can now visit the site of Jamestown.

✓ Stop and Check

Write What problems did the Jamestown colony face? What recommendations would you give to solve these problems?

Find Details As you read, add additional information to the graphic organizer on page 87 in your Inquiry Journal.

Relations between the Powhatan and the Colonists

In addition to being a salty swamp, the location of Jamestown was also in Powhatan territory. The Powhatan Confederacy was an alliance of about thirty tribes. They were led by Chief Wahunsonacock (wah hun SAHN uh kahk), also called Chief Powhatan. He was an intelligent leader who had been successfully increasing the strength and territory of his people when the colonists arrived. Historians are not sure exactly how many tribes Chief Powhatan ruled, but he had thousands of warriors at his command. For the struggling Jamestown colony, the Powhatan could be much-needed allies or dangerous enemies.

As an experienced soldier, Captain John Smith knew Jamestown could not survive a full-force attack from the Powhatan, so he wisely chose to avoid conflict as much as possible. He and Chief Powhatan respected one another. Although there were a few conflicts, the relationship was mostly peaceful, and the Jamestown colony was able to get food through trade with the Powhatan.

Colonists traded with the Powhatan for food.

Unfortunately, Smith was injured in a gunpowder accident. His injury forced him to return to England. Then, in 1618, Chief Powhatan died. Power passed to one of his brothers, who ruled briefly before passing the title again to another brother, named Opechancanough (oh pun CHAN kun awf). He was angry about the growth of the Jamestown colony into native lands, and he waged wars against the colony for the next several decades.

✓ Stop and Check

Think What made it possible for the colonists to trade with the Powhatan?

(t)McGraw-Hill Education; (b)Lanmas/Alamy

The Real Story of Pocahontas

The most famous story about Jamestown and the Powhatan is the story about Chief Powhatan's daughter, Pocahontas. Her real name was Matoaka; Pocahontas was her nickname and meant "the playful one." According to legend, when she was around 13 years old, her father captured Captain John Smith and planned to execute him. Pocahontas saved Smith's life by convincing Powhatan to let him go.

Historians are uncertain if these events happened at all. Captain Smith was known to exaggerate stories. Some historians suggest that the incident was not an attempted execution and that Smith misunderstood a ceremony making him a sub-chief under Powhatan. What is more certain is that Pocahontas was curious and friendly toward the colonists. This improved relations between the two groups. She later married John Rolfe, a successful Jamestown farmer. This marriage brought peace between the settlers and the Powhatan, who had been growing more hostile since Captain Smith returned to England. Pocahontas died of illness in 1617 while visiting England with her husband.

Pocahontas saving John Smith

Pocahontas

 Stop and Check

COLLABORATE

List Make a list of facts and myths about Pocahontas. Compare your list with a partner's list.

Find Details As you read, add additional information to the graphic organizer on page 87 in your Inquiry Journal.

(bkgd)McGraw-Hill Education; (t)Library of Congress Prints and Photographs Division [LC-USZC4-3368]; (b)Williams, S.W., ed. "Pocahontas." Page 183 in Queenly Women, Crowned and Uncrowned. Cincinnati: Cranston and Stowe, 1885.

The Legacy of the Colony

In 1612, John Rolfe introduced tobacco to the colony. It grew well in Virginia and quickly became a **cash crop**. The colony would grow in population and size due to the wealth gained from the new crop. Unfortunately, tobacco is hard on the soil, and so the colonists needed more and more land to grow it. This caused conflicts with the Powhatan and was one of the reasons for the Powhatan Wars. The value of tobacco, however, made the colony strong and the colonists wealthy enough to protect themselves.

Tobacco required a lot of labor, so indentured servants were brought from England to work. Their employers paid for them to travel there, and the indentured servants worked under contract for five to seven years until they repaid their debt. The colonists wanted even more expansion, however, and eventually began purchasing African slaves to work on tobacco farms.

Tobacco farming

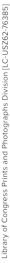
Library of Congress Prints and Photographs Division [LC-US262-76385]

Slavery in the English colonies began in the early 1600s.

This means that the cruel practice of slavery in North America has its roots in England's first permanent colony. The slave trade had already been established by other countries, and in 1619, a Dutch ship entered the port of Jamestown carrying African slaves. Twenty of them were exchanged for food. Since slavery had not yet been established in the colony, these first Africans may have been treated more like indentured servants. Records at the time listed them as servants, not slaves. Some apparently gained freedom after working a certain number of years.

This situation would not last. As the contracts on indentured servants ended and the **demand** for tobacco and other crops grew, planters needed more workers. Some planters attempted to enslave American Indians, since the relationship had become much worse after the departure of Captain John Smith and the death of Chief Powhatan. The American Indians knew the land well and had friends and family to help them, so attempts to enslave them were unsuccessful. African slaves, however, did not have the same networks of friends or family in the unfamiliar land of North America. Escaping was more difficult. By 1650, the number of slaves in the Virginia colony had grown to about 300.

Another important legacy of Jamestown was the first representative government set up by Europeans in the Americas. In 1619, the Virginia Company had the colonists establish their own government, the House of Burgesses. By this time, the Virginia colony had expanded into eleven settlements. Each was allowed to elect two representatives, or burgesses, to speak for them when the House met in Jamestown. Since most of the burgesses were wealthy white tobacco growers, one of their first laws was simply to settle the price of tobacco.

The House of Burgesses

The House of Burgesses had been around for only five years when King James took control of the colony from the Virginia Company. The company had been losing money, and the increasing attacks by the Powhatan, led by Chief Opechancanough, made King James think the colony needed more direct control. He sent royal governors to represent him in leading the colony. Despite this, the House of Burgesses continued to meet every year. Even if the burgesses were no longer in control, they liked being able to discuss what needed to be done and to be united when dealing with the royal government.

Jamestown remained the capital of the Virginia colony until 1699, after the statehouse burned down. By this time, many of the people had moved to other settlements, so they decided to rebuild in a better location. Williamsburg became the new capital, and Jamestown was eventually abandoned.

✓ Stop and Check

Think Aside from being the first successful English colony in America, what other "firsts" can be traced back to Jamestown?

What Do You Think? If you had been in charge of Jamestown, what would you have done differently?

How Did Early European Settlers Compete with One Another and American Indians?

Competition among European Nations

Spain, France, and England had different approaches to colonizing North America. Each nation's monarchy hoped that the New World would bring wealth and greater global power. The three major colonies employed different economic and governmental systems. The colonies of New Spain and New France appointed governors who reported back to the controlling government in Europe and carried out the king's and queen's orders. The English colony at Jamestown, on the other hand, was governed in its early years by a group of people who were elected to represent each settlement in the colony. The three nations competed for land and trade. Spain and France also sought to convert native people to Catholicism, the primary religion in those countries.

HSS.5.2.3, HSS.5.2.4, HSS.5.3.1, HSS.5.3.2, HSS.5.3.5, HAS.CS.5

110 **Lesson 2** How Did Early European Settlers Compete with One Another and American Indians?

1545
Spain finds the largest silver deposits yet discovered in the Americas.

1649
The Iroquois Confederacy defeats the Huron Confederacy in the Beaver Wars.

1718
Jean-Baptiste Le Moyne de Bienville founds the city of New Orleans.

1550	1600	1650	1700	1750	

1608
Samuel de Champlain founds Quebec City.

anada.

F

G

K

H

An early map of Quebec City in modern-day Canada

Laurent

Spain established territories in South America, the Caribbean, Central America and Mexico, as well as the southern and western parts of North America. Spanish settlers quickly learned to use the resources of their new colony to increase the wealth of Spain. The Spanish did not want land in the Americas to be taken by the French or the English. So, to further expand, Spanish rulers offered large portions of land to those willing to move to New Spain. These areas, called **encomiendas**, included any American Indian villages on the land. The American Indians living in an encomienda were forced to work for its owner in exchange for housing and food.

While the early English relationship with the Powhatan in the Jamestown colony involved some instances of cooperation, Spain's relationship with the American Indians was based on conquest. The Spanish also wanted to convert all native peoples to Catholicism.

New Spain's wealth and power came in part from its gold and silver mines. Spanish settlers also built ranches and sugar cane plantations. Many of the workers in the mines and on the plantations were American Indians. Disease, mistreatment, and dangerous working conditions resulted in the deaths of 24 million American Indians in just one hundred years. To replace the shrinking workforce, the Spanish brought slaves to New Spain. By 1570, more than 200,000 Africans were enslaved on the plantations of New Spain.

A mission was a common type of settlement in New Spain.

One Spanish colonist named Bartolomé de Las Casas was so upset at how colonists were treating American Indians that he decided to help them. He became a **missionary**, or a person who teaches his or her religious beliefs to people with different beliefs.

Eventually, many more missionaries from Spain came to the Americas to teach the native peoples about Catholicism. But rather than helping the native peoples, the Spanish missionaries forced them to work and give up their own religion. These native peoples and Spanish missionaries lived in settlements called missions. As Spain began claiming the West Coast, these missions became part of their strategy to prevent Russia and England from settling land in present-day California.

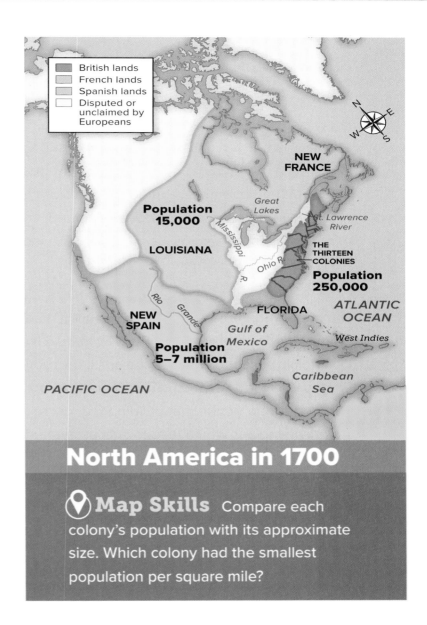

British lands
French lands
Spanish lands
Disputed or unclaimed by Europeans

NEW FRANCE

Great Lakes

St. Lawrence River

Population 15,000

LOUISIANA

Mississippi

THE THIRTEEN COLONIES

Ohio R.

Population 250,000

NEW SPAIN

Rio Grande

FLORIDA

ATLANTIC OCEAN

Gulf of Mexico

West Indies

Population 5–7 million

Caribbean Sea

PACIFIC OCEAN

North America in 1700

 Map Skills Compare each colony's population with its approximate size. Which colony had the smallest population per square mile?

✓ Stop and Check

Think How did New Spain treat American Indians?

Find Details As you read, add new information to the graphic organizer on page 95 in your Inquiry Journal.

(t)McGraw-Hill Education

French Trappers and Traders

When French settlers began to colonize North America, they were interested in finding gold and a route to Asia. Their settlements along the St. Lawrence River in Canada would not help them with either of those goals. What Canada did offer was many fur-bearing animals. The forests of Europe had been overhunted, but Europeans still desired hats made from beaver fur. To meet European demand, French settlers began to export beaver pelts across the Atlantic. The money raised through the fur trade helped pay for more expeditions into North America.

As French explorers continued to explore Canada, the king of France wanted to organize the colony to ensure it made money. He chose Samuel de Champlain (sham PLAYN) to lead New France. In 1604, Champlain sailed to New France as its first governor. Champlain's strategy in North America differed greatly from that of the Spanish conquistadors. He felt that building friendly relationships with groups of American Indians would lead to successful trade. He believed these alliances would allow him to travel freely and keep the French settlements safe from attack. Within his first year in New France, Champlain learned to speak the Huron language. New France and the nearby Huron and Algonquin groups traded with each other and maintained friendly relations.

PRIMARY SOURCE

In Their Words... Samuel de Champlain

We departed on the following day, pursuing our way up the river as far as the entrance to the lake. In it are many beautiful low islands covered with very fine woods and meadows with much wild fowl and animals to hunt, such as stags, fallow deer, fawns, roebucks, bears, and other kinds of animals which come from the mainland to these islands.

—from a diary entry of Samuel de Champlain, 1609

TEXT: De Champlain, Samuel. The Works of Samuel de Champlain, Vol. 2. Edited by H.P. Biggar. Translated by John Squair. Collated by J. Home Cameron. Toronto: The Champlain Society, 1925.; PHOTO: (bkgd)McGraw-Hill Education; (inset)North Wind Picture Archives/Alamy Stock Photo

Marquette and Jolliet

French explorers' efforts to find the Northwest Passage led them to further explore North America's waterways. In 1673, Jacques Marquette and Louis Jolliet headed south in a canoe on the uncharted Mississippi River. They encountered many groups of American Indians living on the banks of the Mississippi. While some American Indians were hostile, the Illinois and other groups helped Marquette and Jolliet.

Marquette and Jolliet claimed the land drained by the Mississippi River for France. Marquette later set up a mission in present-day Illinois, and Jolliet continued to explore North America.

La Salle and Louisiana

In 1682, René-Robert Cavelier Sieur de La Salle led an expedition down the Mississippi River. La Salle claimed the Mississippi and its tributaries, or smaller branching rivers and streams, for France. He named the region *Louisiana* after the French king, Louis XIV. La Salle wanted to build a fort at the mouth of the Mississippi and attack the Spanish in northern Mexico. La Salle and several hundred settlers, however, got lost and ended up in present-day Texas. By 1687, only 36 of La Salle's settlers remained alive.

Bark canoes were sturdy enough to withstand ocean waves and light enough to be carried.

✓ Stop and Check

Talk Why did Champlain develop friendly relationships with American Indians he encountered in New France?

New Orleans

   French colonists slowly began to settle parts of the Louisiana Territory. They built forts in strategic locations to protect new settlements from the Spanish and English. Louis XIV instructed a Canadian naval officer, Pierre Le Moyne Sieur d'Iberville, to build forts at the mouth of the Mississippi. The series of forts he built in present-day Mississippi and Louisiana further established Louisiana as a French possession. One such fort, Fort La Boulaye, lay just south of the future site of the city of New Orleans. When he died of yellow fever, Iberville's younger brother, Jean-Baptiste Le Moyne Sieur de Bienville, continued his work.

PORT OF NEW ORLEANS.

Ships anchored at the Port of New Orleans, about 1800

In Their Words... Pierre Le Moyne Sieur d'Iberville

If France does not take possession of this part of America, which is the finest, to have a colony strong enough to resist those that England possesses... these colonies which are becoming very extensive, will increase to such an extent that in less than a century, they will be strong enough to seize upon the whole continent of America, and to expel all other nations.

—from *The Argument to Settle Louisiana*, 1698

In 1701, Bienville became governor of Louisiana at the age of 21. He built Fort Louis on Mobile Bay and lived there until 1711. In 1718, Bienville founded New Orleans. The Louisiana Territory was much easier to farm than the rest of New France. Settlers built plantations on the fertile soil and grew indigo, rice, and tobacco. Successful plantations brought in more money from trade with American Indians, which allowed the farmers to increase the size of the plantations. The growing plantations required more and more workers. In 1720, a ship carrying about 200 slaves landed in New Orleans. In the decade that followed, the colony imported more than six thousand slaves. Eventually, more than half of the people of New Orleans were slaves.

 Stop and Check

COLLABORATE

Talk Why was it important that France built forts in Mississippi and Louisiana?

TEXT: Pierre le Moyne Sieur d'Iberville. 1669. Quoted in Parliamentary Debates on the Subject of the Confederation of the British North American Provinces, 3rd Session, 8th Provincial Parliament of Canada (Quebec: Hunter, Rose & Company, parliamentary printers, 1865), 324.; PHOTO: (t)McGraw-Hill Education; (b)North Wind Picture Archives/Alamy

New Alliances, New Conflict

As European colonial powers sought to rapidly expand in North America, they came into contact with more and more native peoples. Reactions to the Europeans varied. Some groups of American Indians were friendly, and some were hostile. Before the Europeans arrived, the people living in North America already traded with one another, had military agreements, and shared cultures. The settlers' arrival often complicated the existing relationships between groups of American Indians.

In 1609, Huron and Algonquin leaders approached Samuel de Champlain asking to form a military alliance. The Huron and Algonquin had long been enemies of the Iroquois. Eventually, Algonquin commanders convinced Champlain to lend them French troops in their fight with the Iroquois.

Iroquois armies did not yet have guns and gunpowder. As a result, Champlain's men easily defeated the Iroquois. To thank the French, the Huron and Algonquin helped grow French fur traders' business in the region. After the battle with the Iroquois, France formed a permanent alliance with the Huron and Algonquin. The Iroquois confederacy, meanwhile, sought revenge.

A colonial trading post

North Wind Picture Archives/Alamy Stock Photo

The Iroquois' chance came in 1634, when a smallpox outbreak weakened the Huron confederacy. Smallpox was a disease brought to North America by Europeans. At the same time, beaver populations in Canada dropped significantly. Historians believe that this was the effect of the overhunting of the animal by fur traders. Because of the beavers' role in the conflict, the war between the Iroquois, the French, and the Huron and Algonquin confederacies is called the Beaver Wars.

In 1642, the Iroquois blocked the Huron from accessing the rivers they used to trade with the French and other native peoples. The Huron economy had become dependent on trade. The Huron nearly starved as a result of the Iroquois blockade. By 1649, the Iroquois had defeated the Huron. The Iroquois' conflicts with the French and Algonquin would continue well into the 18th century.

French soldiers fight alongside Huron warriors.

✓ Stop and Check

COLLABORATE

Talk Why did the Huron and the Algonquin side with Champlain in 1609?

What Do You Think?
Did the relationships France and Spain had with the American Indians they encountered make a difference in the outcomes of their settlements?

(t)McGraw-Hill Education, (b)Bettmann/Getty Images

Resources from the New World Enrich Europe

Though many French explorers were disappointed not to find gold in Canada, they did discover another valuable resource. People across Europe were fond of hats made from pelts, or the skins of animals with the fur still on it. Unlike North America, parts of Europe were overpopulated. Some of the continent's forests had been cleared to expand cities. The larger animals that lived there became rare.

Meanwhile, large animals thrived in North America. The French colony made money by hunting and trapping mammals such as moose, elk, deer, and caribou. Beaver fur held special value. European clothing makers used the beaver's thick fur to make felt, which is a smooth, leathery fabric. Beaver hats were especially popular in the cold winters of Northern Europe. An oil naturally produced by beavers was even used to make perfumes. Hat makers had long used the fur of the European beaver to make hats, but overhunting and habitat destruction caused that species to become scarce by the 17th century. French traders were able to replace European beaver fur with an American version.

Just as in Europe, American beaver numbers decreased significantly as a result of overhunting. The animal was eventually saved by a change in fashion trends. Silk prices dropped at the beginning of the 19th century, and Europeans exchanged their beaver hats for silk ones. This allowed the beaver population to make a comeback. Today, beavers are one of the most important national symbols of Canada.

European clothes makers regarded beaver fur as a fashionable and useful material.

(bkgd)McGraw-Hill Education; (inset)Leemage/Corbis Historical/Getty Images

In the 1500s, Spain rose to become one of the world's most powerful empires. Its American colonies were key to the empire's growth. Spanish colonists mined large amounts of silver and gold in South America and Mexico. In 1545, Spanish colonists exploring in the mountains of Peru found the largest silver deposit yet discovered in the Americas. From American gold and silver, the Spanish made coins. Silver and gold coins were important to Spain's economic success because Spain produced very few goods that could be sold to other countries. Spanish traders exchanged coins for foreign goods. With this new wealth, the Spanish built ships and armies to further expand the Spanish Empire.

Spain used profits from the colonies to fund an armada, a large fleet of warships.

Other European powers tried to prevent the growth of Spain's territories. French leaders hired private sea captains to attack Spanish treasure ships as they returned to Spain. Eventually, Spain's dominance came to an end. The value of gold and silver was based on the fact that these metals were very rare. As more and more gold became available, Spanish coins were not as valuable as before. Nations that produced goods began to catch up with Spain economically. Without the ability to buy armies to protect and expand its empire, Spain's influence in the world shrank. In the 1700s, England, France, and the Netherlands fought to take Spain's place as Europe's most powerful nation.

✓ Stop and Check

Talk What caused Spain's power to decrease?

Seeking Religious Freedom

In England in the 1600s, it was a crime to belong to any church other than the Church of England. Members of the church called Separatists, however, wanted to set up their own churches and make their own rules. As a consequence, many members of the church were arrested and fined.

In the early 1600s, a group of Separatists decided to move to the Netherlands to escape persecution. This group later became known as the Pilgrims. Eventually, the Pilgrims decided to leave the Netherlands. Historians disagree over exactly why the Pilgrims left, but some reasons include Pilgrim parents' concerns that their children would lose their English identity and fear of war breaking out between Spain and the Netherlands.

The Pilgrims decided to venture to the New World, not to enrich themselves or to explore, but to find a safe place to practice their religion. They asked the English government permission to settle in Virginia, and the London Company agreed to pay for their passage. In return, the Pilgrims had to send resources such as timber, fish, and furs back to the company.

Pilgrims departing on the *Mayflower* in 1620

(bkgd)McGraw-Hill Education/Jill Braaten; (t)McGraw-Hill Education; (inset)Photos.com/Getty Images

HSS.5.3.1, HSS.5.3.2, HSS.5.3.3, HSS.5.4.1, HSS.5.4.2, HSS.5.4.3, HSS.5.4.4, HSS.5.4.5, HSS.5.4.6, HSS.5.4.7

Time Line

1620
Pilgrims on the *Mayflower* arrive at Plymouth in what is now Massachusetts.

1630
Puritans establish settlement at Boston.

1636
Providence colony is established in what is now Rhode Island.

1675-1676
King Philip's War

1692
Salem Witch Trials

| 1620 | | | 1640 | | | 1660 | | | 1680 | | | 1700 |

1636–1637
Pequot War

1700s
First Great Awakening

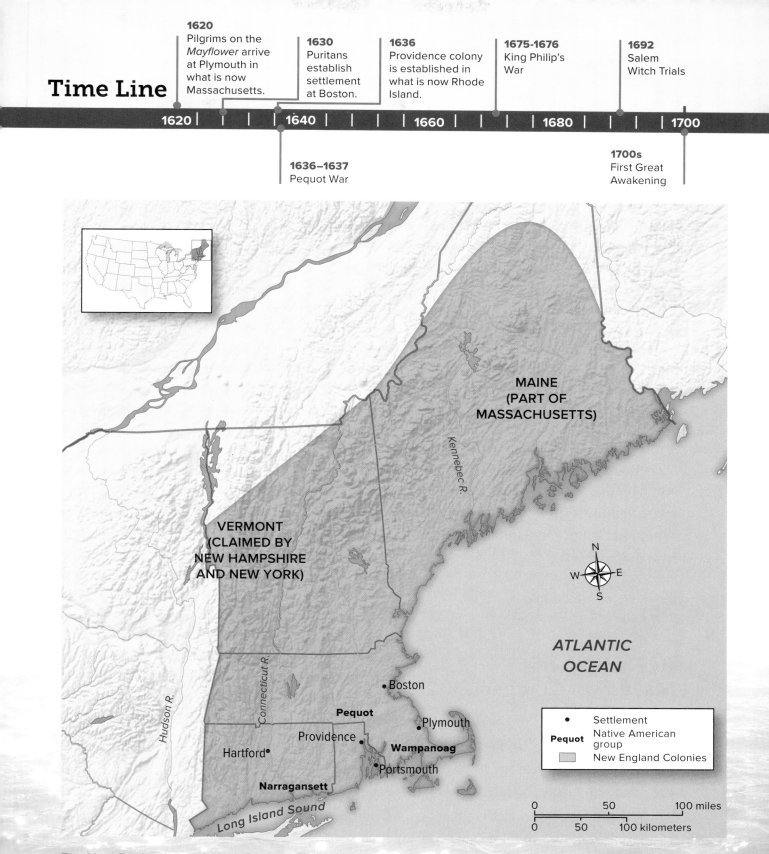

MAINE
(PART OF MASSACHUSETTS)

Kennebec R.

VERMONT
(CLAIMED BY NEW HAMPSHIRE AND NEW YORK)

ATLANTIC OCEAN

N
W E
S

Hudson R.

Connecticut R.

• Boston

Pequot

• Plymouth

Providence •

Hartford •

Wampanoag

• Portsmouth

Narragansett

Long Island Sound

•	Settlement
Pequot	Native American group
	New England Colonies

0   50   100 miles
0 50 100 kilometers

The New England colonies were the northernmost English colonies.

The Pilgrims

In September of 1620, 102 men, women, and children set sail from Plymouth, England, on a ship named the *Mayflower*. These Pilgrims faced a number of hardships on their 66-day voyage across the Atlantic Ocean, including storms and rough seas, disease, and hunger.

When they finally caught sight of land, they realized that they had not landed in Virginia as they had planned. Instead, they were hundreds of miles north, at Provincetown in northern Cape Cod, Massachusetts. The Pilgrims were changing the rules of their original agreement by settling in a different area. Led by William Bradford, the colonists drew up a new contract for their community. This document, called the Mayflower Compact, provided the outline of a new government. This was one of the first steps toward self-government in colonial North America.

The Pilgrims did not decide on a location for their settlement right away. In the early days, they lived on board the *Mayflower*. They eventually chose Plymouth, named by Captain John Smith a few years earlier. They arrived in late December, at the start of a brutal winter. They were without experience, low on supplies, and utterly unprepared for the weather. Half of the Pilgrims died that winter due to starvation, disease, and the cold.

PRIMARY SOURCE

In Their Words...
Mayflower Compact, 1620

Having undertaken, for the glory of God, and advancement of the Christian faith, and honor of our king and country, a voyage to plant the first colony in the northern parts of Virginia, do by these presents solemnly and mutually in the presence of God and one of another . . . [we] combine ourselves together . . . for the general good of the colony: unto which we promise all due submission and obedience. . . .

William Bradford

"The Mayflower Compact." In The Signers of the Mayflower Compact, by Henry Whittemore, p. 5. New York: Mayflower Publishing Co., 1899.

The new colony seemed doomed. But in the spring, they befriended a Pawtuxet man named Squanto, who had been living with the Wampanoag people. Squanto spoke English and taught the Pilgrims how to survive. He showed them how to plant corn and use fish to fertilize the soil. He taught them how to trap animals, catch fish, and find oysters. William Bradford called Squanto "a special instrument sent from God." The Pilgrim settlement thrived and grew.

An artist's interpretation of what the *Mayflower* looked like

✓ Stop and Check

COLLABORATE

Talk Why did the Pilgrims draft a new formal agreement about how their colony would be run?

Find Details As you read, add new information to the graphic organizer on page 103 in your Inquiry Journal.

Perspectives
The Mayflower Compact

When the Pilgrims wrote the Mayflower Compact, it was the first government framework written in the land that is now the United States. It was signed by only some of the colonists—the men. At the time, women rarely held positions of authority in civic or religious life. As a result, they did not have the opportunity to sign such important documents. The purpose of the document was to bind the Pilgrims together. However, the Mayflower Compact did not include any laws. Instead, those who signed it were pledging to follow the laws that would later be enacted by the Pilgrims' small system of self-government.

The Pilgrims signing the Mayflower Compact

(bkgd)McGraw-Hill Education; (inset)SuperStock/Getty Images

You Decide

Working in small groups, you will establish a new settlement.

- Give your settlement a name.
- Tell the location of your settlement.
- Indicate why you are moving to the settlement.

Work together to develop a system of laws for the settlement.

- Consider what principles are most important to your group.
- Think about the kinds of rights and protections you need.
- Write your new laws as a compact, and give the document an official title.
- Sign the compact.

Reflect

What did developing a plan for your new community teach you about the importance of self-government?

- Who helped make the decisions about the settlement's laws and rules?
- How did you come to an agreement about the laws?
- How did you resolve conflicts with other members of your group?

Make Connections

Consider how the development of your settlement compares with the development of the Plymouth settlement. What was similar, and what was different?

✓ Stop and Check

COLLABORATE

Talk Do you think the Pilgrims would have written a different compact if women had been included in the drafting? Would this have been better for the colony as a whole?

What Do You Think? Should women have been allowed to help set up the Pilgrims' community and make laws?

The Puritans

The Pilgrims were not the only group to flee religious persecution in England. A group of Puritans made their own journey to North America in 1629. Unlike the Pilgrims, the Puritans planned to land in Massachusetts. When they arrived in 1630, they founded the Massachusetts Bay Colony. They named their first settlement Boston. Another difference between the Pilgrims and the Puritans was that the Puritans had not separated from the Church of England.

The Puritans believed God had chosen them to create a religious community that was purer than the ones in England. The Puritans worked hard to show that their community was a success. They also worked hard just to survive. While most Puritans were farmers, they also made most of what they needed, however, such as flour, barrels, horseshoes, cabinets, saddles, and shoes.

Because of the abundance of good lumber in New England, shipbuilding eventually became an important part of the economy. The industry was successful in part because of slave labor. Slaves were also put to work in shops and on farms. Massachusetts was the first colony to legalize slavery in 1641. By 1750, it was legal across all of the original thirteen colonies. Massachusetts did not outlaw slavery until 1783.

The Puritans organized their villages so that each one had a school and a common building that served as both meeting house and church.

A saltbox house was a common type of home in Puritan villages.

Puritan leaders wanted each settlement to be "a city upon a hill," which meant its residents had to live up to high moral standards. In an effort to enforce their rules, Puritan leaders required each family to sign a covenant with the church. If a family broke the **covenant**, it had to leave the settlement.

Puritan children were taught the value of hard work from an early age. Young children were expected to work around the house. They also learned to read, because the Puritans believed everyone should be able to read the Bible.

By age twelve, girls did the same chores as women, such as churning butter, spinning and dyeing cloth, and making soap and candles. Girls usually did not get any additional schooling.

Boys helped with the farm animals, chopped wood, and picked vegetables before going to school. At school, some had the chance to learn another language, such as Latin or Greek. Boys also began to learn a trade, such as blacksmithing or printing

Life for Puritan women consisted mostly of managing the home and raising children. Most women were not allowed to own property, and they were supposed to be obedient to men. They were not allowed to participate in town government. Only men could vote in town meetings, in which they decided issues and made laws.

Although the Puritans founded the Massachusetts Bay Colony on the principles of religious freedom, they were not tolerant of **dissension** among their own members. Roger Williams told leaders they should not take land that belonged to the American Indians. He also thought that the colony should allow other religions to be practiced. Believing Williams's ideas were dangerous, Puritan leaders banished him. In 1636, Williams founded Providence, now the capital of Rhode Island.

In 1637, Anne Hutchinson was put on trial for arguing that people should be allowed to interpret the Bible themselves. Hutchinson was forced to leave Massachusetts. She founded a new settlement, now Portsmouth, Rhode Island.

Anne Hutchinson on trial

In 1692, the Puritans' strict moral codes led to one of the darkest episodes in their history. Three girls in Salem fell mysteriously ill. They blamed three women for using witchcraft on them, and other accusations soon followed. From June to September, the Puritans tried and hanged 19 people for witchcraft. Finally, a higher court stepped in to stop the trials.

Events like these left some Puritans yearning for more independence from the church. In the 1700s, ministers like John Wesley, Jonathan Edwards, and George Whitefield began to preach in a dramatic, emotional style. They emphasized the importance of faith over actions. They and their followers created the Baptist and Methodist churches, which focused on ordinary people who had not been attending church regularly. This movement, called the First Great Awakening, led many away from Puritanism.

✓ Stop and Check

Talk If the Puritans left England because people were intolerant of their religion, why didn't the Puritans tolerate other religious views in their colony?

North Wind Picture Archives/Alamy

American Indian Relations

The New England colonists had both positive and negative encounters with local American Indians. The Pilgrims' relationship with Squanto and the Wampanoag people made the difference between the survival and extinction of their new colony.

Squanto teaches the Pilgrims to farm.

To give thanks for their survival, the Pilgrims and Wampanoag had a three-day festival to celebrate the good harvest. This feast would later be called the first "thanksgiving." The Wampanoag brought deer, and the Pilgrims brought turkey, goose, duck, and a variety of vegetables and fruits.

Not all relationships between New England colonists and local American Indians were friendly, however. In 1637, the Pequot people of Connecticut and the English settlers went to war over trade disputes. The settlers were allied with the Narragansett and Mohegan people. These two peoples disliked the Pequot for their strict control of trade in the previous decades. At first, the two sides seemed evenly matched in what came to be called the Pequot War. The English had superior weapons, but the Pequot had knowledge of the land. In the end, however, the English defeated the Pequot. Many of the Pequot people taken prisoner by the English were sold into slavery.

Despite the promising beginning to the Pilgrims' relationship with the Wampanoag, Narragansett, and Mohegan peoples, the colonists soon became enemies with these groups. The American Indians were angered by the increasing number of new colonists who were settling on their lands. By 1675, these tensions resulted in a bloody conflict called King Philip's War.

"King Philip" was the name that English settlers gave to the Wampanoag leader, Metacomet. Metacomet's father, Massasoit, had helped the Pilgrims survive their first harsh winters. However, the colonists' desire for more and more territory changed their relationship with the Wampanoag for the worse.

Thousands of people died in King Philip's War. Metacomet was eventually killed, and his family was sold into slavery. In their brutal conquest of the American Indians, the English showed they were capable of seizing land and maintaining power. The war marked the end of any resistance to English colonization of New England.

Metacomet, also called King Philip, of the Wampanoag people

✓ Stop and Check

Talk What caused the tensions that led to King Philip's War?

What Do You Think?
Why did King Philip's War mark the end of resistance to English settlement of New England?

The First Thanksgiving at Plymouth
by Jennie Augusta Brownscombe

A Region of Diversity

The English Middle Colonies—New York, New Jersey, Pennsylvania, and Delaware—were quite diverse, or varied. These colonies were home to people of many different ethnic backgrounds and religions. They became known for tolerance of these differences. They also became known as centers of **commerce**. Their central location and fine ports made them ideal for trading and distributing goods both north and south. Outside the port cities, fertile soil and a mild climate encouraged farming of wheat, corn, and other grains. Farming was so successful that growers were usually able to produce a surplus, or more than they needed. They could sell the surplus to the other colonies. For this reason, the Middle Colonies were sometimes called the "breadbasket" of colonial America.

A crossroads of ideas as well as trade, these successful colonies helped establish important American principles such as trial by jury and freedom of the press. They were also home to some of the most influential colonial figures. Among them was author, inventor, and thinker Benjamin Franklin.

HSS.5.3.1, HSS.5.4.1, HSS.5.4.1, HSS.5.4.2, HSS.5.4.3, HSS.5.4.4, HSS.5.4.5, HSS.5.4.6, HSS.5.4.7, HAS.CS.5

134 **Lesson 4** What Shaped Life In the Middle Colonies?

Time Line

1624
Dutch traders found New Netherland.

1664
English take New Netherland from the Dutch, renaming it New York.

1732
Benjamin Franklin begins publishing *Poor Richard's Almanack*.

1600   1650   1700   1750

1638
Swedish and other traders found New Sweden.

1682
William Penn arrives in Pennsylvania.

1735
John Peter Zenger found not guilty of libel.

1738
First Great Awakening continues.

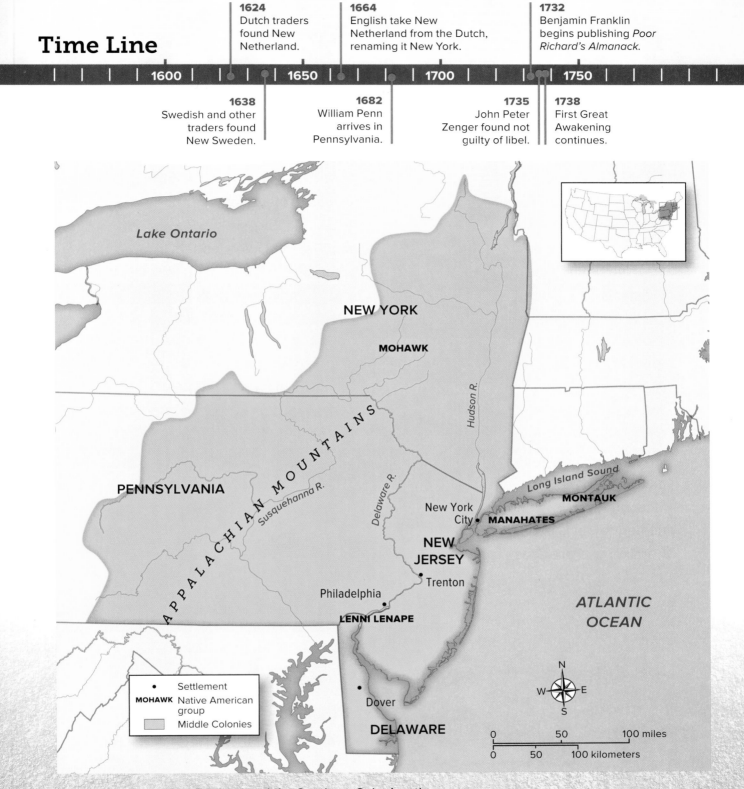

Located between New England and the Southern Colonies, the Middle Colonies became the commercial center of colonial America.

New York and New Jersey

England and the Netherlands were at war in Europe for much of the late 1600s. In 1664, English King Charles II decided to try to gain control of New Netherland to expand his colonies in North America. He put his brother, the Duke of York, in charge of seizing the Dutch colony and putting it under English rule.

The Duke of York sent a fleet of English warships to New Netherland. English troops reached the colony in August 1664. The English commander, Colonel Richard Nicolls, demanded that the Dutch leaders in New Netherland surrender the colony immediately. Peter Stuyvesant, the Dutch governor, wanted to fight the English. The Dutch colonists refused. They saw no chance of victory against the powerful English navy. They thought it best to surrender on reasonable terms. Nicolls became the governor of England's new colony. England changed the name from New Netherland to New York, in honor of the Duke of York. New Amsterdam became New York City.

The Duke of York soon granted some of the colony's land to two friends. The friends, Lord John Berkeley and Sir George Carteret, received the land west of the Hudson River. Their holdings became New Jersey, named for an island between England and France that Carteret had previously governed.

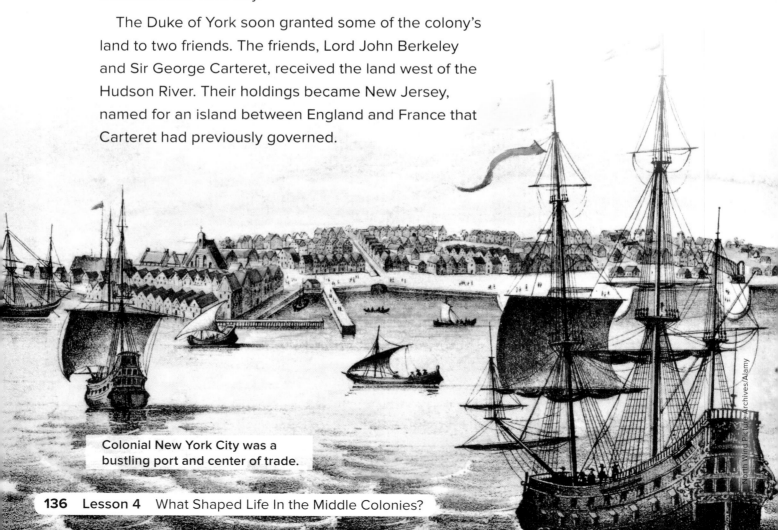

Colonial New York City was a bustling port and center of trade.

Dutch governor Peter Stuyvesant (in the yellow sash)
surrenders New Netherland to the English.

Under English rule, the colonists in what had been New Netherland
were allowed to live much as before. People continued to speak Dutch,
particularly north of New York City. They could continue worshipping in
their own churches. Most of those who held land were allowed to keep it.
The practice of granting farmland to settlers continued. The English also
agreed not to place troops in people's houses without paying for them.

People had come to the colony from all over Europe because the
colony was tolerant of religious and ethnic differences. Women, too, had
more rights here than elsewhere. They could own property, keep shops,
and engage in the fur trade. The Dutch had also been active in the
African slave trade and brought slaves to the colony to build the
settlements or help farm the land. Though slaves had few rights, under
the Dutch they did have a path through which many could become free.
Those working directly for the Dutch West India Company could gain
what was called "half-freedom," supplying slave labor only at certain
times of the year.

(t)McGraw-Hill Education; (b)North Wind Picture Archives/Alamy Stock Photo

One way in which the English differed from the Dutch was in their treatment of slaves. This was partly because English authorities feared rebellion from the growing number of slaves. They passed a law preventing slaves from gathering in groups of more than two. They also made it more difficult for slaves to win freedom and much easier to force freed slaves back into slavery.

English authorities also feared criticism, which they said might lead to unrest. In 1733, a colonist named John Peter Zenger printed newspaper articles that strongly criticized the governor of New York. Arrested and put on trial, Zenger was defended by a well-known lawyer named Andrew Hamilton. Hamilton insisted on a trial by jury, which is a group of peers who decide if someone is innocent or guilty. He then argued that newspapers must have the freedom to print material critical of the government. The judge disagreed, but the jury did not, and Zenger was found not guilty. The trial helped establish two important American principles: the right to a trial by jury and freedom of the press.

PRIMARY SOURCE

In Their Words... Andrew Hamilton

The question before the Court and you, Gentlemen of the jury, is not of small or private concern. It is not the cause of one poor printer, nor of New York alone, which you are now trying. No! . . . It is the cause of liberty.

—from his Summation at the trial of John Peter Zenger, 1735

✓ Stop and Check

Talk What main characteristics of the Middle Colonies dated back to the Dutch and continued after the colony became English? Discuss your ideas with a partner.

Find Details As you read, add additional information to the graphic organizer on page 111 in your Inquiry Journal.

Zenger, John Peter. The Tryal of John Peter Zenger, of New-York, Printer, Who was Lately Try'd and Acquitted for Printing and Publishing a Libel Against the Government: With the Pleadings and Arguments on Both Sides. London: Printed for J. Wilford, 1738.

Pennsylvania and Delaware

William Penn came from a wealthy English family. His father had even lent the King of England a large sum of money. In 1681, the king repaid the debt by granting land in North America to Penn. The land was called Pennsylvania in his father's honor.

Some years before, Penn had joined the Society of Friends, or Quakers. Some of the members of this Christian group had been jailed and even killed for their beliefs. They believed that each person could have a direct relationship with God. They also thought that all people should be treated fairly. They believed women were equal to men in God's eyes and allowed them to take on roles much larger than those in other religions. Quakers were against war and refused to join the military. In time, they would become strong opponents of slavery.

Penn himself had been jailed more than once for his beliefs. He wanted a place where Quakers and others could worship without fear. He called his colony a "Holy Experiment" to prove that people of many faiths and backgrounds could live together peacefully. Penn explained his plans in his publication *Frame of Government* and made them part of the Charter of Privileges under which the Pennsylvania colony was governed. In addition to freedom of religion and trial by jury, the charter set up an elected **assembly** that could propose and pass laws. However, not all colonists had the right to vote. In addition, a strict moral code limited some personal activities; for example, the performance of plays was banned.

William Penn

When the king gave Penn the land for his colony, a native people called the Lenape were living on it. Penn insisted on paying the Lenape for the land. He believed that American Indians should be treated justly. His sons, however, did not share those views. After he died in 1737, they used a false document to claim that the colony was entitled to a "Walking Purchase" of more Lenape land—the distance a man could walk in one-and-a-half days. They then hired the fastest runners in the colony to cover twice as much land as the Lenape had thought they would.

When Penn founded Pennsylvania, he planned its main "towne," or capital city. He called it *Philadelphia*, Greek for "city of brotherly love." He located it where the Schuylkill (pronounced SKOOL kil) River and Delaware River meet. This seemed like a good spot for a trading port, since ships could sail down the Delaware into the Atlantic Ocean or northwest on the Schuylkill to the interior part of the colony. Penn had lived through some terrible disasters in London, and so he wanted a city where disease and fire could not spread so easily. He created a grid of wide, tree-lined streets with many small parks and gardens. On them, he planned brick and stone buildings that would not burn.

A man dressed as a colonial-era blacksmith

People from all over Europe came to Philadelphia. Many came because they could earn a living much more easily than in their native lands. They also appreciated the rights they could enjoy there. As trade grew, the city prospered. People who specialized in different goods and crafts—butchers, bakers, silversmiths, cabinetmakers, and blacksmiths—opened busy shops.

Outside Philadelphia, many immigrants came to farm the land. Among them were German settlers who practiced the Mennonite religion. Some belonged to a strict set of Mennonites called the Amish. These people dressed plainly and lived very simple lives. Their descendants are sometimes called the Pennsylvania Dutch, but that does not mean they are from the Netherlands. It refers to their German background and the language they spoke; *deutsch* (pronounced DOYCH) is the German word for "German."

South of Philadelphia along the Atlantic coast was the area known as Delaware. Swedish traders had come there in 1638 and claimed it as part of their colony of New Sweden. They built a settlement called Fort Christina near what is now the city of Wilmington, Delaware. Insisting that the Swedes took Dutch lands, Peter Stuyvesant had captured New Sweden in 1654 and made it part of New Netherland. Ten years later, it became an English possession along with the rest of New Netherland.

When the English king granted Pennsylvania to William Penn, Penn was worried because the land had no Atlantic coastline. Ships sailing from the port of Philadelphia had to go down the Delaware River to reach the ocean, and the river sometimes froze in winter. Penn asked the Duke of York to sell him the area we now call Delaware, which did have an Atlantic coastline. The Duke agreed. However, the Swedish, Dutch, and Finnish colonists who already lived in the area did not like the idea of being controlled by Pennsylvania. They wanted to make laws for themselves. So in 1702, Penn allowed Delaware to create its own lawmaking assembly.

✓ Stop and Check

Talk In what ways did government in Pennsylvania support people's rights and freedoms? In what way did it fail to support them? Discuss your views with a partner.

By the 1700s, Philadelphia had become a busy port and one of the largest cities in the English colonies.

Life in the Middle Colonies

The English may have claimed the Middle Colonies, but the people who settled there came from many places besides England. The diversity of backgrounds and religions helped make the Middle Colonies unique. Only a small number of colonists were wealthy landowners and traders. Many more were shopkeepers, craft workers, and small farmers. They had to work hard, but there were often great opportunities if they did. Farming was especially difficult, with land to clear and weather to worry about. Yet even small farmers could become prosperous in the Middle Colonies.

Many endured difficulties hoping for a brighter future. In the cities, young boys often signed up as apprentices, or trainees learning a craft. They had to promise to work for several years with the master training them. To get to America, some people signed indenture agreements. They promised to work as servants for a certain number of years in exchange for having the cost of their trip to America paid. At the end of that period, they usually got a piece of land, a suit of clothes, or a set of tools—and their freedom. African slaves found it harder and harder to become free. However, the movement to end slavery was growing.

Religion was important in most colonists' lives. Some, like Quakers, Jews, and Mennonites, came to the colonies to practice their religion more freely. Others were attracted to new religious movements. In 1738, George Whitefield, an English preacher, arrived to lead a Protestant movement known as the First Great Awakening, because it awakened strong religious feelings. Traveling through the colonies, Whitefield drew huge crowds of people from many different churches and backgrounds.

George Whitefield's dramatic sermons drew large crowds.

Preachers were not the only public speakers that colonists went to hear. Political speeches were also well attended. And by the 1700s, printers were distributing newspapers that often contained political news—and criticism. *The New York Gazette*, New York's first newspaper, began publication in 1725. It was put out by a master printer that William Penn originally brought to Pennsylvania to print religious materials.

Colonists attending a political discussion

Words were central to the life of Philadelphia's most famous resident, Benjamin Franklin. Franklin opened his Philadelphia print shop in 1728. He married a woman who ran a bookshop. In 1731, he helped found America's first library. A year later, he began publishing *Poor Richard's Almanack*, a magazine famous for its proverbs, or wise sayings—such as "There are no gains without pains" and "Well done is better than well said." Franklin also wrote many other works, including his autobiography.

Did You Know?

Ben Franklin was also a scientist and an inventor. You may have heard about his experiment with a kite in a lightning storm, which helped us understand how electricity works. Franklin was also the first person to use the terms "battery," "conductor," "positive charge," and "negative charge."

Connect to Science   Do Internet research to find out one thing that Benjamin Franklin invented.

(t)McGraw-Hill Education, (c b)North Wind Picture Archives/Alamy

✓ Stop and Check

COLLABORATE

Talk   What do the details about Benjamin Franklin show about life in the Middle Colonies? Discuss your ideas with a classmate.

How Did Economics Impact People in the Southern Colonies?

An Agricultural Economy

Life in the rural Southern Colonies differed sharply from life in the colonies to the north. The South provided the ideal **environment** for crops like rice, cotton, tobacco, and indigo. This was due to its rich soil, high humidity, and long growing season. However, the production of these crops required large areas of land and intense labor.

During the colonial period, the primary function of a colony was to produce raw goods for the mother country—England. The mother country would then, in turn, ship back to the colonies finished products. The original thirteen colonies lacked valuable resources like gold. What they could offer were agricultural goods. For New England and the Middle Colonies, this initially meant lumber and non-cash crops, such as wheat. For the Southern Colonies, it meant cash crops like tobacco and cotton.

As the colonies grew, the demand for domestic goods grew faster than Britain could keep up with. In response, the northern colonies began producing more valuable finished goods such as furniture, iron, and ships. Meanwhile, Southerners became more adept at producing cash crops. In time, finding the labor needed to produce crops like cotton and tobacco became a difficult problem for the Southern Colonies.

HSS.5.3.1, HSS.5.3.2, HSS.5.3.5, HSS.5.4.1, HSS.5.4.2, HSS.5.4.3, HSS.5.4.5, HSS.5.4.6, HAS.CS.5

(bkgd)McGraw-Hill Education, (inset)Ken Karp/McGraw-Hill Education

Time Line

1634 Lord Baltimore founds Maryland.

1663 King Charles II grants proprietors land in Carolina.

1732 James Oglethorpe founds Georgia.

1770 About 500,000 African slaves are living in the Southern Colonies.

1600   1650   1700   1750   1800

1640 First recorded case of slavery in Virginia

1715 Yamasee War begins.

MARYLAND (1634)

Potomac River

Chesapeake Bay

NANTICOKE

St. Mary's City

POWHATAN

VIRGINIA (1607)

Williamsburg

James River

FRENCH TERRITORY

TUTELO

TUSCARORA

SECOTAN

NORTH CAROLINA (1729)

CHEROKEE

Savannah River

CATAWBA

WACCAMAW

SOUTH CAROLINA (1729)

HITCHITI

GEORGIA (1732)

Charles Town

ATLANTIC OCEAN

CREEK (MUSKOGEE)

Savannah

YAMACRAW

YAMASEE

FLORIDA (SPAIN)

APPALACHIAN MOUNTAINS

N E S W

0   80   160 miles
0   80   160 kilometers

Virginia and Maryland

Starting with the Jamestown settlement, Virginia was the first colony in the American South. As Virginia's population grew, new settlements appeared west and north of the James River. This rich land was called the Tidewater. The Tidewater, a 75-mile-wide strip of Virginia's coast, often flooded. Despite the presence of salt water, the land is fertile. Settlers were able to make money growing tobacco. By 1700, the colony's population was 70,000.

In Virginia, the Church of England, also called the Anglican Church, was the established church of the colony. An established church is the official church of a nation or state. In Virginia, this meant that everyone had to pay a tax to the Anglican Church, even if they worshipped in another church.

In contrast to Virginia, Maryland was founded for religious reasons. In 1632, George Calvert, Lord Baltimore of England, decided to create a community especially for Roman Catholics. King Charles I granted Calvert land north of Virginia on which to start a colony. Calvert named the new colony "Maryland" in honor of the king's wife, Queen Henrietta Maria.

George Calvert died before he could visit the colony. As a result, his son Cecilius became the second Lord Baltimore. Cecilius decided to stay in England to make sure that the king continued to support a separate colony of Maryland. He sent his brother Leonard Calvert to Maryland in his place. Lord Leonard Calvert became the first governor of Maryland.

A tobacco field

In 1634, Leonard Calvert, along with about 300 colonists, arrived at St. Clement's Island in Maryland. Calvert bought a village from the Yoacomoco, a group of American Indians. The village became known as St. Mary's City. Calvert promised to trade fairly with the Yoacomoco and to protect them from their enemies.

On the land that the Yoacomoco cleared, the Maryland colonists and slaves planted corn and tobacco. As the colony grew, Maryland colonists, like those in Virginia, discovered the profitability of selling tobacco to England. By the late 1600s, plantations—large farms that grow one crop—lined many of the creeks and rivers of Maryland. Chesapeake Bay had a harbor that was deep enough for large ships to use. This made it easy to transport goods to other colonies and to England.

Most of the settlers who came to Maryland from England were Catholic. Many of Maryland's other settlers, however, came from Virginia and were members of the Church of England. Soon, Anglicans in Maryland outnumbered the Catholics. This meant that Catholics might have faced persecution. Fortunately, Maryland's charter—the Maryland Toleration Act, passed in 1649—protected them. This protection did not extend to Jews or to all Christians, but it was a significant stepping stone toward religious freedom in the colonies.

George Calvert, Lord Baltimore

Stop and Check

COLLABORATE

Talk Why did the people of Virginia and Maryland grow tobacco?

Find Details As you read add additional information to the graphic organizer on page 119 in your Inquiry Journal.

The Carolinas and Georgia

England kept adding to its North American colonies. The new king, Charles II, set his sights on land south of Virginia. In 1663, he gave a charter to eight **proprietors**. Seven years later, they founded their first settlement, the port city of Charles Towne.

From the beginning, Carolina had two regions. In the southern part, Charles Towne's natural harbor, warm climate, and natural resources made it a center for agriculture and trade. The southern part of Carolina also had large areas of low, marshy land—ideal for growing rice. Wealthy colonists built plantations outside the city. There they grew tobacco, rice, and indigo—a plant used to make blue dye.

Colonists who settled in northern Carolina grew tobacco and sold forest products, such as timber and tar. The economy in northern Carolina grew slowly due primarily to the lack of a good harbor, which made trade difficult. By 1729, the differences between colonial life in the north and in the south resulted in the colony splitting into North Carolina and South Carolina.

For years, the Tuscaroras had lived in northern Carolina's Coastal Plain. They were an agricultural tribe related to the Iroquois. The colonists had a habit of cheating the Tuscaroras in trade deals and moving in on their land. Tensions erupted in 1711 when Chief Hancock, a Tuscarora leader, killed a local surveyor. A surveyor is someone who determines land boundaries. The chief believed the surveyor had stolen Tuscarora land when he measured boundaries. The Tuscaroras then attacked settlements in the disputed area, named New Bern, killing more than 130 people. The colony's government sent troops to attack the Tuscaroras and forced them to surrender in 1713. Similarly, conflicts arose with the Yamasee, a tribe that had once been an ally to North Carolina. The Yamasee claimed the colonists owed them money. With a large army, the Yamasee attacked colonists in 1716. With help from the Cherokees, however, the colonists eventually defeated the Yamasee in 1717.

A rice field

Wasana Fromthong/EyeEm/Getty Images

Georgia, the last of the thirteen colonies created by the British, was founded in 1732. James Oglethorpe, a respected British general and member of the English Parliament, planned to use Georgia as a home for debtors. In England, debtors (people who owe money they can't repay) were sent to prison, often with their entire families. Oglethorpe thought that instead of wasting away in prison, debtors would be better off trying to make a fresh start for themselves as colonists.

James Oglethorpe

But it was Oglethorpe's military experience, rather than his plan for dealing with debtors, that most interested King George II. The King worried about an invasion of South Carolina by the Spaniards from Florida or by the French from Louisiana. When Oglethorpe suggested that the new colony could help protect South Carolina, the King listened and granted Oglethorpe his charter. In November of 1732, a group of 114 men, women, and children left London bound for the newest English colony in America. It was called Georgia after King George II.

Oglethorpe understood that the colony's success depended on establishing peaceful relations with the American Indians in the area. A Creek group—the Yamacraw—lived near Yamacraw Bluff, where Oglethorpe planned to build his first settlement. Oglethorpe befriended the Yamacraw's leader, Chief Tomochichi. He agreed to sell Oglethorpe Yamacraw Bluff. It was here that Oglethorpe built his settlement and named it Savannah.

Initially, Georgia's growth was slow. Oglethorpe's plan to settle Georgia with English debtors failed because few debtors took up the offer. In the beginning, colonists grew corn and tobacco. Later, rice and indigo became important crops.

✓ Stop and Check

Write How did land features affect the economies and population of North and South Carolina?

Find Details As you read, add additional information to the graphic organizer on page 119 in your Inquiry Journal.

Life in the Southern Colonies

Most Southern colonists lived on small farms with their families. Southern colonists who had once been indentured servants often ended up owning smaller farms. Every family member worked to keep the farm running. Religion was an important part of colonists' lives. Because colonists spent most of their time working, they often combined work with play. An entire community, for example, would get together to build houses for newly married people. Colonists held plowing and corn-husking competitions. At quilting bees, neighbors sewed together pieces of cloth to make a bedspread. When they were not helping their parents, children played with simple toys, such as balls, dolls, marbles, kites, and jump rope. In the evening, families often read books aloud, played music, or sang together.

Those who owned plantations, especially large plantations, lived a wealthy lifestyle. They hired workers or used slaves to keep the plantation running. Large plantation owners had great influence on government. Their view that the economy of the South would suffer without slaves was widely accepted in the region.

Large plantations were like small villages. Plantations often had a flourmill, a blacksmith, and a carpenter's shop. The planter's family lived in the center of the plantation, in a section called "the big house." Most plantations of the 1700s, however, were much smaller than the one shown in the diagram, with the average planter owning about 20 slaves. Male family members helped the planter manage the land and crops. The women worked to feed and care for everyone on the plantation. Most children on plantations were educated at home.

A plantation in the Southern Colonies

By 1750, slaves had been living in the Southern Colonies for more than a hundred years. Although many slaves worked on small farms, most worked on large plantations.

In contrast to plantation owners, slaves lived in small, poorly made cabins near the crop fields. The work on plantations started at sunrise and ended at sundown. The overseer was the man hired by the plantation owner to oversee, or manage, work in the fields. The overseer told slaves what to do. The overseer also harshly punished people.

Slaves on Southern tobacco plantations did the backbreaking work of planting tobacco, caring for it, and then harvesting it. In South Carolina, slaves often had to move tons of dirt to build rice fields and irrigation canals. To help overcome the harshness of their lives, slaves often turned to family. On Sundays, usually the only day of the week they did not work, some slave parents could visit their children who had been sold away from them. However, this was only if the children lived on neighboring plantations. When families were together, they told stories and sang songs that mainly taught about values and beliefs. The

A colonial-style cabin

stories about Africa gave children a sense of a different past. Sadly, these slave families were not officially recognized under the law.

Not all African Americans in the Southern Colonies were enslaved. About five percent were free. Some had been freed, while others had escaped. Some bought their freedom by working paid jobs. Free African Americans lived in cities and towns. They also lived in the backcountry— the eastern foothills of the Appalachian Mountains. There, many lived in friendship with local American Indians.

✓ Stop and Check

Talk How did the economy of the Southern Colonies affect the lives of the various people living there?

Find Details As you read, add additional information to the graphic organizer on page 119 in your Inquiry Journal.

An Inhumane System

The type of work assigned to slaves depended on the economy of the colony in which they lived. In the North, many of the slaves worked in New England's busy shipyards. In Rhode Island and New York, slaves did farm work. It was rare for a Northerner to own more than one slave. Northern farms were small, and it was not profitable to use large numbers of slaves there.

Southern farms, on the other hand, were often huge and grew cash crops. The major cash crop of the Southern Colonies in the 1600s was tobacco. Both rice and tobacco required many workers to plant, tend, and harvest the crop. Most Southern plantations had about 20 slaves. South Carolina was unusual. By 1720, slaves made up more than half of the population of the colony.

The possibility of slave rebellions was a constant fear for colonial leaders. Leaders in states with large enslaved populations were especially concerned. In part to ease those worries, colonies and later states wrote laws defining the status of slaves and the rights of their owners. These laws were called slave codes. The purpose of the slave codes was to place harsh restrictions on slaves and give owners absolute power over them. The slave codes varied from colony to colony. Most prevented the slaves from learning to read and write. Most states also prevented them from leaving the plantation without permission, testifying in court, or gathering together without a white person being present.

Slave auction block

Slaves had been kidnapped, forced to work, separated from their families, and punished harshly. Slaves resisted their situation by slowing their work, running away, and on occasion rebelling violently.

Despite the hardships they suffered through, slaves managed to build a culture. They orally passed down African traditions, introduced African words into the English language, and told stories to their children to teach them about life. They also created many work songs and spirituals that are still sung to this day.

PHOTO: McGraw-Hill Education; TEXT: Slave Songs of the United States, compiled by William Francis Allen, Charles Pickard Ware, and Lucy McKim Garrison, 59. New York: A. Simpson & Company, 1867.

In Their Words... African Slaves

Slaves working in the fields often sang work songs to relieve their boredom and to take their minds off their exhaustion. These songs sometimes had a "call and response" structure, in which one person sang a verse and the others responded with a chorus. Many lyrics featured Christian themes and dialect, or language that is specific to a region or group of people. The songs often focused on the peace and relief that a person could find in the afterlife.

Here are lyrics for two songs sung by slaves in the South:

I Don't Feel Weary

Chorus
I don't feel weary and noways tired,
O glory hallelujah

Verses
Just let me in the kingdom
While the world is all on fire
O glory hallelujah

Going to live with God forever
While the world is all on fire
O glory hallelujah

And keep the ark a-moving
While the world is all on fire
O glory hallelujah

In the Mansions Above

Chorus
Good Lord, in the mansions above,
Good Lord, in the mansions above,
My Lord, I hope to meet my Jesus
In the mansions above.

Verses
If you get to heaven before I do,
tell my Jesus I'm a-comin' too,
To the mansions above.

My Lord, I've had many trials here below;
My Lord, I hope to meet you
In the mansions above.

Fight on, my brother, for the mansions above,
For I hope to meet my Jesus there
In the mansions above.

 Stop and Check

Write How did the colony where slaves lived affect the kind of work they had to do?

Find Details As you read, add additional information to the graphic organizer on page 119 in your Inquiry Journal.

The Triangular Trade and Slavery

England, Africa, and the Americas

Triangular trade is the term used to describe the trade routes between England, Africa, and the Americas during the 1700s. Shipowners wanted their ships to carry cargo on every voyage so that they could cover the costs of travel. The triangular trade was designed for traders to sell products and pick up cargo at each stop. In the first stage, ships from England left bound for West Africa. The ships carried goods, such as guns, cloth, ironware and rum, all made in England. Upon reaching the African coast, these goods were traded for African men, women, and children kidnapped by slave traders or purchased from African chiefs.

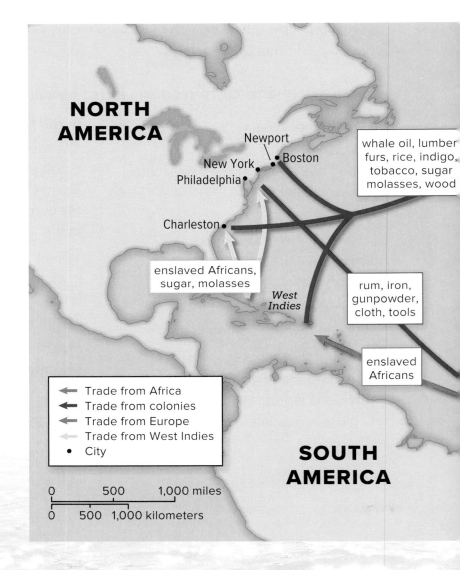

NORTH AMERICA

Newport
Boston
New York
Philadelphia

Charleston

whale oil, lumber furs, rice, indigo, tobacco, sugar molasses, wood

enslaved Africans, sugar, molasses

West Indies

rum, iron, gunpowder, cloth, tools

enslaved Africans

SOUTH AMERICA

← Trade from Africa
← Trade from colonies
← Trade from Europe
← Trade from West Indies
• City

0   500   1,000 miles
0   500 1,000 kilometers

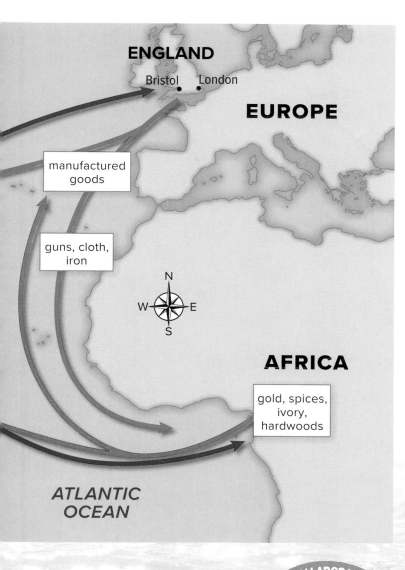

ENGLAND

Bristol   London

EUROPE

manufactured
goods

guns, cloth,
iron

N
W E
S

AFRICA

gold, spices,
ivory,
hardwoods

ATLANTIC
OCEAN

In the second stage, European traders bought African slaves. Family members were separated. Traders held slaves until a ship appeared. Traders then sold the slaves to a European or African captain. The captain went through the long process of filling the ship.

When the ship was filled, the "Middle Passage"—the journey to the Caribbean Islands or North America—began. The journey was horrific. Many Africans died. Some committed suicide.

In the Americas, slaves were sold at auctions to the highest bidders. Two-thirds of African slaves were taken to the Americas. With the money made from the sale of slaves, goods such as sugar, cotton, and tobacco were purchased in North America and the Caribbean Islands and shipped back to England for sale.

✓ Stop and Check

COLLABORATE

Talk Why do you think people called the journey from Africa to the Americas the "Middle Passage"?

Map and Globe Skills

The Thirteen Colonies: Then and Now

The United States has steadily grown in population since the Constitution was ratified in 1788. Historians estimate that around four million people lived in the United States in 1790. In 2015, the nation had a population over 320 million. The maps in this section will allow you to investigate some of the changes that occurred in the two centuries since the writing of the Constitution.

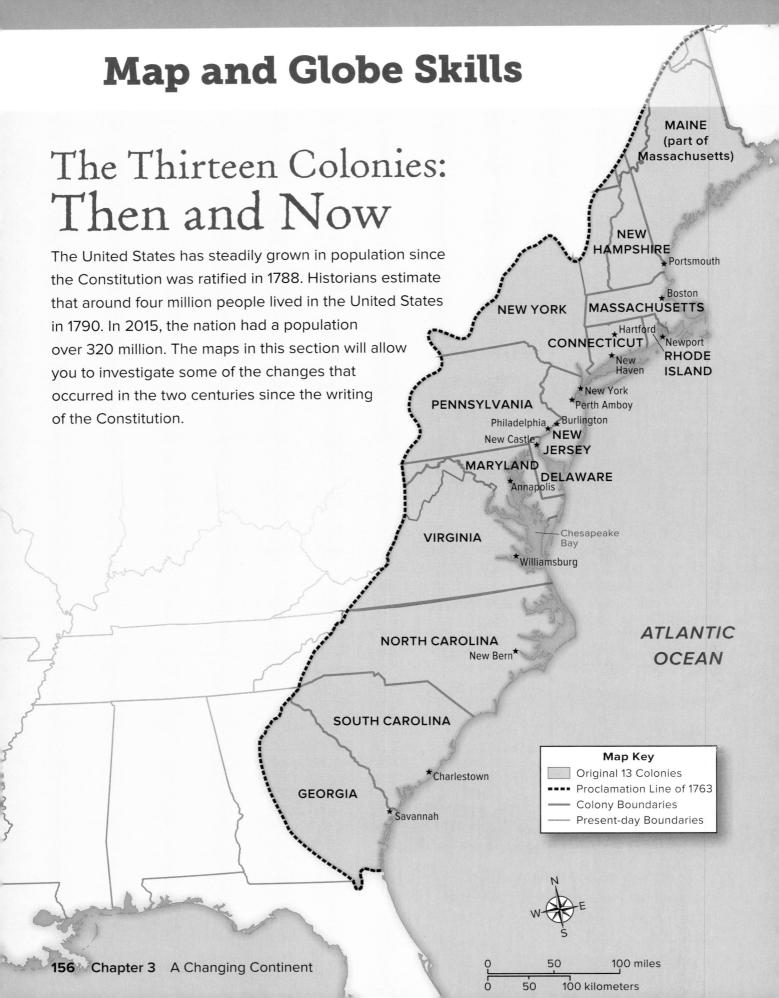

MAINE
(part of Massachusetts)

NEW HAMPSHIRE

★ Portsmouth

NEW YORK

MASSACHUSETTS

★ Boston

★ Hartford

CONNECTICUT

★ Newport

★ New Haven

RHODE ISLAND

★ New York

★ Perth Amboy

PENNSYLVANIA

Philadelphia ★

★ Burlington

New Castle ★

NEW JERSEY

MARYLAND

DELAWARE

★ Annapolis

VIRGINIA

Chesapeake Bay

★ Williamsburg

ATLANTIC OCEAN

NORTH CAROLINA

New Bern ★

SOUTH CAROLINA

★ Charlestown

GEORGIA

★ Savannah

Map Key

- Original 13 Colonies
- ▪▪▪▪ Proclamation Line of 1763
- Colony Boundaries
- Present-day Boundaries

N W E S

0   50   100 miles

0   50   100 kilometers

Connecticut

1790 Population: 237,946
2015 Population: 3,590,886
★ **Capital:** Hartford

Delaware

1790 Population: 59,096
2015 Population: 945,934
★ **Capital:** Dover

Georgia

1790 Population: 82,548
2015 Population: 10,214,860
★ **Capital:** Atlanta

Maryland

1790 Population: 319,728
2015 Population: 6,006,401
★ **Capital:** Annapolis

Massachussettes

1790 Population: 378,787
2015 Population: 6,794,422
★ **Capital:** Boston

New Hampshire

1790 Population: 141,885
2015 Population: 1,330,608
★ **Capital:** Concord

New Jersey

1790 Population: 184,139
2015 Population: 8,958,013
★ **Capital:** Trenton

New York

1790 Population: 340,120
2015 Population: 19,795,791
★ **Capital:** Albany

North Carolina

1790 Population: 393,751
2015 Population: 10,042,802
★ **Capital:** Raleigh

Pennsylvania

1790 Population: 434,373
2015 Population: 12,802,503
★ **Capital:** Harrisburg

Rhode Island

1790 Population: 68,825
2015 Population: 1,056,298
★ **Capital:** Providence

South Carolina

1790 Population: 249,073
2015 Population: 4,896,146
★ **Capital:** Columbia

Virginia

1790 Population: 747,610
2015 Population: 8,382,993
★ **Capital:** Richmond

✓ Stop and Check

Think Using the Thirteen Colonies map and the information for each state, note which states have different capitals than they had in 1788. What reasons might a state have for moving its capital?

Connections in Action!

Back to the EQ

Think about the Chapter EQ, **"How Did European Settlements Impact North America?"**

- **Talk** with a partner about what you learned in the chapter. Choose two settlements to compare and contrast. Consider each settlement's relations with local American Indians, its location, its economy, and its form of government.

- Which settlement was more successful and in what ways? What do you think led to its success?

- **Share** your ideas with the class. Then have a discussion about the different types of settlements and governments in early America.

More to Explore

How Can You Make an IMPACT?

Compare and Contrast

Work as a group to organize your notes about each early North American settlement. To help you discuss the settlements, fill in a five-column chart with the headings Origin, Parent Country, Relations with American Indians, Successes, and Failures.

Write an Encyclopedia Entry

Use your research to write an encyclopedia entry about one early North American settlement. Include the story of its founding, information about its relations with local American Indians, and facts and statistics about its population, economy, location, and so on.

Word Play

Using the words from the chapter Word Bank, create lists of synonyms, or words that have the same or nearly the same meaning. For example, synonyms for *assembly* may include *council* and *congregation*. Keep your list handy and add to it as you read the next chapters.

McGraw-Hill Education

The Road to War

ESSENTIAL EQ QUESTION

Why Would a Nation Want to Become Independent?

In this chapter, you'll read about the conflicts that arose between the American colonies and Great Britain. You'll learn about how colonists were divided between wanting independence and wanting reconciliation with Great Britain, and you'll discover what ultimately led them down the road to war.

Step into the Time Chronological Thinking

Look at the time line. What was happening in other parts of the world while the American colonists were beginning to rebel against British rule?

1754
The French and
Indian War
begins.

1763
Treaty of Paris ends the
French and Indian War.
1763
Proclamation of 1763 sets aside
land west of the Appalachians
for American Indians.

Americas

| 1730 | 1740 | 1750 | 1760 |

World Events

1736
Ṣafavid Empire ends in
Persia (modern-day Iran).

1735
Qianlong
becomes
emperor of
China.

1740–1741
Cold weather and poor
harvests kill more than a
third of the population in
Ireland.

1760
George III
becomes ruler of
Great Britain.

HSS.5.3.3, HSS.5.4.7, HSS.5.5.1, HAS.CS.1

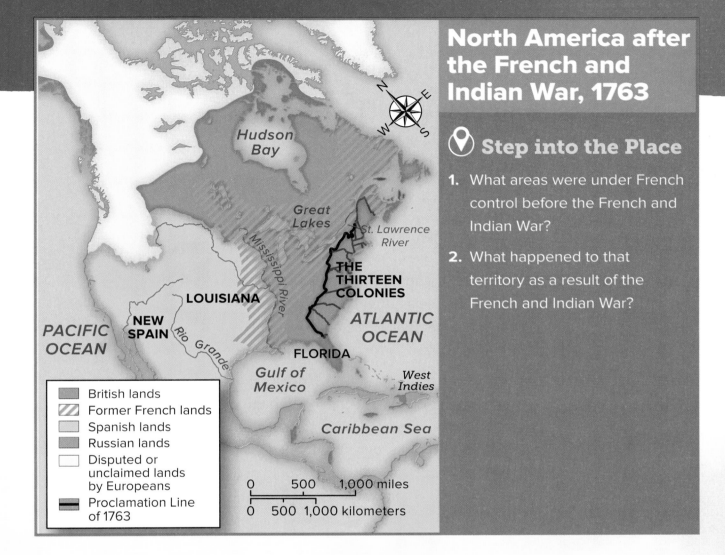

North America after the French and Indian War, 1763

Map legend:
- British lands
- Former French lands
- Spanish lands
- Russian lands
- Disputed or unclaimed lands by Europeans
- Proclamation Line of 1763

Map labels: Hudson Bay, Great Lakes, St. Lawrence River, THE THIRTEEN COLONIES, Mississippi River, LOUISIANA, NEW SPAIN, Rio Grande, PACIFIC OCEAN, FLORIDA, Gulf of Mexico, ATLANTIC OCEAN, West Indies, Caribbean Sea

Scale: 0 500 1,000 miles / 0 500 1,000 kilometers

Step into the Place

1. What areas were under French control before the French and Indian War?

2. What happened to that territory as a result of the French and Indian War?

Timeline:

1765 Parliament passes the Stamp Act and the Quartering Act.

1767 Parliament passes the Townshend Acts.

1769–1770 British captain James Cook explores Australia and New Zealand.

1770

1772 Samuel Adams forms the first Committee of Correspondence.

1773 Colonists protest the Tea Act with the Boston Tea Party.

1774 Joseph Priestley of Great Britain becomes the first scientist to publish a description of the chemical element oxygen.

1774 The First Continental Congress meets.

1775

Connect Through Literature

excerpt from

Johnny Tremain

by Esther Forbes

Salt Water Tea

On Sundays, the boys might relax a little, breakfast when they pleased, only they must turn up clean and shining in time to go to church with Aunt and Uncle and listen to the inflammatory Reverend Sam Cooper. Doctor Cooper was putting more politics than gospel into his sermons that fall and more fear of "taxation without representation' than God into his congregation.

England had, by the fall of 1773, gone far in adjusting the grievances of her American colonies. But she insisted upon a small tax on tea. Little money would be collected by this tax. It worked no hardship on the people's pocketbooks: only threepence the pound. The stubborn colonists, who were insisting they would not be taxed unless they could vote for the men who taxed them, would hardly realize that the tax had been paid by the East India Company in London before the tea was shipped over here. After all, thought Parliament, the Americans were yokels and farmers—not political thinkers. And the East India tea, even after that tax was paid, would be better and cheaper than any the Americans ever had. Weren't the Americans, after all, human beings? Wouldn't they care more for their pocketbooks than their principles?

Shivering—for the last week in November was bitterly cold—Johnny built up the fires in the attic. From the back window, he could see that the roofs of the African Queen were white with frost.

A sharp rat-tat on the shop door below woke Rab.

"What time's it?" he grumbled, as people do who think they are disturbed too early Sunday morning.

"Seven and past. I'll see what's up."

It was Sam Adams himself. When either cold or excited, his palsy increased. His head and hands were shaking. But his strong, seamed face, which always looked cheerful, today looked radiant. Sam Adams was so pleased that Johnny, a little naively, thought he must have word that Parliament had backed down again. The expected tea ships had not sailed.

"Look you, Johnny. I know its Lord's Day, but there is a placard I must have printed and posted secretly tonight. The Sons of Liberty will take care of the posting, but Mr. Lorne must see to the printing. Could you run across and ask him to step over? And Rab—where's he?"

Rab was coming down the ladder.

"What's up?" said Rab sleepily.

"The first of the tea ships, the *Dartmouth*, is entering the harbor. She'll be at castle Island by nightfall."

"So they dared send them?"

"Yes."

"And the first has come?"

"Yes. God give us strength to resist. That tea cannot be allowed to land."

When Johnny got back with Mr. Lorne, Rab had Mr. Adams's text in his hands, reading it as a printer reads, thinking first of spacing the capitals, not of the meaning.

"I can set that in no time. Two hundred copies? They'll be fairly dry by nightfall."

"Ah, Mr. Lorne," said Adams, shaking hands, "without your printer the cause of liberty would be lost forever."

"Without you"—Mr. Lorne's voice shook with emotion—"there would not have been any belief in liberty to lose. I will, as always, do anything—everything you wish."

"I got word before day. It's the *Dartmouth* and she will be as far as Castle Island by nightfall. If that tea is landed—if that tea is paid—everything is lost. The selectmen will meet all day today and I am calling a mass meeting for tomorrow. This is the placard I will put up."

He took it from Rab's hand and read:

> Friends! Brethren! Countrymen! That worst of Plagues, the detested tea shipped for the Port by the East India Company, is now arrived in the Harbour: The hour of destruction, of manly opposition to the machinations of Tyranny, stares you in the Face; Every Friend to his Country, to Himself, and to Posterity, is now called up to meet at Faneuil Hall, at nine o'clock this day [that, of course, is tomorrow Monday], at which time the bells will ring to make united and successful resistance to the last, worst, and most destructive measure of Administration . . . Boston, Nov. 29, 1773.

Then he said quietly: "Up to the last moment—up to the eleventh hour, we will beg the Governor's permission for the ship's return to London with their cargo. We have twenty days."

Johnny knew that by law any cargo that was not unloaded within twenty days might be seized by the custom-house and sold at auction.

"Mr. Lorne, needless to say the Observers will meet tonight. There are private decisions to be made before the mass meeting tomorrow at nine."

Johnny pricked up his ears. Ever since he had come to Mr. Lorne's (and Rab said he might be trusted with anything possible with men's lives) he had now and then summoned the members of the Observers' Club. They were so close to treason they kept no list of members. Rab made Johnny memorize the twenty-two names. They met in Rab and Johnny's attic.

"Johnny," said Mr. Lorne, anxious and over-anxious to please Mr. Adams, "start right out."

"No, sir, if you please. Noon will be better. That will give the members time to get home from church. And as usual, Johnny, make no stir. Simply say, 'Mr. So and So owes eight shillings for his newspaper.'"

Johnny nodded. That meant the meeting would be tonight at eight o'clock. If he said one pound eight shillings, it would mean the next night at eight. Two pounds, three and six would mean the day after at three-thirty. It gave him a feeling of excitement and please to be even on the fringes of great, secret, dangerous events.

Think About It

1. How would you describe Johnny's role in the resistance?

2. Why do you think the Sons of Liberty used Johnny in this role?

3. Why is Sam Adams so determined to stop the arrival of the tea?

People You Should Know

James Logan

The son of Chief Shikellamy of the Oneida people, James Logan was a respected figure in the Pennsylvania colony. His good relationship with the white settlers in the area of the Ohio River Valley lasted until 1774. At that time, a trader murdered Logan's family during the Yellow Creek Massacre. This treachery sparked the conflict that came to be called Lord Dunmore's War between the American Indians and European settlers. Later, he helped the British army during the American Revolution.

Sarah Bradlee Fulton

Called "Mother of the Boston Tea Party," Sarah Bradlee Fulton used her own kitchen as a meeting place for the men who dumped tea into Boston Harbor on December 16, 1773. She and other "Daughters of Liberty" showed similar resistance to the British throughout the revolution that was to come. She organized women to nurse wounded soldiers after the Battle of Bunker Hill and acted as a courier, crossing enemy lines and risking her own life during the Revolutionary War.

North Wind Picture Archives

William Pitt, the Elder

PONTIAC.

Chief Pontiac

A British leader, William Pitt was a mastermind of Great Britain's strategy in the Seven Years' War, which included the French and Indian War. Pitt convinced Parliament to put him in charge, to give him almost unlimited resources, and to let him completely restructure the British military in order to win the conflict. His strategies worked, and Great Britain won the war. They also left Britain with tremendous debt that Britain wanted the colonists to help pay for. Later, Pitt spoke out against Britain's taxing the colonists without allowing them to be represented in Parliament.

A chief of the Ottawa people of the Great Lakes region, Pontiac forged an alliance to beat back the British in the conflict known as Pontiac's War (1763–1766). His alliance included almost all of the American Indian tribes between Lake Superior and the lower Mississippi. His strategy was fairly successful at first, but years of fighting took their toll. Pontiac signed a peace treaty with the British in 1766.

What Caused the Conflict between Great Britain, France, and the American Indians?

Conflict in the Ohio River Valley

In the early 1700s, England and France were each creating colonial empires in North America. England, which became Great Britain in 1707, established thirteen colonies between the Atlantic Coast and the Appalachian Mountains. These British colonies had a large, growing population and a vigorous economy based on farming and trade. The colonies of New France consisted of two areas: what is now Canada and also Louisiana in the Mississippi River Valley. New France was far larger than the British colonies in total land area but much smaller in population. Most colonists in New France were involved in the fur trade.

By the mid-1700s, the British and French colonists were coming into conflict. The French fur traders wanted to preserve the forested wilderness as it was. As the British colonists needed more land for farming, the French feared that British farmers would cut down the trees, ruining the **habitat** of fur-bearing animals.

(t)McGraw-Hill Education

HSS.5.3.1, HSS.5.3.2, HSS.5.3.3, HSS.5.3.4, HSS.5.3.5, HSS.5.3.6, HSS.5.5.1, HAS.HI.3

168   Lesson 1   What Caused the Conflict between Great Britain, France, and the American Indians?

Time Line

1754
War breaks out between British and French settlers in the upper Ohio River Valley.

1763
The Treaty of Paris ends the French and Indian War.

1763–1764
Ottawa leader Chief Pontiac leads resistance to the British.

1766
Pontiac and the British agree to a peace treaty.

1750 | | | 1755 | | | 1760 | | | 1765 | | | 1770 | | | 1775 | | | | |

1759
A British victory at the Battle of Quebec is a turning point in the war.

Ivy Close Images/Alamy

In 1757, the Oneida, Seneca, and other tribes crossed Lake Champlain to aid the French.

American Indian groups were drawn into this struggle. They wanted to protect their ways of life. As a result, they became allies with either the French or the British. The Algonquin and Huron (also called Wyandot) groups sided with the French. These American Indians also wanted to preserve the forested wilderness and forest animals from British settlers. In addition, the French had aided the Algonquin and Huron in their struggles with their traditional enemies, the Iroquois Confederacy. The Iroquois sided with the British because they were angry at the French for helping their enemies.

The focus of the struggle between the French and the British, and their American Indian allies, was the upper Ohio River Valley. In firm control of the territories of New France, French settlers had spread southward into the Great Lakes region. They established a major outpost there at Detroit in 1701. By the 1750s, farmers and traders from the British colonies of Virginia and Pennsylvania had begun to cross the Appalachian Mountains, moving into the lands beyond. To halt this advance, the French built a line of forts from Lake Erie to western Pennsylvania. The British saw the forts as a threat and decided to try to drive the French out.

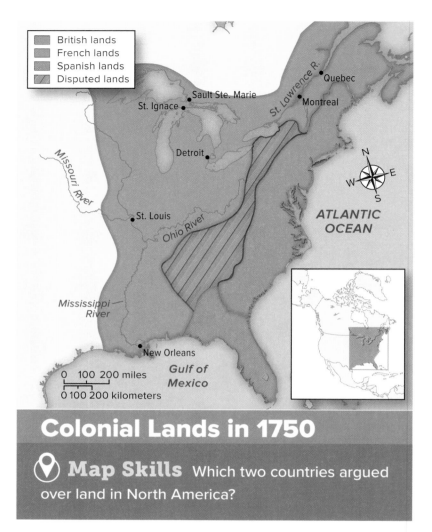

Legend:
- British lands
- French lands
- Spanish lands
- Disputed lands

St. Lawrence R.
Quebec
Sault Ste. Marie
St. Ignace
Montreal
Detroit
Missouri River
St. Louis
Ohio River
ATLANTIC OCEAN
Mississippi River
New Orleans
Gulf of Mexico

0 100 200 miles
0 100 200 kilometers

Colonial Lands in 1750

 Map Skills Which two countries argued over land in North America?

✓ Stop and Check

Think How did France's choice of allies among American Indians cause the Iroquois to become allies of the British?

Find Details As you read, add additional information to the graphic organizer on page 137 in your Inquiry Journal.

The Battle at Fort Duquesne

Robert Dinwiddie was the lieutenant governor of the British colony of Virginia. He wanted to convince the British government in London of the seriousness of the French threat in the Ohio Valley. So, in early 1754, Dinwiddie sent 22-year-old George Washington with a small force to strengthen a British **outpost** at the site of what is now the city of Pittsburgh. As Washington neared the fort, he discovered that French troops had already seized it and renamed it Fort Duquesne (doo KAIN).

Washington quickly built a temporary post in the area and named it Fort Necessity. From this base, Washington's troops launched a successful attack against the French on May 28, 1754. But the French counterattacked on July 3, forcing Washington to surrender. He and his men were allowed to return to Virginia, and the French destroyed Fort Necessity. The French and Indian War had begun.

An early map of Fort Duquesne, later renamed Fort Pitt

Back in Virginia, Washington found his defeat had not harmed his reputation. The colonial government thanked him for his efforts, and he was named head of Virginia's militia on the frontier. Washington remarked in a letter to his brother, "I have heard the bullets whistle; and believe me, there is something charming in the sound."

Stop and Check

COLLABORATE

Talk How did Washington's expedition into the Ohio Valley support Robert Dinwiddie's views about the French? Discuss your opinion with a partner.

The French Gain the Upper Hand

The early phase of the war was marked by French victories. Their American Indian allies taught the French how to make surprise attacks from behind trees and rocks. By contrast, British troops, who marched into battle in formation, were easy targets. Such British tactics resulted in disaster in 1755 when General Edward Braddock led another group of British troops against Fort Duquesne. Colonel George Washington rode alongside Braddock. On July 9, the French and their allies ambushed the British force in the wilderness. British losses were severe. Some 900 of their 1,400 troops were killed or wounded, including nearly all the officers. Braddock himself was fatally wounded. Now in command, Washington was able to lead the remaining British forces to safety.

The French continued to be victorious. In 1756, their commander Louis-Joseph de Montcalm led a force of French soldiers and American Indians in the capture of an important British post, Fort Oswego, in the Great Lakes region. Montcalm reported that he had taken 1,600 prisoners and seized 100 cannon, six armed vessels, and a two-year supply of food. "All this cost us only 30 men killed and wounded," he said. Montcalm's victory gave the French full control of Lake Ontario. The following year, he captured another British post, Fort William Henry, which was near present-day Lake George, New York.

An engraving depicting the evacuation of Fort Duquesne, 1758

✓ Stop and Check

Think What was the major cause of French success in the early part of the French and Indian War?

The Print Collector/Alamy

The Turning Point

News of French victories shocked the British colonies. The colonists begged the British Prime Minister, William Pitt, for more help. Pitt believed that the war in North America was critical to the overall struggle between Great Britain and France. The two nations were also at war in Europe. Pitt convinced the British government to pour more money, troops, and other supplies into the conflict. In addition, the British navy blockaded ports in New France, cutting off shipments of food and other supplies to French colonists. Finally, both British soldiers and American colonial militias became skilled in fighting the way American Indians did in the wilderness. All of these factors changed the course of the war.

In 1758, British troops defeated the French at Louisbourg, Nova Scotia. Several months later, Colonel John Bradstreet led the British to victory over the French in a battle at Fort Frontenac on Lake Ontario. In November, the British finally retook Fort Duquesne. They renamed it Fort Pitt in honor of the British prime minister. In 1759, Sir William Johnson forced the French to surrender Fort Niagara. British General Jeffery Amherst then defeated the French at Fort Ticonderoga near Lake Champlain in upstate New York.

Then and Now

The city of Pittsburgh, Pennsylvania, was built around Fort Pitt. The land where Fort Pitt used to be is now a public park, though the brick outline of the old fort is still intact. The site is also home to the Fort Pitt Museum, which presents the story of western Pennsylvania's essential role in the French and Indian War as well as the American Revolution.

Fort Pitt in 1758 (background) and Fort Pitt Block House today (top-right)

(t)McGraw-Hill Education; (bkgd)White, Edward, ed. "Fort Pitt and Pittsburgh in 1759." Frontispiece in 150 years of Unparalleled Thrift...Image copyright 1908 by Pittsburgh Photo Engraving Company, Historic Pittsburgh Book Collection/Historic Pittsburgh.org.; (inset)Amy Cicconi/Alamy

The climax of the war came in June 1759 when the British moved against the French stronghold at Quebec. The city of Quebec is located on steep cliffs above the St. Lawrence River. Both the river's strong currents and the fortress's cannon protected it. A British assault at the end of July failed. British commander James Wolfe decided on a daring plan—a surprise attack.

During the early hours of September 13, 1759, Wolfe landed an advance force in darkness. These soldiers climbed the steep cliffs and captured a French outpost. By morning, Wolfe's entire force was assembled on the Plains of Abraham outside the city. Like Wolfe, French commander Montcalm also decided to take a risk. He attacked immediately instead of waiting for reinforcements. The two armies both numbered about 4,500 men. However, Wolfe's troops were professional soldiers, while Montcalm's were volunteers. The battlefield was not forested wilderness, but open country. The careful musket fire of Wolfe's troops halted the advance of the French and then caused them to retreat. Both Montcalm and Wolfe were fatally wounded in the battle.

On September 18, the French surrendered Quebec City. A year later, the French surrendered their last stronghold, Montreal. The British now controlled New France.

British troops attack Quebec.

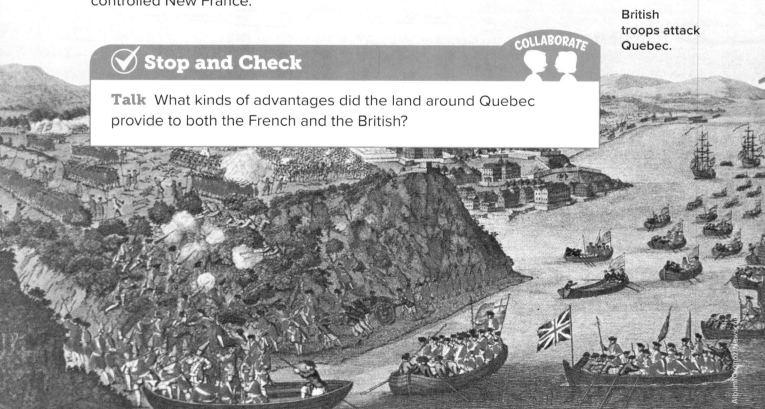

✓ Stop and Check

COLLABORATE

Talk What kinds of advantages did the land around Quebec provide to both the French and the British?

Outcomes and Aftermath

The French tried to retake Quebec in 1762 but failed. In Europe, meanwhile, Great Britain and France continued their war. Spain aided the French and, in return, France agreed to give Spain much of the Louisiana Territory. By 1763, the French were ready to negotiate a peace treaty with Great Britain. The Treaty of Paris was signed on February 10, 1763.

In October 1763, news of the Treaty of Paris reached North America. The defeated French could no longer aid American Indians in their resistance to British settlers. However, Great Britain wanted to keep down the cost of defending its American colonies. To stop British settlements in the Ohio River Valley, British King George III issued the Proclamation of 1763. This official order set aside all British land west of the Appalachian Mountains for American Indians. This decision satisfied the native peoples but angered American colonists hungry for land.

North America, 1750 and 1763

Map Skills Which European power lost the most land in North America from 1750 to 1763? Which two European powers gained the most land?

McGraw-Hill Education

By 1760, although the British were defeating the French in North America, their control over the lands was not firm. Some of the American Indian allies of the French decided to resist British rule. The most important leader of this resistance was Pontiac. He was a member of the Ottawa, an Algonquin-speaking group whose homeland was in what is now northern Michigan and parts of Canada. As French outposts in Ottawa territory were surrendered to the British, Pontiac agreed not to attack British troops if they treated him with respect. His experience with the British convinced Pontiac, however, that they were a threat. Soon, settlers would follow these troops, Pontiac correctly believed. The settlers would want to turn Ottawa hunting grounds into farms.

In 1762, Pontiac organized almost every American Indian group from Lake Superior to the lower Mississippi River Valley. The plan, which Pontiac announced in early 1763, was for each group to attack the nearest British outpost. Then, all the American Indians would combine in a general attack on the British settlements. Pontiac himself was to attack Detroit. Although his attack on Detroit failed, the American Indians were successful in seizing many other British outposts and destroying frontier settlements. British troops struck back, though, and by 1764 American Indian resistance to the British in the Great Lakes region had ended.

As a result of the French and Indian War, British colonists saw themselves in a new way. They had helped fight a powerful enemy and had won. They also proved that they had strong leaders, such as George Washington. They had learned that the British colonies could unite in a common effort. This gave them a feeling of strength.

PRIMARY SOURCE

In Their Words... Pontiac

It is important for us, my brothers, that we exterminate from our lands this nation which seeks only to destroy us. You see as well as I that we can no longer supply our needs, as we have done from our brothers, the French.

—from a speech by Pontiac to the Ottawa people in May 1763

TEXT: Pontiac. 5 May 1763. Quoted in Michigan Society of the Colonial Wars, M. Agnes Burton, ed., Journal of Pontiac's Conspiracy, 1763 (Detroit, MI: Clarence Monroe Burton, 1912), 38.
PHOTO: North Wind Picture Archives/Alamy

The colonists also saw their relationship with Great Britain in a new light. They were angry with the British government for the Proclamation of 1763. Many colonists ignored the order and continued to cross the Appalachians to settle in the lands reserved for American Indians. The colonists knew that they could rely very little on British protection from American Indian attacks. In the end, the effect of the French and Indian War would be to unite the colonists in opposition to British government policy. Soon, this would lead them to fight for their own independence.

George Washington leads an attack on a French encampment.

PRIMARY SOURCE

In Their Words... George Washington

The Virginia troops showed a good deal of bravery, and were nearly all killed; for I believe, out of three companies that were there, scarcely thirty men are left alive. ... I luckily escaped without a wound, though I had four bullets through my coat, and two horses shot under me.

—from George Washington's letter to his mother about Braddock's defeat, July 18, 1755

✓ Stop and Check

Talk Why didn't the British colonists obey the Proclamation of 1763? Were they right or wrong to disobey it?

TEXT: Washington, George. George Washington to his mother, Mary Ball, 14 July 1755. In Some Old Historic Landmarks of Virginia and Maryland... by W.H. Snowden, p. 121. Alexandria, VA: G.H. Ramey & Sons, 1904.
PHOTO: (t)McGraw-Hill Education, (b)North Wind Picture Archives/Alamy

What Were the Views of the Patriots, Loyalists, and the British?

New Taxes

Great Britain's 1763 victory in the French and Indian War came at a great cost. The war doubled Britain's debt, which reached 122 million pounds in 1763. Adding to the cost were the British troops left behind to protect the colonies from further conflict. King George III, who had been on the throne for only three years, struggled to find ways to pay the massive debt.

George III was a young king determined to make his mark as a strong ruler. He surrounded himself with advisors who agreed he should rule the colonies with a firm hand. British citizens already paid high taxes. The advisors argued that it was only fair to tax colonists to help pay for Britain's protection during and after the war.

Parliament, the British legislature, passed the Sugar Act in 1764. It forced the colonists to pay a tax on all sugar products. An older British tax on sugar products already existed, but the British government had never enforced it. With the new Sugar Act, any colonist who refused to pay was arrested and fined. However, the Sugar Act did not bring in enough money to make a significant impact on Britain's debt.

(t)McGraw-Hill Education

HSS.5.5.1, HSS.5.5.4, HAS.HI.1, HAS.HI.4

178 Lesson 2 What Were the Views of the Patriots, Loyalists, and the British?

Time Line

1763 February Treaty of Paris ends the French and Indian War.

1763 October Proclamation of 1763 sets aside land west of the Appalachians for American Indians.

1764 Parliament passes the Sugar Act.

1765 Parliament passes the Stamp Act.

52 | 1763 | 1764 | 1765

In the 1760s and 1770s, the British Parliament passed tax laws that made many colonists unhappy.

One year later, Parliament passed the Stamp Act. It forced colonists to buy stamps for all printed documents. This included everyday paper products such as letters, newspapers, pamphlets, and even playing cards.

Many colonists were furious. They disagreed with Britain's **imposing** the tax on them. Colonists complained that Parliament passed the new tax laws without colonists' consent, or agreement. One strong opponent of the tax laws was Samuel Adams of Massachusetts. Adams sent protest letters to newspapers and addressed delegates from the colony's assembly. In one letter, he stated, "If our trade may be taxed, why not our lands? Why not . . . everything we possess or use?"

A British stamp used on printed documents

Chart Skills

GDP is the Gross Domestic Product, the total value of all goods and services a country produces in a year. When a country owes more in debt than it produces in a year, it can take a long time for the country to pay down its debt.

Source: ukpublicspending.co.uk

The Growth of Britain's Debt

Year	British Debt as a Percentage of GDP
1700	23
1710	34
1720	83
1730	76
1740	68
1750	107
1760	132
1770	126

✓ Stop and Check

Talk How did Britain plan on paying the war debt?

Find Details As you read, add additional information to the graphic organizer on page 145 in your Inquiry Journal.

Photo Researchers, Inc/Alamy

The Colonies Respond

Colonists were still British citizens. Since the British government had spent money to protect these citizens, Parliament believed that the colonists should pay for the French and Indian War in the form of taxes. Many colonists saw the Stamp Act as taxation without representation. That meant they were forced to pay taxes approved by officials they had not elected. Colonists who demanded that Americans have more control of their government were known as Patriots.

Before these tax laws, only colonial legislatures had taxed colonists. Colonists had accepted those taxes because they had elected the officials. These officials, they argued, were the only ones who should be allowed to tax goods. To make matters worse, the tax money collected from the colonists went to Britain instead of the colonial governments.

Every colony protested the new tax law. In Boston, some colonists formed a group to protest the Stamp Act. They called themselves the Sons of Liberty. Samuel Adams actively participated in this group. The Sons of Liberty met under an elm tree that Adams called "The Liberty Tree." As tensions continued between the colonies and Great Britain, many Patriots began talking about breaking away from Great Britain and becoming independent.

Colonists protesting in the streets

Not all colonists were Patriots, however. A third of all colonists remained loyal to King George III. These people were called Loyalists. Many of them were wealthy, but others were ordinary people. Some business leaders were Loyalists. Philadelphia merchant Thomas Clifford complained that independence would "assuredly prove unprofitable." Many Loyalists wished to remain British citizens or were fearful that independence would lead to chaos.

In October 1765, representatives from nine colonies met in New York City and formed the Stamp Act Congress. The representatives declared that Parliament had no right to tax the colonists, since colonists were not allowed to vote for members of Parliament. These laws, they argued, were against British legal traditions.

Parliament created more conflict by ignoring colonists' concerns. On November 1, the Stamp Act took effect. In turn, angry colonists staged a **boycott.** Boycotting means refusing to do business with—or to buy goods from—a person, group, or country. Colonists refused to use the new stamps.

Colonial women joined the protest. They formed a group called the "Daughters of Liberty." They made a kind of cloth known as "homespun" and found other ways to replace British goods with homemade items.

Colonists refused to purchase British goods, such as tea. The boycott began to hurt British merchants. Because of the boycott, Parliament in 1766 voted to cancel the Stamp Act.

This teapot was made for sale in the colonies to celebrate the cancellation of the Stamp Act.

Smithsonian National Museum of American History, Kenneth E. Behring Center

✓ Stop and Check

COLLABORATE

Talk Why were colonists' different types of protests effective?

Perspectives

Views from a Patriot and a Loyalist

Colonists who demanded that Americans have more control of their government were known as Patriots. Colonists who wanted to remain loyal to the British government were called Loyalists. The following quotations show the points of view of George Mason, a Patriot, and Joseph Galloway, a Loyalist.

"We claim nothing but the liberty and privileges of Englishmen, in the same degree, as if we had still continued among our brethren in Great Britain: these rights have not been forfeited by any act of ours, we can not be deprived of them without our consent, but by violence and injustice."

—George Mason, to the Committee of Merchants in London, June 6, 1766

George Mason

Joseph Galloway

"The protection of America has, in no small degree, contributed to this burden of the mother country. To the large sums of money that have been expended from the English treasury and the parental care of a British Parliament, we in a great measure owe our present freedom...."

—Americanus (pseudonym for Joseph Galloway), letter to the *New York Gazette*, 15 August 1765, reprinted two weeks later in the *Pennsylvania Journal* (29 August 1765)

What Do You Think?
Whose argument do you think is more convincing? Why?

TEXT: (t)Mason, George. George Mason to the Committee of Merchants in London, 6 June 1766. In The Life of George Mason, 1725-1792, Volume 1, ed. Kate Mason Rowland, no. 3. New York: G.P. Putnam's Sons, 1892.; (b)Galloway, Joseph. "Americanus." Letter to The New-York Gazette, 15 August 1765.; PHOTO: (t)McGraw-Hill Education, (r)Bettmann/Getty Images

The Townshend Acts

Parliament gave in to colonial pressure when it **repealed** the Stamp Act in 1766, but the break from taxes did not last long. In 1767, Parliament found another way to raise taxes. It passed the Townshend Acts, which were named for the treasurer of the British government, Charles Townshend. Parliament believed colonists would be more accepting of a tax on factory-made goods imported from Great Britain. These included common imports such as tea, paper, glass, lead, and paint. Again, colonists were angry. They demanded Britain cancel the Townshend Acts. They also organized a boycott of the newly taxed items as well as any colonial businesses that continued to sell or use taxed goods.

Goods Taxed Under the Townshend Acts

tea
paper
glass
lead
paint

After the passage of the Townshend Acts, a Pennsylvania farmer named John Dickinson began writing a series of letters to the people of Great Britain. Although he was a Patriot, Dickinson was against independence and argued in favor of peaceful protest of Britain's taxes. Some other Patriots agreed with him. In fact, there were many among the British, Patriots, and Loyalists who did not wish to go to war. But in the coming years, relations between the colonists and Great Britain would become only more tense.

Britain feared the boycotts could lead to violence, and so they acted on these fears. Britain sent troops to Boston, which was the center of colonial protests. What happened next would push the two sides even closer to war.

✓ Stop and Check

Think Based on what you have read about colonists' protests, do you think Britain was justified in sending troops to Boston?

Colonial boycotts affected the economy in Britain as well as in the colonies.

Around the World

How Did the Boycott Hurt Britain's Economy?

The French and Indian War had left Britain not only with debt but also with an economic **recession**. Colonists' boycott of British goods weakened trade in a struggling British economy. British businesses and factories suffered losses from fewer products being exported to the colonies. So, like the colonists, British merchants began organizing to pressure Parliament to end the Stamp Act. Parliament took the merchants' concerns more seriously than the colonists' concerns. It canceled the Stamp Act.

What Do You Think? What was similar about colonists' and British merchants' organizing efforts? What was different about them?

The Boston Massacre

Tensions were high between colonists and British soldiers in Boston in early 1770. The people of Boston were not happy with the increase in the number of British soldiers in the city. Because of the Quartering Act, some residents were forced to allow British officers to stay in their homes. On March 5, the conflict turned deadly. Historians debate the specific details, but all accounts begin the same way. A group of colonists gathered at the Customs House, where taxes on imported goods were paid to Great Britain. British soldiers arrived. An exchange of angry words and insults quickly turned physical. The colonists hurled snowballs and ice at the soldiers. Some of the soldiers lost control and fired their **muskets** into the crowd. Five colonists were killed as a result of these actions. Among them was Crispus Attucks, a man who had escaped from slavery.

The incident became known as the Boston Massacre. Samuel Adams and the Sons of Liberty used the event as fuel to add to the growing movement for colonial self-government.

HSS.5.5.1, HSS.5.5.2, HSS.5.5.3, HAS.HI.3

Time Line

1765
Parliament passes the Stamp Act and the Quartering Act.

1767
Parliament passes the Townshend Acts.

1772
Samuel Adams forms the first Committee of Correspondence.

1773
Parliament passes the Tea Act.

1774
The First Continental Congress meets.

1760 | | | | | | | 1765 | | | | | | | 1770 | | | | | | | 1775 | | | | | |

The conflict between the colonists and the British troops turned deadly in Boston in early 1770.

Samuel Adams
AND THE COMMITTEES OF CORRESPONDENCE

A portrait of Samuel Adams

Samuel Adams was a key figure in the colonists' quest for freedom. He was among the founders of the Sons of Liberty, a group that was organized to protest the Stamp Act. It continued to speak out against British rule. Anti-British feeling spread slowly throughout the colonies. Adams realized that the colonists needed a way to communicate. Having previously written letters to newspapers to protest the Stamp Act, Adams knew that the fastest and most reliable way to communicate was through letters. In 1772, he formed a 21-person committee to communicate the Patriots' plans and progress. He adapted this idea from a committee that was formed in 1764 to protest new British rules about currency and customs.

By forming the committee, Adams—and other Sons of Liberty—could stay up-to-date with the events in the colonies. Thus, the Committee of Correspondence was born. Within a few months, more than 80 similar Committees of Correspondence formed throughout the colonies. A few years later, a volunteer rider for the Boston Committee of Correspondence would also make history. His name was Paul Revere.

Samuel Adams continued to be an influential figure during the Revolutionary War and in the early republic. In 1776, he signed the Declaration of Independence. Later, he was elected governor of Massachusetts. During his time in government, he fought for the rights of boys and girls to receive free and equal education.

✓ Stop and Check

Talk What did Samuel Adams do to show his opposition to the way Britain was ruling the colonies? How did his actions help the colonists?

Find Details As you read, add new information to the graphic organizer on page 153 in your Inquiry Journal.

The Boston Tea Party

Some of the colonists' protests worked. Parliament repealed the Townshend Acts. However, it also passed the Tea Act in 1773. The Tea Act gave the British East India Company the exclusive right to sell tea in the colonies without paying export taxes. This allowed the company to sell its tea at a price cheaper than that of other merchants' tea. Colonial tea merchants could no longer compete. Further, colonists still had to pay taxes when they bought the tea. This upset Samuel Adams, the Sons of Liberty, and other colonists for two reasons. First, it was another tax that they had not voted to approve. Second, it hurt local businesses because it gave a British company a **monopoly** on tea.

In late November 1773, three ships from the East India Company landed in Boston Harbor. Some Boston residents decided to protest the Tea Act by refusing to let the ships unload their cargo. Governor Thomas Hutchinson wanted to honor the new law and decided that the ships were to remain in the harbor until the tea was sold.

The angry colonists threw British tea into Boston Harbor.

The Sons of Liberty broke open 342 tea chests.

A few weeks later, on the night of December 16, 1773, the Sons of Liberty took action. About 50 members, some dressed as Mohawk Indians, boarded the ships. They broke open the tea chests and dumped the contents of the chests into the harbor. This act of **vandalism** became known as the Boston Tea Party. Similar protests happened in New York and in Annapolis, Maryland, but only the city of Boston would face immediate consequences.

Parliament wanted to punish the colonists for their actions. It closed Boston Harbor until the colonists paid for the tea they had destroyed. It also banned town meetings and sent more soldiers to live in the city. This series of acts was known as the Coercive Acts. The Patriots called them the Intolerable Acts, because they found the actions hard to tolerate, or live with. Instead of breaking the protestors' spirits, these acts unified the anti-British colonists in their struggle. Representatives from the colonies decided to meet to discuss what to do next. Their meeting would be called the First Continental Congress.

COLLABORATE

✓ Stop and Check

Talk How did the passage of laws after the Boston Tea Party motivate the colonists to take action?

Cayman/Alamy

The First Continental Congress

On September 5, 1774, representatives from the colonies met in Philadelphia to discuss the Coercive Acts. Their goal was to plan a response to these laws. Fifty-six men represented 12 of the 13 colonies. Each colony was granted one vote. After rejecting a plan to **reconcile** with the British government, the First Continental Congress decided to write a petition, or written request, to King George III. In the document, members of the congress outlined complaints about the way the British government had been treating them. They reminded the king of their status as British citizens. They demanded that they be given the same rights—including the right to representation—that were granted to other British citizens. Then they asked the king to repeal the Coercive Acts and other laws they felt were unfair to the colonists. Lastly, they proposed an end to trade with Britain until their demands were met.

Attendees of the First Continental Congress met at Carpenters' Hall in Philadelphia.

PRIMARY SOURCE

In Their Words... The First Continental Congress

The foundation of English liberty, and of all free government, is a right in the people to participate in their legislative council: and as the English colonists are not represented, and from their local and other circumstances, cannot properly be represented in the British parliament, they are entitled to a free and exclusive power of legislation in their several provincial legislatures, where their right of representation can alone be preserved, in all cases of taxation and internal polity, subject only to the negative of their sovereign, in such manner as has been heretofore used and accustomed.

—from the *Declaration of Rights and Grievances*, October 14, 1774

Stop and Check

Think How does having a common goal unite a large group of people?

TEXT: Declaration and Resolves of the First Continental Congress, Res. 4, October 14, 1774. Documents Illustrative of the Formation of the Union of the American States. Government Printing Office, 1927. House Document No. 398. Selected, Arranged and Indexed by Charles C. Tansill.; PHOTO: (t)McGraw-Hill Education, (b)Zack Frank/Shutterstock.com

Connections in Action!
Back to the EQ

Think about the Chapter EQ, **"Why Would a Nation Want to Become Independent?"**

- **Talk** with a partner about what you learned in the chapter. Take sides. One of you should make the case for independence. The other should make the case against it.

- If you are for independence, which important events convinced you that independence was necessary? If you are against independence, which events prove that the colonies should remain part of Great Britain?

- **Share** your ideas with the class. Then have a class discussion about why a nation would want to become independent or not.

More to Explore

How Can You Make an IMPACT?

Television Interview

Work with a partner. One of you will play the part of someone who witnessed the Boston Tea Party. The other will play a television interviewer. Together, develop questions that give your viewers answers about *who was involved*, as well as *where, when, why,* and *how* the Boston Tea Party happened. Act out the interview for your class.

Letter to the Editor

Imagine you are a colonist in New England. Write a letter to the editor of your local newspaper about how Parliament's taxes affect your daily life. Your letter should persuade readers to take some kind of action. Use evidence from the text to support your claims.

Word Play

Choose three words from the chapter Word Bank. Write a short story in which each of the terms is a key word. Keep in mind that you can use different forms of a word as needed to fit your story—for example, *vandal* in place of *vandalism* and *boycotted* instead of *boycott*.

Chapter 5

The American Revolution

What Does the Revolutionary Era Tell Us about Our Nation Today?

In this chapter, you'll read about important events and people in the American Revolution. You'll think about why these events and people are important, the impact they had during the Revolution, and how the Revolution still impacts our nation today.

Step into the Time Chronological Thinking

Look at the timeline. What was going on in the rest of the world during the same years as the American Revolution?

1775
Revolutionary War begins at Lexington and Concord in Massachusetts.

George Washington becomes the leader of the Continental Army.

1776
Continental Congress signs the Declaration of Independence.

1777
Continental Army wins the Battle of Saratoga.

1778
French and American governments sign the Treaty of Alliance.

Americas

| 1775 | 1776 | 1777 | 1778 |

World Events

1776
Wolfgang Amadeus Mozart's Serenade No. 7 is first performed in Salzburg, Austria.

1778
Tây Sơn Dynasty is established in Vietnam.

HSS.5.5.2, HSS.5.5.3, HSS.5.6.1, HAS.CS.1

The Original Thirteen British Colonies

Step into the Place

1. Which of the cities or settlements identified on the map are not located in one of the original Thirteen Colonies?

2. Which original colonies' boundaries have changed the most since the American Revolution? Which ones have changed the least?

1779
British army shifts focus to Southern states.

1781
Continental Army defeats British at Yorktown, Virginia.

1783
Peace of Paris formally ends Revolutionary War.

1779 — **1780** — **1781** — **1782** — **1783**

1780
Hundreds are killed during the Gordon Riots in London.

1781
Sir William Herschel discoveres the planet Uranus.

1782
The city of Bangkok is founded as the capital of Siam.

1783
Laki volcano erupts and causes famine in Iceland.

McGraw-Hill Education

Connect Through Literature

Selections from
Paul Revere's Ride

By Henry Wadsworth Longfellow

Paul Revere was a Patriot who, along with Samuel Prescott and William Dawes, rode from Boston to Lexington and Concord to warn of a British attack. This poem written 100 years later, celebrated that famous ride.

Listen, my children, and you shall hear
Of the midnight ride of Paul Revere,
On the eighteenth of April, in Seventy-five;
Hardly a man is now alive
Who remembers that famous day and year.

He said to his friend, "If the British march
By land or sea from the town to-night,
Hang a lantern aloft in the belfry arch
Of the North Church tower as a signal light,—
One, if by land, and two, if by sea;
And I on the opposite shore will be,
Ready to ride and spread the alarm
Through every Middlesex village
and farm, For the country folk to be up and to arm."
Then he said, "Good night!" and with muffled oar
Silently rowed to the Charlestown shore . . .

You know the rest. In the books you have read,
How the British Regulars fired and fled,—
How the farmers gave them ball for ball,
From behind each fence and farmyard wall,
Chasing the Red Coats down the lane,
Then crossing the fields to emerge again
Under the trees at the turn of the road,
And only pausing to fire and load.

So through the night rode Paul Revere;
And so through the night went his cry of alarm
To every Middlesex village and farm,—
A cry of defiance and not of fear,
A voice in the darkness, a knock at the door,
And a word that shall echo forevermore!
For, borne on the night-wind of the Past,
Through all our history, to the last,
In the hour of darkness and peril and need,
The people will waken and listen to hear
The hurrying hoof beats of that steed,
And the midnight message of Paul Revere.

Think About It

1. What was the purpose of Paul Revere's ride?

2. How do you think a poem helps people remember Paul Revere's story differently than an informative article in a book would?

3. Longfellow describes Revere's warning as "a cry of defiance and not fear." How is a "cry of defiance" different from a "cry of fear"?

TEXT: Longfellow, Henry Wadsworth. "Paul Revere's Ride." The Atlantic Monthly 7, no. 39 January 1861: 27-29. Boston: Ticknor and Fields, 1861.; PHOTO: (bkgds)McGraw-Hill Education; (inset)Ed Vebell/Archive Photos/Getty Images

People You Should Know

John Hancock

Peter Salem

John Hancock, from Boston, Massachusetts, was an important Patriot during the American Revolution. Hancock was a very wealthy man, and he used his money to support the revolution. He was the president of the Second Continental Congress, and he also served twice as the governor of Massachusetts. As president of the Continental Congress, he was the first person to sign the Declaration of Independence.

Peter Salem was an African-American soldier in the American Revolution. He was born into slavery in 1750. In 1775, he was freed by his owner so he could serve in the militia. Peter Salem fought in the Battle of Concord. He also fought at the battles of Bunker Hill and Saratoga. Salem spent nearly five years fighting for the freedom of the American colonies. He is buried in Framingham, Massachusetts. In 1882, the town erected a monument to Peter Salem and declared June 17 Peter Salem Day.

Mercy Otis Warren

Haym Salomon

Mercy Otis Warren was born in Massachusetts in 1728. She is considered the first American woman to write primarly for a public audience, rather than herself. She wrote about politics and what was happening in the American colonies. During the American Revolution, she was an adviser to many political leaders, including Patrick Henry, George Washington, Thomas Jefferson, and John Adams. Mercy Otis Warren's writings had an important effect on the shaping of our nation.

Haym Salomon, a Jewish American businessman, was a strong supporter of the American Revolution. He realized that a major obstacle to the success of the United States would be its lack of money. He stepped in to arrange loans and funding from France. When that wasn't enough, he lent huge amounts of his own money to keep the revolution alive. He also gave money to founding fathers, such as Thomas Jefferson, to ensure those men could continue to do their important work. By the end of the war, Salomon was completely broke, but the young nation did not repay him.

How Did the American Revolution Start?

The Battles of Lexington and Concord

By 1775, the colonists were tired of British taxes and oppression. After some violent encounters with British troops, the colonists began stockpiling arms and gunpowder in Lexington and Concord, two towns near Boston, Massachusetts.

Paul Revere Rides

On April 18, 1775, British General Thomas Gage ordered 700 soldiers from Boston to seize and destroy colonial war supplies and to arrest patriot leaders Samuel Adams and John Hancock. Gage's plan was to make a surprise attack on Lexington and Concord, so he gave his troops orders not to allow any colonists to leave Boston that night.

Little did General Gage know that a small group of patriots had learned of his plan to attack the two towns. Under cover of night, Paul Revere, William Dawes, and Samuel Prescott set out to warn the people in the area. Revere arrived at Lexington around midnight. When a guard for Adams and Hancock asked him not to make so much noise, Revere told him, "You'll have noise enough before long. The regulars [British troops] are coming!"

Paul Revere set out at night to warn of Britain's plan to attack Lexington and Concord.

HSS.5.5.4, HSS.5.6.1, HAS.CS.4

December 1773
Boston Tea Party dumps tea into Boston Harbor.

May 1775
Second Continental Congress meets in Philadelphia.

June 1775
Battle of Bunker Hill

1773 | 1774 | 1775 |

April 1775
Fighting begins at Lexington.

An engraving of the Battle of Lexington

Library of Congress Prints & Photographs Division [LC-DIG-pga-00995]

Battle at Lexington

When the British troops reached Lexington, Captain John Parker was waiting with the local **militia**. The militia was a group of volunteer soldiers, like the minutemen, who fought only in an emergency. John Robbins, one of the colonial militiamen, described the sight of the British advancing: "There appeared a number of the King's troops . . . at the distance of about sixty or seventy yards from us . . . and on a quick pace toward us. . . ."

The First Shots

Captain Parker's orders to the militia were very simple, "Don't fire unless fired upon, but if they mean to have a war, let it begin here."

As the distance between the two groups grew smaller, someone in one of the groups fired a shot. To this day, no one knows which side fired first, but other shots quickly followed. Even though the battle lasted only a few minutes, eight militiamen were killed. The British succeeded in taking Lexington and marched on to Concord.

Arriving in Concord

Doctor Samuel Prescott, one of the men working with Paul Revere, had warned Concord of the impending attack. The townspeople moved most of the arms and gunpowder to nearby towns. When the British arrived, they found only the few supplies the townspeople of Concord had not had time to hide.

By now the church bells were ringing loudly to alert the local farmers of the British attack. The Concord **rebels** turned on the British troops. Minutemen, local farmers, and townspeople fired at the British troops from behind fences, houses, and trees.

The British troops were forced to retreat back to Boston, 18 miles away. By the time they reached safety, more than 90 British soldiers had been killed and 174 were wounded. With these two battles, the war for American independence had begun!

The British heard that the Americans were holding large amounts of weapons at Concord.

Routes to Lexington and Concord

📍 **Map Skills** Working with a partner, use the information provided in the map to determine who traveled the greatest distance to get to Lexington: Paul Revere, William Dawes, or the British. Use the scale to determine how many miles each traveled.

✅ Stop and Check

Perspectives Why is it important that some colonists found out about the British plans ahead of time?

Find Details As you read, add additional information to the graphic organizer on page 167 in your Inquiry Journal.

The Second Continental Congress

The leaders of the thirteen colonies had known a war with Great Britain was possible. They had already met in 1774, in the First Continental Congress, to decide what to do about the recent taxes set by the British government. Great speakers such as Patrick Henry had given fiery speeches to urge the leaders to prepare to separate from Great Britain. The Second Continental Congress met in Philadelphia on May 10, 1775, just days after the battles of Lexington and Concord. Participants sent from each of the thirteen colonies had to decide how to respond to what had happened.

They decided that they had to prepare for war. First, they made the militia that had stood up to the British in Massachusetts part of an official American army. To lead that army, they nominated a veteran of the French and Indian War and a member of the Congress: George Washington. Washington did not think he was up to the task of commanding the entire army, but he agreed to do his best.

The Second Continental Congress Voting for Independence by Robert Pine and Edward Savage

In Their Words... George Washington

Though I am truly sensible of the high Honor done me in this Appointment, yet I feel great distress, from a consciousness that my abilities and Military experience may not be equal to the extensive and important Trust: However, as the Congress desire it I will enter upon the momentous duty, and exert every power I Possess In their service and for the Support of the glorious Cause.

—address to the Continental Congress, June 16, 1775

The Second Continental Congress was not just a single meeting. It began as a series of meetings during the spring and summer of 1775. Besides establishing a Continental Army, the delegates also elected a president—John Hancock—and drafted the Olive Branch Petition. This was an attempt to resolve the conflicts between the colonies and Great Britain. However, King George refused to receive the Congress's peace offering.

As Great Britain's grip on the colonies weakened, the Continental Congress became the unofficial government. The war was far from over, but the colonists were learning how to govern themselves. The delegates would continue to meet throughout the war and even afterwards to make important decisions for the thirteen colonies.

Stop and Check

Connect to Now Is the Second Continental Congress anything like our government today? Using what you know, discuss with a partner how the Second Continental Congress is similar or different.

TEXT: "Washington Accepts his Appointment as Commander of Continental Army." Journals of the Continental Congress, vol. 2. June 16, 1775.; PHOTO: (t)McGraw-Hill Education; (b)Yale University Art Gallery

Soldiers of the American Revolution

The Minutemen

The citizen soldiers in the local militia didn't have uniforms. Instead, they wore their own clothes. Because the minutemen were the first ones to arrive for battle, many of the colonies made an effort to arm them with muskets and other supplies. Minutemen had the advantage over British troops of being familiar with frontier hunting and knowing what the local land was like.

Hat

Since Minutemen provided their own clothing, they wore whatever hat they owned. Styles varied greatly among the Minutemen.

Waistcoat and Coat

A sleeveless and collarless waistcoat was worn over a man's shirt. Waistcoats were usually made of linen or wool. Men wore a coat over the waistcoat. These overcoats were usually made of heavy linen or wool.

Breeches

Knee breeches were common in the 18th century. These came just below the knee and were closed with ties or buttons. Breeches were made of leather, wool, or linen.

Musket

A good soldier could load and fire his musket three times per minute. Muskets weren't very accurate and didn't work well in wet weather.

The Redcoats

The British redcoats were all issued uniforms and muskets. Because battlefields of the 18th century could be smoky and confusing, the soldiers wore red. This way, British soldiers wouldn't have trouble separating friend from foe. The red-coats had the advantages of military training and better equipment over the colonial minutemen.

Hat

Hats identified which regiment a soldier belonged to.

Musket

The British Short Land Pattern musket was standard issue. Soldiers would affix a bayonet, or attachable blade, to the musket's muzzle for close combat.

Buttons

There could be as many as three dozen buttons on a soldier's uniform. Buttons often had the name of the soldier's regiment inscribed on them. Buttons had to be polished regularly.

Facings

These visible linings along the edges of the soldier's coat were colored to show the regiment he belonged to.

✓ Stop and Check

Perspectives Based on what you've just read about British and colonial fighters, who do you think had the advantage in battle? Discuss your opinion with a partner.

The Battle of (Not) Bunker Hill

On June 18, 1775, James Warren, a Boston colonist, explained the conflict in Boston to his wife, Mercy Otis Warren, "It is impossible to describe the confusion in this place, women and children are flying into the country, armed men going to the field, and wounded men . . . fill the streets."

British general Thomas Gage decided to occupy the hills around Boston. Word about the British plan spread quickly. Colonel William Prescott and General Israel Putnam led one thousand colonial troops to hills north of Boston, across the Charles River. The original plan was to fortify Bunker Hill, which means to build earthen walls around it. This way, the colonists could fire cannons at the British troops stationed across the Charles River in Boston. Instead, the colonists decided to protect Breed's Hill, which was closer to the river. The colonists worked all night to build a fort for protection.

The Battle Begins

British troops crossed the Charles River by boat and marched up Breed's Hill. The militia and civilians, or ordinary citizens, waited, hidden behind the walls they had built. The colonists did not have much ammunition, or musket balls and gunpowder. Officers told them not to waste ammunition by firing at British soldiers who were too far away. Historians say that either Colonel Prescott or General Israel Putnam said, "Don't shoot until you see the whites of their eyes."

Then and Now

A 221-foot granite obelisk in Charlestown, Massachusetts, commemorates the Battle of Bunker Hill. The cornerstone was placed in 1825 on the fiftieth anniversary of the battle by the Marquis de Lafayette, a hero of the American Revolution. The monument was completed in 1842.

A British Victory

Twice, the British charged up the hill only to be stopped by the militia. Both times they were forced down by American fire. After a third try, the British overwhelmed the colonists. The British won what became known as the Battle of Bunker Hill, but the victory was costly. More than a thousand soldiers were killed or wounded in the battle. Great Britain was one of the most powerful nations on Earth, but winning a war against the American colonists wasn't going to be easy.

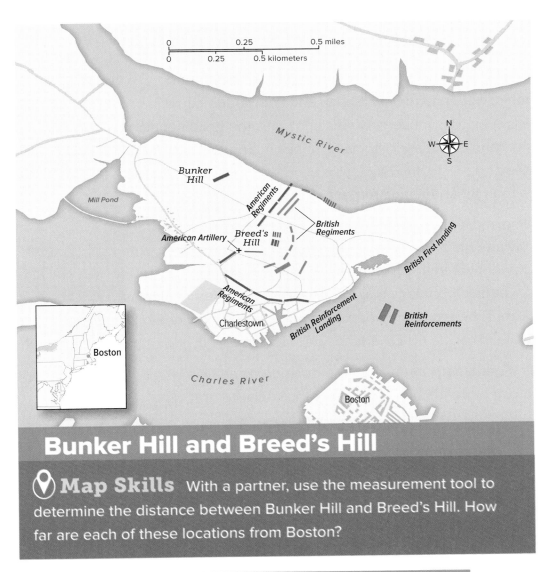

Bunker Hill and Breed's Hill

Map Skills With a partner, use the measurement tool to determine the distance between Bunker Hill and Breed's Hill. How far are each of these locations from Boston?

Stop and Check

Perspectives How might the large number of casualties have changed the way the British viewed the colonists?

Why Is the Declaration of Independence Still Important Today?

Enlightened Thinking

Many European philosophers in the seventeenth and eighteenth centuries wanted to understand how reason and knowledge could improve people's lives. This movement was known as the Enlightenment. Thinkers such as John Locke and Thomas Hobbes in England and Jean-Jacques Rousseau (roo-SOH) in France also used these ideas to change the way people thought about government.

Before this time, most people in Europe believed that kings and queens had a divine right to rule. This right allowed the **monarchs** to rule with absolute power over their subjects. As Enlightenment ideas spread, however, people began to believe that the main duty of government was to protect its citizens. In return, the people would give their consent to be governed by a ruler. This idea is called the *social contract*.

The Enlightenment greatly influenced the American men who wrote the Declaration of Independence. The idea of the social contract is particularly important in the Declaration of Indpendence.

HSS.5.5.2, HSS.5.5.3, HSS.5.5.4, HAS.HR.2

210 **Lesson 2** Why Is the Declaration of Independence Still Important Today?

Time Line

April 1775
Battles of Lexington and Concord

January 1776
Thomas Paine publishes *Common Sense.*

July 1776
Congress agrees on Declaration of Independence.

| 1775 | 1776 | 1777 |

May 1776
Second Continental Congress begins meeting.

August 1776
Members of Congress begin to sign Declaration of Independence.

THE DECLARATION COMMITTEE.

The Committee of Five was appointed to draft the Declaration of Independence.

Common Sense

Thomas Paine was living in London when he met Benjamin Franklin. Franklin advised Paine to emigrate to North America to build a new life there. When Paine arrived in Philadelphia in November 1774, the colonies were edging toward revolution. He got a job as the editor of *Pennsylvania Magazine*.

After fighting broke out in Lexington and Concord, Paine wrote a 50-page pamphlet titled *Common Sense*. He published it in January 1776. He argued that government should be a social contract, as other Enlightenment thinkers had suggested. Paine also believed that the colonies had lived through so much tyranny that there could be no **reconciliation** with Great Britain. Paine put his argument into such simple language that ordinary people easily understood his ideas. His powerful pamphlet got many colonists talking about independence.

PRIMARY SOURCE

In Their Words... Thomas Paine

. . . and that the *elected* might never form to themselves an interest separate from the *electors*, prudence will point out the propriety of having elections often; because as the *elected* might by that means return and mix again with the general body of the *electors* in a few months, their fidelity to the public will be secured by the prudent reflection of not making a rod for themselves. And as this frequent interchange will establish a common interest with every part of the community, they will mutually and naturally support each other, and on this, (not on the unmeaning name of king,) depends the *strength of government, and the happiness of the governed*.

—from *Common Sense*, published in January 1776

Writing the Declaration

In June 1776, Richard Henry Lee of Virginia told the Second Continental Congress, "These United colonies are, and of a right, ought to be, free and independent States." The Congress nominated five members to outline the colonies' reasons for wanting independence from Great Britain. The members of the committee were John Adams of Massachusetts, Benjamin Franklin of Pennsylvania, Robert Livingston of New York, Roger Sherman of Connecticut, and Thomas Jefferson of Virginia.

The committee chose Jefferson to write the first draft. He wrote for two weeks. Then Franklin and Adams made minor changes before presenting the declaration to the full Congress on June 28, 1776. The other members of the Congress argued about the wording of the document. One of the most controversial issues was language Jefferson had included about the evils of slavery. Representatives from the Southern Colonies, whose economies depended on slavery, wanted that language removed. John Adams later said, "I knew his southern brethren would never . . . [allow the section] to pass in Congress." Jefferson ultimately agreed to take out the section, and the Southern members gave their approval, leading to Congress's voting in favor of the Declaration.

Thomas Jefferson was born in Virgina.

(bkgd)McGraw-Hill Education; (r)kittimages/iStockphoto/Getty Images; (inset)Stocktrek Images/Getty Images

 Stop and Check COLLABORATE

Talk What prompted Congress to remove the language about slavery from the Declaration of Independence?

Find Details As you read, add new information to the graphic organizer on page 175 in your Inquiry Journal.

Signing the Declaration

After two days of debating the details of the Declaration, the members passed the final version on July 4, 1776. Word spread. The document was reprinted in newspapers and posted in meetinghouses and churches. On August 2, the members began to sign the Declaration. John Hancock, the president of the Congress, signed first. The rest of the 56 members signed beneath his signature. Each man knew he was risking his life and his property by putting his name on the Declaration. But the signers believed so strongly in independence that they took the risk. They could only hope that the colonists' Continental Army would be strong enough to beat the British.

John Hancock was the first delegate to sign the Declaration of Independence.

Citizenship

A Call for Unity

The members knew that signing the Declaration of Independence would be viewed by the British government as an act of treason. This meant each man who signed put his life at risk. The members needed to be unified as they bravely met this danger. After signing, Ben Franklin is believed to have remarked, "We must all hang together, or assuredly we shall all hang separately."

Even though not every member of the Second Continental Congress wanted the colonies to gain independence from Great Britain, they did indeed "all hang together." John Dickinson argued that the colonies should reconcile with Great Britain. He refused to sign. After Congress passed the Declaration, however, Dickinson showed his support for the new nation by joining the Pennsylvania militia. He did this even though he had disagreed with the other delegates on the question of independence.

Structure of the Declaration

Preamble

The first paragraph is the inspirational introduction to the document.

List of Grievances

This list of 27 complaints against King George outlines why the colonists want their independence from Great Britain.

Declaration of Independence

The concluding paragraph states in firm terms that the colonies are declaring themselves free and independent from Great Britain.

✓ Stop and Check

Think Why was it important to list 27 reasons the colonists wanted to be free from King George and Great Britain?

Does the Declaration Still Matter?

More than 240 years after the Declaration of Independence was signed, it still inspires people in the United States and around the world to believe in the ideal of self-government. Part of the document's success is a result of how well Jefferson made his case. The document argues that freedom belongs to everyone and no tyrant deserves the right to rule.

Though the words are still powerful today, some of their meanings have changed. For example, our understanding of the important phrase "all men are created equal" has grown to include women, African Americans, American Indians, and people of all other backgrounds.

The phrase "Life, Liberty, and the Pursuit of Happiness" is often used today, too. It means that all people have natural rights, or rights they are born with. No government can take these rights away.

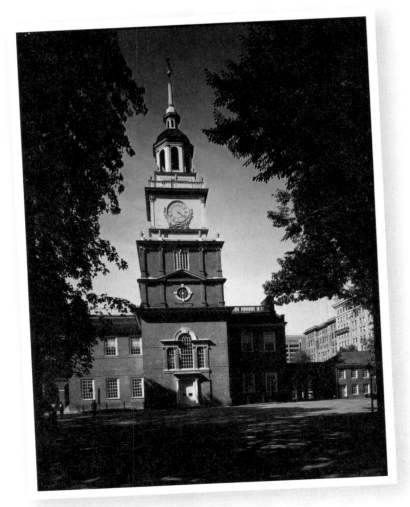

Another key phrase from the Preamble argues that a government derives its power from the "consent of the governed." This idea, taken from John Locke, describes the social contract that continues to exist between a ruler and the people: Each gains power from the other.

Independence Hall in Philadelphia, Pennsylvania, site of the Second Continental Congress

The statement "It is their right, it is their duty, to throw off such government" argues that the colonies are justified in their revolution. Because King George III was considered a tyrant, the Declaration states that it is the right and, more importantly, the duty of the colonists to "throw off" his rule over them.

What about the rest of the British people? The Declaration states that they will be considered "Enemies in War, in Peace Friends." This means that if the British continue to fight, the Americans will fight back. If they make peace, the Americans will be their friends.

PRIMARY SOURCE

In Their Words... Thomas Jefferson

We hold these truths to be self-evident, that all men are created equal, that they are endowed by their Creator with certain unalienable Rights, that among these are Life, Liberty and the pursuit of Happiness.—That to secure these rights, Governments are instituted among Men, deriving their just powers from the consent of the governed, . . .

—from the Preamble to the Declaration of Independence

✓ Stop and Check

Talk Why has the meaning of the phrase "all men are created equal" changed over the years?

McGraw-Hill Education

Field Trip to Philadelphia

In 1777, Philadelphia, Pennsylvania, was the largest city in North America. It was centrally located among the new American states. This location made it a good place to hold meetings that included leaders from each state. In the city today, you can still tour Philadelphia's past.

Liberty Bell

The Liberty Bell originally hung in the belfry of Independence Hall. It now resides in its own building nearby. The bell was rung for the First Continental Congress and the battles of Lexington and Concord. On July 8, 1776, the bell was rung before the public reading of the Declaration of Independence.

Elfreth's Alley

Near Independence Hall is Elfreth's Alley, the oldest street in the country. People have lived and worked in Elfreth's Alley since 1702.

Franklin Court

Visitors can view many objects that once belonged to Benjamin Franklin in Franklin Court. The area includes a working print shop as well as a post office once run by Franklin, who was America's first Postmaster General.

Betsy Ross House

According to legend, Betsy Ross made the first United States flag after a visit from George Washington in June 1776. During this visit, Ross showed Washington a 5-pointed star made from a folded square of cloth with a single cut of the scissors.

(bkgd)McGraw-Hill Education; (t)Jean-Pierre De Mann/robertharding/Alamy; (b)Photographs in the Carol M. Highsmith Archive, Library of Congress, Prints and Photographs Division.

Stop and Check

Talk Why was Philadelphia an ideal place for the Second Continental Congress to meet?

What Do You Think? Why is the
Declaration of Independence still important today?

Strengths and Weaknesses of the Two Sides

The American Revolution presented challenges for both the British and the Americans. Neither side was prepared to fight a war that would last eight years. They would often have shortages of equipment, soldiers, and the money to pay for both. While a wealthy and powerful nation like Britain would seem to have a great advantage, both sides had their strengths and weaknesses.

The war was very expensive for Britain. All soldiers and supplies had to be sent by ship across the Atlantic Ocean. Britain financed the war by raising taxes on citizens living in Britain. Many British people disagreed with the war because they did not want higher taxes.

The American army received its funding from the Second Continental Congress. Congress, however, often did not have enough money to pay soldiers or buy supplies or food for them. As a result, it was difficult to keep men from deserting, or leaving the army. Some people, known as **profiteers**, took advantage of the poor wartime economy to hoard goods and sell them at high prices. However, the war had tremendous support from civilians in the colonies. To help with the war effort, civilians made musket balls and blankets. They gathered food and supplies to send to the front.

(t)McGraw-Hill Education

Time Line

April 1775
Battles of Lexington and Concord

July 1776
Congress agrees on Declaration of Independence.

January 1777
After a series of losses in New York, George Washington's Continental Army triumphs over British twice in New Jersey.

1777–1778
Washington's Continental Army endures a brutal winter at Valley Forge in Pennsylvania.

February 1778
Americans and French sign Treaty of Alliance.

October 1777
British suffer a major defeat at the Battle of Saratoga.

1775	1776	1777	1778	1779	

Courtesy of the U.S. Navy Art Collection, Washington, D.C. U.S. Naval History and Heritage Command [NH 73927-KN]

French ships (on the left) battle the British Navy during the Revolutionary War. France's entry into the war on the American side was a defining moment of the war.

The British had more soldiers, including American Indians and paid German **mercenaries**, or people who fight for money. The British soldiers were also better trained and armed than the American soldiers. However, the British soldiers were trained to fight only in open battlefields. Americans were more familiar with the land where they lived. The Americans took advantage of this British weakness to surprise the British in different kinds of terrain such as the swamps of the south and the forests of the north. The Americans' more plain-looking clothes helped them blend into the landscape, while the British soldiers' red coats made them easy targets.

Ultimately, the British failed to recognize both their own weaknesses and the Americans' strengths. One of their biggest mistakes was underestimating the Americans' willingness to risk everything to win their independence.

British soldiers were trained to fight only in open battlefields. Their red coats made them easy targets.

Washington on the Offensive

After the Battles of Lexington and Concord and the signing of the Declaration of Independence, the Americans suffered some major setbacks. The Continental Army lost important battles in New York state. By the middle of 1776, George Washington's soldiers had been driven into Pennsylvania.

Washington needed victories to boost his soldiers' morale. He was concerned that many would leave his army and go home when their term of service ran out. On Christmas night, 1776, he led 2,400 soldiers across the Delaware River from Pennsylvania into New Jersey.

The army reached Trenton at dawn and attacked at once, surprising and defeating German mercenaries who were fighting for the British. A few days later, Washington won another victory when his soldiers left their campfires burning near Trenton so the British would not be aware that they had snuck away to attack Princeton successfully. It became clear that the Americans had a chance of winning the war after all.

✓ Stop and Check

Talk How did Washington prove in 1776 and 1777 that he was capable of defeating the British troops?

Find Details As you read, add new information to the graphic organizer on page 183 in your Inquiry Journal.

Commander-in-Chief George Washington led the Continental Army.

(t)McGraw-Hill Education, (b)Library of Congress, Prints and Photographs Division (LC-USZC4-2737)

The Battle of Saratoga

In 1777, the British decided to try to capture the Hudson River Valley, cutting off New York and New Jersey from the states in New England. British General John Burgoyne believed this would fatally weaken the American army. His army invaded the valley from its base in Canada.

British General Burgoyne surrenders at Saratoga, New York.

Part of Burgoyne's plan depended on help from Mohawk and Iroquois scouts. Burgoyne's army became bogged down in terrain made difficult by forests and swamps. The Mohawk and Iroquois began to lose confidence in British promises that they could prevent more colonists from taking their lands. As the scouts drifted away, Burgoyne had no information about where the Americans were or what they were doing.

The Americans, on the other hand, were prepared. General Thomas Gates planned an attack on British forces near Saratoga, New York. The American fighting force was three times the size of that of the British. Gates also sent expert riflemen to attack British troops as they moved through New York. By the time the British forces reached Saratoga, they had been badly weakened.

Even though his troops were weakened and outnumbered, Burgoyne was sure he could still defeat the Americans. He chose to attack at Freeman's Farm near Saratoga. Before the British could attack, however, a Polish engineer named Tadeusz Kościuszko (tah-DEH-oosh kohsh-CHOOSH-koh) helped the Americans fortify the walls around Freeman's Farm and the surrounding roads. Kościuszko helped protect the Americans and their supply lines from the British attack in this first Battle of Saratoga. General Gates was also able to obtain fresh troops to strengthen his lines of defense against the British.

Then and Now

The battlefields of Saratoga are now part of a National Park. When you visit, you can go on a self-guided tour. You can see a monument, a 155-foot tall obelisk to the American victory. You can also take a walk through Victory Woods, the site of General Burgoyne's last encampment before surrendering.

Throughout September 1777, American riflemen who were hidden in the hillsides shot at any British soldier who tried to fetch water from the Hudson River. This further weakened the British troops. On October 7, American General Benedict Arnold's forces drove back a portion of Burgoyne's soldiers who had been scouting the area to gain information. This battle became known as the Second Battle of Saratoga.

By mid-October, Burgoyne's troops were greatly reduced in number. As a result of the Americans' preparedness, the British were cut off from receiving more supplies. They were running out of food. Finally, after two more months of fighting, Burgoyne decided to surrender to Gates on October 17. The victory at Saratoga changed the direction of the war.

Biography

Tadeusz Kościuszko

Born in Poland, Tadeusz Kościuszko emigrated to the United States in 1776. He immediately joined the American fight for independence. Because he was a skilled engineer, Kościuszko was asked to help fortify the meeting place of the Continental Congress. In 1777, he joined General Gates in upstate New York. There, he helped fortify Freeman's Farm and the American supply lines. He went on to prove his bravery and cleverness at several more battles during the war before being promoted to the rank of brigadier general. After the Revolution, he was granted American citizenship.

 Stop and Check

Think Why did it matter that the American forces were able to fortify Freeman's Farm and the surrounding roads before the British attacked?

A Turning Point

The Americans' victory at the two Battles of Saratoga proved to the rest of the world that the Americans were capable of defeating the British. In 1777 and 1778, Benjamin Franklin, who was then the American Ambassador to France, worked with French officials to create the Treaty of Alliance. As a result of this treaty, France sent troops, warships, and supplies to the United States.

Individual Europeans agreed to come to the aid of the United States, too. Baron Friedrich von Steuben of Prussia helped to train American soldiers to fight together. Casimir Pulaski of Poland trained soldiers to fight on horseback and became a general. He gave his life in battle for American independence. The Marquis de Lafayette of France became a valuable member of Washington's staff. He would prove his worth at the Battle of Yorktown.

Since it was allied with France, Spain also joined America's struggle with Great Britain. In 1779, the governor of the Spanish territory of Louisiana closed the port of New Orleans to British ships and opened it to American ships. Spain also made loans to support the American war effort. Spanish Colonel Bernárdo de Galvez led a force to fight the British in the South.

Casimir Pulaski

✓ Stop and Check

Talk Why was the Battle of Saratoga a turning point in the Revolutionary War?

(t)McGraw-Hill Education; (b)Bettmann/Getty Images

Winter at Valley Forge

Despite the great victory at Saratoga, the Continental Army elsewhere suffered a number of defeats, including two near Philadelphia in late 1777. Washington's 11,000 men set up camp that winter at Valley Forge, Pennsylvania. The site seemed easy to defend, should the British attack. It was also close to good roads, which would allow the army to get supplies.

American soldiers suffered during the brutal winter at Valley Forge.

Bettmann/Getty Images

That winter, however, was a time of cold, hunger, and loneliness for the Patriot soldiers. Often the only food was "fire cakes," which were made of a paste of flour and water baked hard over a campfire. Many soldiers gave up and went home. At least 2,500 died of diseases that winter, including smallpox, typhoid, and influenza. Those who lived faced frostbite and starvation. The Marquis de Lafayette later wrote, "The unfortunate soldiers were in need of everything; they had neither coats, hats, shirts, nor shoes, their feet and legs froze."

Washington begged the Continental Congress and the state governors for supplies. He described the terrible sufferings of his army. His letters were answered with promises, but very little help arrived.

Washington held his army together with little but the force of his own leadership. He used the time at Valley Forge wisely, however. Groups of 100 soldiers took turns training with Baron von Steuben. Then each trainee taught another 100 men what he had learned. By the spring, more money became available due to the alliance with France. While Washington's troops came to Valley Forge a barefoot, ragged band, they marched away in 1778 as professional soldiers.

 Stop and Check

Talk What happened to the soldiers of the Continental Army at Valley Forge?

What Do You Think? How did the talents of individual Europeans like von Steuben, Pulaski, and Kościuszko strengthen the cause of American Independence?

What Was It Like to Live During the American Revolution?

Women of the Revolution

The Revolutionary War impacted the lives of more than just the soldiers and generals waging war. The Revolutionary War changed the lives of women, African Americans, American Indians, and every civilian in the colonies.

American women supported the war in many ways. Mercy Otis Warren and Hannah Winthrop recorded and wrote letters about the events of the Revolution so everyone knew what was happening. Phillis Wheatley, a freed African American, wrote poetry that inspired many people. Other women tended farms or minded shops while their husbands were away fighting in the army.

Some women followed their husbands to war and did whatever they could to help. Earning the nickname "Molly Pitcher," Mary Ludwig Hays carried pitchers of water to men on the battlefield. Legend has it that she took her husband's place at a cannon when he became too exhausted to fight during the Battle of Monmouth in 1778.

McGraw-Hill Education

HSS.5.6.3, HSS.5.6.4, HSS.5.6.7, HAS.HI.2

230 Lesson 4 What Was It Like to Live During the American Revolution?

THE HEROINE OF MONMOUTH.

MOLLY PITCHER — The wife of a Gunner in the American Army, who when her husband was killed, took his place at the gun, and served throughout the battle. (June 28ᵗʰ 1778.)

Molly Pitcher helps load a cannon at a battle in New Jersey.

Still other women remained loyal to the British crown. Either for religious reasons, or because their families' businesses depended on British trade, Loyalist men and women wanted reconciliation with Great Britain. Some of them even worked actively against the revolution.

There were also women who worked actively to help create the new United States. Abigail Adams exchanged many letters with her husband, John, in which they discussed important issues facing the Continental Congress. Abigail asked her husband to remember women's rights as he helped to create the new government.

PRIMARY SOURCE

In Their Words... Abigail Adams

I long to hear that you have declared an independency— and by the way in the new Code of Laws which I suppose it will be necessary for you to make I desire you would Remember the Ladies, and be more generous and favorable to them than your ancestors. Do not put such unlimited power into the hands of the Husbands. Remember all Men would be tyrants if they could. If particular care and attention is not paid to the Ladies we are determined to foment a Rebellion, and will not hold ourselves bound by any Laws in which we have no voice, or Representation. That your Sex are Naturally Tyrannical is a Truth so thoroughly established as to admit of no dispute, but such of you as wish to be happy willingly give up the harsh title of Master for the more tender and endearing one of Friend. Why then, not put it out of the power of the vicious and the Lawless to use us with cruelty and indignity with impunity.

—from a letter to John Adams, March 31, 1776

TEXT: Adams, Abigail. Abigail Adams to John Adams, 31 March 1776. In Familiar Letters of John Adams and His Wife Abigail Adams, During the Revolution: With a Memoir of Mrs. Adams, ed. Charles Francis Adams, no. 91. New York: Hurd and Houghton, 1875.;

✓ Stop and Check

Talk Why did Abigail Adams ask John Adams to "remember the ladies"?

COLLABORATE

The Secret War

Life during the Revolutionary War was filled with divisions and intrigue. Many Loyalists spied on the Patriots for the British. Some who helped the British made it appear that they were instead helping the Patriot cause. Benedict Arnold was an American general who eventually turned **traitor**. He gave important information about a planned invasion of Canada to the British. He later fled to England, but people started calling any traitor a "Benedict Arnold" because of his treachery.

The Patriot side had its own spies. Nathan Hale was attempting to spy on the British in 1776 when he was captured. He was hanged without a trial. Reportedly, his famous last words were "I only regret that I have but one life to lose for my country."

One of the most successful American spies was James Armistead, a man born into slavery. He volunteered to spy for General Lafayette, managing to become a servant to the British general Cornwallis. Armistead smuggled important information to Lafayette, which helped the Continental Army win the Battle of Yorktown. After the war, Lafayette helped Armistead win his freedom.

Nathan Hale was put to death for being a Patriot spy.

✓ Stop and Check

Think With a partner, discuss why people call someone who betrays them a "Benedict Arnold."

Find Details As you read, add new information to the graphic organizer on page 191 in your Inquiry Journal.

(t)McGraw-Hill Education; (b)Yale University Art Gallery

African Americans Join the Cause

This man is dressed as a soldier of the First Rhode Island Regiment.

The words "all men are created equal" in the Declaration of Independence gave hope to African slaves. Many supported the revolution because they believed those famous words might one day apply to them.

In all, about 5,000 African American soldiers served in the Continental Army. The First Rhode Island Regiment, formed in 1778, consisted mainly of African Americans. These included men freed from slavery in exchange for their service. Another African American freed from slavery in exchange for fighting was Peter Salem. He lived in Massachusetts and fought in the Battles of Concord and Bunker Hill.

African Americans also served in the Continental Navy. A 14-year old free African American named James Forten was captured in 1781 during his service as a powder boy. The British offered him his freedom, but he turned down the offer saying, "No, I'm a prisoner for my country and I'll never be a traitor to her." He was held for seven months as a prisoner of war.

American Indians Choose Sides

During the Revolutionary War, American Indians had to decide whom to support. As the colonies grew bigger, they began to take more and more land from the American Indians. The British promised to protect American Indians' land from the Americans who wanted to settle there. Most of the Iroquois Confederacy, led by Chief Joseph Brant, sided with the British. The Oneida and Tuscarora supported the American cause.

Brant's Indian loyalists fighting for the British attacked American settlements in New York's Mohawk Valley. They also provided scouts to help the British troops. The Iroquois eventually lost faith in the British and stopped participating in the war.

However, Americans would continue to regard American Indians as enemies. As a result, many Americans felt no guilt about taking more lands from native peoples after the war.

> **✓ Stop and Check** COLLABORATE
>
> **Think** Why did many American Indians at first side with the British during the Revolutionary War?
>
> Why did many African Americans choose to fight with the colonists?

Iroquois chief Joseph Brant supported the British army during the war.

The Hardships of War

Wartime Shortages
Paper Dollars Equaling One-Dollar Coin, 1777–1781

The amount of paper Continental dollars needed to equal a one-dollar coin rose dramatically during the Revolutionary War.

Congress had trouble paying for the war. To afford expensive supplies, they began to print more and more dollars, called "Continentals." They printed so many Continentals, however, that the money began to lose value due to **inflation**. Soon the bills were nearly worthless. A pair of shoes that had cost a few Continental dollars at the start of the war cost 5,000 Continental dollars by the end.

Because their money lost almost all of its value, people had trouble buying the food and supplies they needed. Even for the wealthy, goods that had once been imported from Great Britain were now hard to find. These shortages led people to hoard food, clothes, and other goods. Some people hoarded to try to support their families. Others did it to make money by charging high prices to others. Laws were passed against this practice, called profiteering, but the laws were difficult to enforce.

✓ Stop and Check

Talk What problems did inflation cause?

What Do You Think? What would it have been like to live during the American Revolution?

Are Women and African Americans of the Revolution Overlooked?

Work with a partner. Design a monument that honors the contributions of women or African Americans during the war. Consider what your monument should look like.

- Make an outline of the ways women and African Americans contributed to the war.
- Who were some individuals you learned about, and how do they represent the larger groups?
- Think about other monuments you have seen, and think about how your monument could compare to them.

Draw or make a model of your monument.

Present your monument to the class. Explain what you have learned about how women and African Americans helped the war effort.

James Armistead, who was a slave, risked his life to spy for the colonists.

Deborah Sampson disguised herself as a man so she could join the Continental Army.

Lesson 5

What Did the Colonists Gain by Winning the War?

The War Moves South

By 1779, the American Continental Army had turned back British attacks in the north and the west. British leaders decided to focus on the Southern Colonies. The Southern Colonies had higher proportions of Loyalists, and the British hoped to have their help in defeating the Americans once and for all. General Charles Cornwallis became the leader of British troops in the South in 1780.

Congress had very little money and almost no supplies for forces in the Southern Colonies. Between 1778 and 1781, the British won battles against American General Nathanael Greene at Savannah, Georgia, and at Charles Town and Camden in South Carolina. At first it seemed as if Cornwallis's strategies were working. However, the colonists' greater knowledge of the land they were fighting for proved to be an advantage.

Soldiers listen as General George Washington gives his final orders.

HSS.5.6.1, HSS.5.6.2, HSS.5.6.7, HAS.CS.5

Time Line

June 1779
Spain declares war on Great Britain.

May 1780
General Charles Cornwallis becomes British commander in the South.

September 1783
Peace of Paris ends American Revolution.

| | 1775 | | | | | | | | 1780 | | | | | | | | 1785 | | | | | |

October 1781
British defeated at Yorktown, Virginia

PRIMARY SOURCE

In Their Words... George Washington

My Lord: I have had the Honor of receiving Your Lordship's Letter of this Date. An Ardent Desire to spare the further Effusion of Blood, will readily incline me to listen to such Terms for the Surrender of your Posts and Garrisons of York and Gloucester, as are admissible. I wish previously to the Meeting of Commissioners, that your Lordship's proposals in writing, may be sent to the American Lines: for which Purpose, a Suspension of Hostilities during two Hours from the Delivery of this Letter will be granted. I have the Honor etc.

The Officers will be indulged in retaining their Side Arms, and the Officers and Soldiers may preserve their Baggage and Effects, with this Reserve, that Property taken in the Country, will be reclaimed. With Regard to the Individuals in civil Capacities, whose Interests Your Lordship wishes may be attended to, until they are more particularly described, nothing definitive can be settled.

I have to add, that I expect the Sick and Wounded will be supplied with their own Hospital Stores, and be attended by British Surgeons, particularly charged with the Care of them. Your Lordship will be pleased to signify your Determination either to accept or reject the Proposals now offered, in the Course of Two Hours from the Delivery of this Letter, that Commissioners may be appointed to digest the Articles of Capitulation, or a Renewal of Hostilities may take place. I have the Honor etc.

— from Letters from George Washington to General Lord Cornwallis, October 17, 1781

Washington, George. George Washington to General Lord Charles Cornwallis, 17 October 1781. George Washington Papers at the Library of Congress, 1741-1799: Series 3e Varick Transcripts.

The Continental Army managed to surprise the British in several raids led by Captain Francis Marion. Marion was called "The Swamp Fox" because his small force of raiders attacked the British unexpectedly and then retreated into the swamps of South Carolina.

Cornwallis pursued the Continental Army through the Carolina backcountry. When the two armies met in March 1781 at Guilford Court House, in North Carolina, Cornwallis lost one-fourth of his men. He declared it a victory because Greene's troops had left the battlefield. The loss, however, crippled the British forces. When word of the battle reached England, Charles James Fox declared in Parliament that "Another such victory would destroy the British army."

Because of the heavy losses, Cornwallis knew his men needed to rest and resupply. He fled north to Virginia to await ships from British headquarters in New York City. This movement would present George Washington with an opportunity.

Key Battles in the Southern Colonies

 Stop and Check

Talk Why was it important that Cornwallis lost so many men as a result of his victory at the Battle of Guilford Court House?

Find Details As you read, add new information to the graphic organizer on page 199 in your Inquiry Journal.

The Battle of Yorktown

George Washington had put the Marquis de Lafayette in charge of a troop of soldiers in Virginia. When Cornwallis marched north to Virginia, Lafayette wrote to Washington, "Were I to fight a battle, I should be cut to pieces. . . . I am not strong enough even to get beaten."

Lafayette did have an important secret weapon, however. James Armistead, who was enslaved in Virginia, volunteered to spy for Lafayette. From a position as Cornwallis's servant, he passed information about Cornwallis's plans and weaknesses.

From the intelligence Armistead provided, Lafayette formed a plan to **blockade** Chesapeake Bay. This prevented Cornwallis from resupplying his troops. Armistead told Cornwallis that the Americans planned to attack New York City, tricking Cornwallis into believing his army was safe at Yorktown.

Meanwhile, Washington's troops and a French army moved quickly and secretly to Yorktown to join Lafayette. By the time Cornwallis realized what had happened, he was surrounded by a force more than twice the size of his own.

French general Jean de Rochambeau, with George Washington, gives orders for the attack on Yorktown.

The British battled the Americans and French at Yorktown for nearly three weeks. American cannons fired into the British camp. The French blockade of Chesapeake Bay continued to prevent Cornwallis from getting any fresh supplies or troops. Finally, on October 19, 1781, Cornwallis surrendered to Washington.

Did You Know?

George Washington and the Comte de Rochambeau, a French general, were in New York when word came that Cornwallis had fled to Virginia. Washington wrote to Lafayette, telling him to keep Cornwallis there. Washington left a few men in New York and began a rapid march south to join Lafayette. After marching his men to Maryland, Washington met up with a French fleet of ships at Chesapeake Bay. The ships carried the Americans and French troops south to Williamsburg, Virginia. From there, Washington's troops joined Lafayette's and surrounded Cornwallis at Yorktown.

Marquis de Lafayette

COLLABORATE

✓ Stop and Check

Talk Why did Washington move quickly from New York to Virginia?

Battle Map of Yorktown

Washington and Lafayette created a plan that trapped Cornwallis on the Yorktown peninsula. A combination of French ships and French and American soldiers kept Cornwallis from getting new supplies.

French ships carried French and American troops south to Williamsburg, Virginia.

Washington's troops met Lafayette's troops to surround the British.

A blockade of French ships prevented the British from getting supplies.

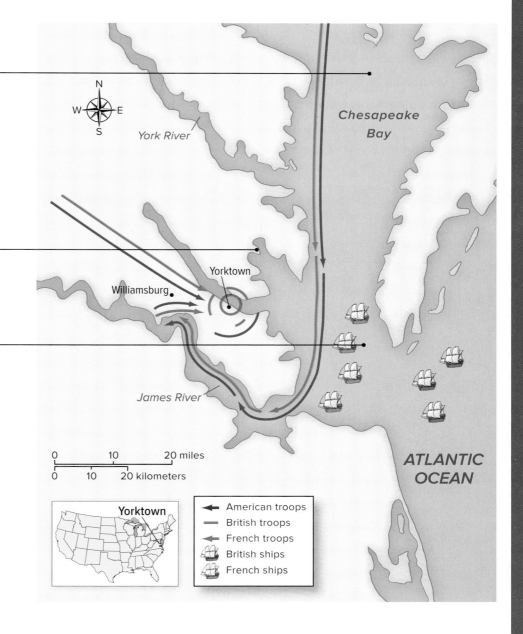

York River

Chesapeake Bay

Yorktown

Williamsburg

James River

ATLANTIC OCEAN

| 0 | 10 | 20 miles |
| 0 | 10 | 20 kilometers |

Yorktown

◄— American troops
— British troops
◄— French troops
🚢 British ships
🚢 French ships

Ending the War

The Battle of Yorktown marked the end of the main British resistance to American independence. There were still British troops in several cities and on the frontier, but the cost of the war had gotten so high that the British people were opposed to supporting the war with their taxes.

The slow process of ending the war began as Britain agreed to **negotiate** a treaty with the United States and its allies, France and Spain. The peace talks took place in Paris. John Adams, Benjamin Franklin, and John Jay were on hand to negotiate for the United States.

The Peace of Paris, as it came to be called, was the treaty that ended the American Revolution. As part of the agreement, Britain had to recognize American independence. The Mississippi River became the nation's new western boundary. Spain regained Florida, and France regained Senegal from the British in Africa. The Continental Congress made the treaty official in April 1783. After eight years of fighting, the 13 colonies were recognized as the United States of America.

A modern reenactment of the battle at Yorktown, Virginia

Nancy Carter/North Wind Picture Archives

TEXT: Treaties and Other International Acts of the United States of America. Edited by Hunter Miller. Volume 2 Documents 1-40 : 1776-1818. Washington: Government Printing Office, 1931.; PHOTO: (bkgd)McGraw-Hill Education; (t)Kean Collection/Archive Photos/Getty Images; (b)National Archives and Records Administration (299805)

John Adams (seated, left), Benjamin Franklin, and John Jay (standing, right) signed the Peace of Paris for the United States.

PRIMARY SOURCE

Peace of Paris, Article I

His Britannic Majesty acknowledges the said United States, viz., New Hampshire, Massachusetts Bay, Rhode Island and Providence Plantations, Connecticut, New York, New Jersey, Pennsylvania, Maryland, Virginia, North Carolina, South Carolina and Georgia, to be free sovereign and independent states, that he treats with them as such, and for himself, his heirs, and successors, relinquishes all claims to the government, propriety, and territorial rights of the same and every part thereof.

✓ Stop and Check

Talk What agreements were part of the Peace of Paris?

No Victory for Some

After the war ended, the 40,000 Loyalists left in the country had to decide what to do. Some moved to Canada, which was still controlled by the British. Others remained in the United States. They tried to make the best of life there, but many were forced to give up their homes and property.

Slaves had hoped the end of the war would mean the end of slavery. To create a united government, however, the Congress agreed to allow slavery to continue in the Southern Colonies in return for Southern support.

American Indians—including the Mohawk and Iroquois—who had sided with the British found that more and more Americans settled on Indian lands. The Americans saw the native peoples as enemies because of the Iroquois alliance with the British. Eventually, the Mohawk and Iroquois signed a peace agreement with the United States.

It would still take many years before the phrase "all men are created equal" could truly include all people in the United States.

North Wind Picture Archives/Alamy Stock Photo

Those African Americans who were free at the end of the Revolutionary War also met with disappointments. They found themselves receiving unequal treatment in many forms. One free African American in Massachusetts, Prince Hall, collected signatures for a petition protesting one form of this discrimination.

TEXT: Hall, Prince. "Petition for Equal Educational Facilities," (October 17, 1787). Quoted in Herbert Aptheker, ed., A Documentary History of the Negro People in the United States: From Colonial Times through the Civil War, Volume 1. (New York: Citadel Press, 1951), 19–20.; PHOTO: McGraw-Hill Education

PRIMARY SOURCE

In Their Words... Prince Hall

. . . we are of the humble opinion that we have the right to enjoy the privileges of free men. But that we do not will appear in many instances, and we beg leave to mention one out of many, and that is of the education of our children which now receive no benefit from the free schools in the town of Boston, which we think is a great grievance, as by woeful experience we now feel the want of a common education. We, therefore, must fear for our rising offspring to see them in ignorance in a land of gospel light when there is provision made for them as well as others and yet can't enjoy them, and for not other reason can be given this they are black.

—from a petition presented to the Massachusetts state legislature, October 1787

 Stop and Check

Talk What happened to Loyalists after the war?

What Do You Think? Did everyone in the United States gain his or her independence as a result of the war?

Connections in Action!
Back to the EQ

Think about the Chapter EQ, **"What Does the Revolutionary Era Tell Us about Our Nation Today?"**

- **Talk** with a partner about the people and events that you read about in this chapter. Consider ways that they contributed to the cause of freedom from Great Britain.

- How do these people and events continue to influence our nation today?

- **Share** your ideas with the class.

(bkgd)Yale University Art Gallery; (tl)Library of Congress Prints & Photographs Division [LC-DIG-pga-00995]; (bl)Library of Congress Prints and Photographs Division [LC-USZC2-2711]; (br)From The

More to Explore

How Can You Make an IMPACT?

Debate in Action

The colonists were divided about whether or not to go to war with Great Britain. If you were a colonist, which side would you have supported? Why?

Take a Stand

Choose a person from this chapter who you think was one of the most important figures in the American Revolution. Make a list of the reasons you think that way. Use evidence from the text to support your opinion. Get together with a partner or small group and talk about your choice. Be prepared to defend your thinking!

Word Play

Choose three words from the chapter Word Bank. For each of those words, find two words that have the same base word. Write the definition for each base word. For example, for the word *revolutionary*, you could use *revolt* and *revolution*. Get together with a partner and switch word lists. Take turns using each new word in a sentence.

Forming a New Government

How Does the Constitution Help Us Understand What It Means to Be an American?

In this chapter, you'll read about how the United States Constitution was developed. You'll learn about the people who created a stronger national government, their opinions about how it should be run, and the pressures that drove them to compromise on important issues. You'll examine how the Constitution has changed over the course of U.S. history to protect the rights of all people.

Step into the Time Chronological Thinking

Look at the time line. What was happening in other parts of the world while the United States Constitution was being developed?

Americas

1776
Declaration of Independence is signed; Congress creates Articles of Confederation.

1777
United States starts operating under Articles of Confederation.

1781
Articles of Confederation is ratified by all 13 states.

1775   1780

World Events

1778
Captain James Cook becomes first European to visit Hawaiian Islands.

1779
War breaks out in South Africa between Dutch settlers and the Xhosa people.

HSS.5.7.1, HSS.5.7.2, HSS.5.7.4, HAS.CS.4

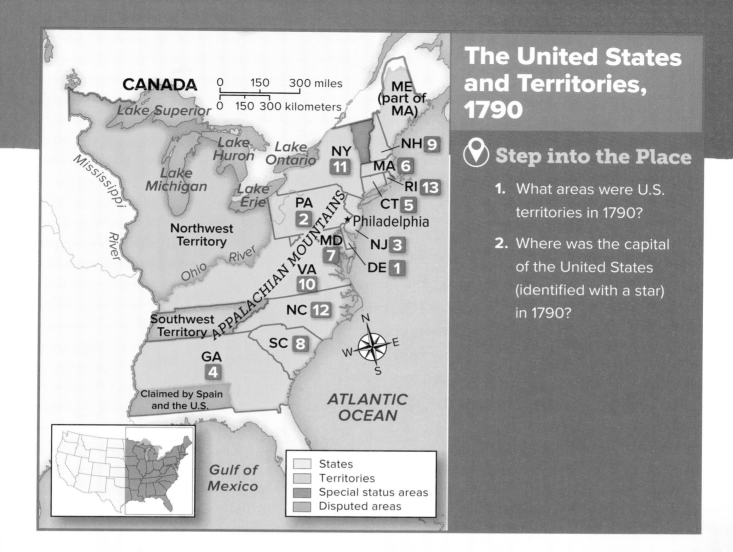

The United States and Territories, 1790

Step into the Place

1. What areas were U.S. territories in 1790?

2. Where was the capital of the United States (identified with a star) in 1790?

Map labels:

CANADA

0   150   300 miles
0 150 300 kilometers

Lake Superior
Lake Huron
Lake Ontario
Lake Michigan
Lake Erie
Mississippi River
Northwest Territory
Ohio River
Southwest Territory
APPALACHIAN MOUNTAINS

ME (part of MA)
NH 9
NY 11
MA 6
RI 13
PA 2
CT 5
★Philadelphia
MD 7
NJ 3
VA 10
DE 1
NC 12
SC 8
GA 4
Claimed by Spain and the U.S.
ATLANTIC OCEAN
Gulf of Mexico

N S E W (compass)

Legend:
- States
- Territories
- Special status areas
- Disputed areas

Once the Constitutional Convention agreed on the Constitution, at least nine states had to agree to it too. One by one, the 13 states signed the document and officially became part of the United States, beginning with Delaware and ending with Rhode Island. Gradually, new states joined the Union, but it took 169 years for the United States to look as it does today.

May 1787
Constitutional Convention convenes in Philadelphia.
July 1787
The Great Compromise is made.
December 1787
States begin to ratify Constitution.

May 1790
Last of 13 original states ratifies Constitution.

1785

1790

1783
Crimea becomes Russian territory following conflict with the Ottoman Empire.

1787
Mozart's opera *Don Giovanni* premiers in Prague.

1789
The French Revolution begins.

1789
Antoine-Laurent Lavoisier develops a way to organize chemical elements, beginning the study of modern chemistry.

Connect Through Literature

A Ship Called the Hamilton

by Virginia Calkins

It was July 23, 1788, and New York City was having a big parade. The Constitution of the United States had finally been ratified by ten states, and the people of New York wanted to celebrate.

Caught up in the excitement were Philip, Angelica, and Alexander, the natural children of Alexander and Betsy Hamilton. Fanny Antil, the orphan whom the Hamiltons had adopted, was excited, too. Baby James was only four months old, a bit too young to understand. The children waited impatiently for the parade to begin. Suddenly they heard the boom of a cannon. That was the starting signal.

A group of trumpeters led the parade. Then came artillerymen pulling a large cannon. Suddenly Philip exclaimed, "Look, everybody!" Coming toward them was a huge float pulled by ten white horses. The float was a replica of a ship, a thirty-two-gun frigate. It had been constructed by shipbuilders and was twenty-seven feet long, large enough for a crew of thirty plus their officers.

As the float came closer, Angelica noticed something familiar about the figurehead at the front of the ship. "That looks like Papa," she said, raising her voice to make herself heard above the cheers of the crowd.

"Yes, child, the figurehead was carved to look like your father," Mrs. Hamilton said. "The banner says that the ship is named the Hamilton."

Philip gave her a puzzled look. "Why did they name it after Father?" he asked.

"The people of New York are grateful to your father for the work he has done for the Constitution," his mother replied. "Remember when he was in Philadelphia last summer?"

Philip nodded. He remembered well.

"He was helping to write the Constitution then," Mrs. Hamilton said. "And remember last winter when he stayed up late night after night writing *The Federalist Papers*? Your father, Mr. Madison, and Mr. Jay wrote those papers to help people understand the Constitution and urge them to support it."

"I wish Father was here," Philip said with a sigh.

"I wish he was, too," his mother replied. "But your father is needed in Poughkeepsie. The State of New York is having a convention to decide whether it will ratify the Constitution, and your father is a delegate."

"Here comes another ship," little Alexander shouted.

This ship was made by sail makers and named the New Constitution. A carved figure of Alexander Hamilton stood on its deck, with papers representing the new Constitution in his right hand and the Articles of Confederation in his left. This was to indicate the change from the Articles of Confederation to the Constitution.

More floats followed. Angelica and Fanny liked the one that featured a beautiful garland of artificial flowers. Three of the flowers were drooping, and Mrs. Hamilton explained that they represented the three states (including New York) that had not yet ratified the Constitution.

The parade continued, with marching bands, tradesmen and merchants, doctors, professors, and public officials. Ten law students carried the ten state ratifications. Three officials carried the new Constitution. More than five thousand people participated in the parade.

When it was over and the Hamiltons turned toward home, Philip declared, "That was wonderful! I hope Father comes home soon so I can tell him all about it."

Eighty miles away in Poughkeepsie, Alexander Hamilton was fighting for ratification. When the convention had begun on June 17, only nineteen of the sixty-five delegates favored ratification. The leaders of the opposition were Governor George Clinton, who was the chairman of the convention, and Melancton Smith, a great debater. Hamilton believed that it was extremely important that New York join the Union. Besides being centrally located geographically, it also was a center of trade and commerce. How could he win over his opponents?

First he persuaded the delegates to debate the Constitution clause by clause, thus taking up time until he heard from New Hampshire or Virginia. At that point eight states had ratified; another would mean that the Constitution would go into effect, with or without New York. Hamilton hoped that another ratification would convince some of the delegates to switch sides.

When an Antifederalist introduced an amendment to make U.S. senators subject to recall by their state legislatures, Hamilton jumped up to object. He insisted that the Senate must be a stable body, not subject to the whims of state legislatures. As the debate dragged on, Hamilton waited anxiously for word from his friends.

Suddenly he heard hoof beats. An express rider brought news that on June 21 New Hampshire had ratified the Constitution. The United States of America had been born!

Still the Antifederalists would not give in. Governor Clinton suggested fifty-five amendments. He was willing to enter the Union on the condition that New York could withdraw if these amendments failed to pass within a reasonable time. Hamilton could not agree to this.

On July 2, a messenger arrived from James Madison. Virginia had ratified! With this large state in the Union, it would be difficult for New York to stand alone.

Word reached Poughkeepsie about the parade being planned in New York City. There were rumors that the city might secede from the state if the convention failed to ratify. On July 23, Melancton Smith and his men switched sides. The next day there was a move for conditional ratification. Hamilton read a letter from Madison to the delegates that said New York could not enter the Union "conditionally." Finally, on July 26, New York ratified the Constitution with a recommendation for a Bill of Rights and other amendments. The vote was 30 to 27.

Alexander Hamilton returned to his family a tired but happy man. Proudly, he showed the ratification document to Betsy and the children. The children were impressed, but they really wanted to tell their father about the parade.

"It was tremendous," Philip related. "There was a ship called the Hamilton."

His father picked up the ratification papers and moved toward the door. "I must bring this document to the Continental Congress at the City Hall," he said. "But I will return soon, and you can tell me about the parade. I want to hear everything, particularly about that ship called the Hamilton!"

Think About It

1. Why was a parade held in New York City on July 23, 1788?

2. What was Alexander Hamilton's tactic to get New York state to ratify the constitution?

3. What are two pieces of evidence that show that New York City was in favor of ratifying the Constitution, even if the rest of the state was not?

People You Should Know

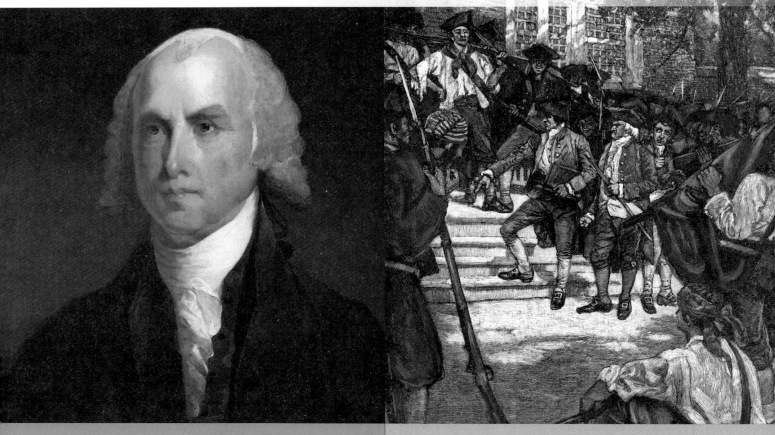

James Madison

Known as the Father of the Constitution, James Madison created policies during the Constitutional Convention that shaped much of the U.S. Government as we know it today. After the convention, he worked with Alexander Hamilton and John Jay to promote ratification of the Constitution in a series of essays called *The Federalist Papers.* As a member of Congress, he supported adding to the Constitution ten amendments, which would later be known as the Bill of Rights. In 1808, he was elected the fourth president of the United States.

Daniel Shays

A decorated veteran of the Revolutionary War, Daniel Shays later held local office in his native Massachusetts. When the economy declined during the years after the war, many people lost their homes and property. Shays led a group of people who protested this treatment. The short-lived but violent revolt came to be called Shays's Rebellion. Shays was arrested and sentenced to death but eventually granted a pardon.

George Mason

Though a respected member of Virginia society, George Mason had never been very interested in holding public office. When the Constitutional Convention convened in 1787, however, he accepted a post as one of Virginia's delegates. He argued against the compromise that ensured slavery would continue in the new nation. He argued for adding a bill of rights to the Constitution, protecting individual freedoms. The U.S. Bill of Rights was based partly on Virginia's state bill of rights, which Mason had written.

Martin Luther King Jr.

Even after the Emancipation Proclamation and the Civil War ended slavery in the United States, African Americans living in the South were still not free. They were separated from white people in public places, and they were treated with injustice and prejudice. In the 1950s and 1960s, Martin Luther King Jr., helped African Americans gain important civil and economic rights with his focus on peaceful protest and his inspiring messages. In one such speech, called the "I Have a Dream" speech, he envisioned a time when all people would live together in peace.

What Was the Articles of Confederation and Why Did It Fail?

One Nation or Thirteen States?

The **Articles** of Confederation was the first written document to establish a United States government. The Second Continental Congress began writing the Articles of Confederation in 1776 and approved it in 1777. However, it was not ratified by all 13 states until 1781. Its writers imagined a nation unlike European countries. They promised a "firm league of friendship" in which each state was guaranteed its "freedom and independence."

The Articles granted new powers to the national government. It created a Confederation Congress to govern the country. The Congress created departments of finance, foreign affairs, war, and the post office. The Congress also signed a peace treaty with Great Britain, formally ending the Revolutionary War.

The Articles allowed the states to continue to run their own governments independently. States retained the right to print their own money. States also had the authority to tax while the Confederation Congress did not. By 1786, many of the thirteen states had written their own constitutions that challenged the authority of the Articles of Confederation. Meanwhile, the Confederation Congress passed laws controlling the growth of the new country.

HSS.5.6.5, HSS.5.6.6, HSS.5.7.1, HSS.5.9, HAS.HI.1, HAS.HI.3, HAS.CS.1, HAS.HR.1, HAS.HR.2

258 Lesson 1 What Was the Articles of Confederation and Why Did It Fail?

McGraw-Hill Education

Time Line

1776
Declaration of Independence signed; Second Continental Congress creates Articles of Confederation.

1781
Articles ratified by all 13 states

1787
Northwest Ordinance is passed; Constitutional Convention begins.

1770

1780

1790

1777
The United States starts operating under the Articles.

1786–1787
Shays's Rebellion

Daniel Shays leads farmers in a rebellion against the government of Massachusetts.

©North Wind Picture Archives

The Northwest Ordinance

Congress organized the settlement of the Northwest Territory under the Articles of Confederation. This territory included land north of the Ohio River and east of the Mississippi River. The government would later divide the Northwest Territory into the states of Ohio, Indiana, Illinois, Michigan, and Wisconsin.

Congress **issued** the Northwest Ordinance to help organize the territory. The law defined a strict structure for the settlements. Areas with small populations could vote on legislators. Regions with at least 60,000 adults could register for statehood.

The Northwest Territory was divided into rectangular townships. Each township included 36 sections. Large companies bought much of the land in the townships. The companies sold smaller portions to settlers for a profit. Arthur St. Clair ran the Ohio Company. The company owned 1.5 million acres of the Northwest Territory. He became the first governor of the Northwest Territory.

In 1783, Congress ruled that, after the Revolutionary War, American Indians no longer held the right to land in the Northwest Territory. The U.S. government began to treat the native peoples as conquered nations. Congress sent soldiers to the territory to remove American Indians by force.

One army officer reported that settlers regularly attacked and killed groups of American Indians without government support. To defend themselves, the Miami, Shawnee, and Delaware peoples formed a military alliance. In 1791, Miami chief Little Turtle led an attack on Arthur St. Clair's troops. Nine hundred of the U.S. troops were killed. It was the worst defeat suffered by U.S. soldiers in the history of war against American Indians. Little Turtle died in one of the battles that followed, but the American Indians' resistance forced the U.S. government to negotiate peace agreements.

The Northwest Ordinance declared that "neither slavery nor involuntary servitude" was allowed in the Northwest Territory. In the mid-1780s, however, most states outside of the territory still permitted white men to own slaves. Even free African Americans had many fewer rights than whites.

Prohibited from worshipping in white churches, African Americans created their own churches. Richard Allen founded the first fully independent African-American church in Philadelphia in 1794, the African Methodist Episcopal (A.M.E.) Church. Communities of African-American worshippers would go on to build A.M.E. churches across the United States.

The Northwest Territory, 1787

 Map Skills About how far is it from the northernmost part of the Northwest Territory to the southernmost part?

✓ Stop and Check

COLLABORATE

Talk If you were living in one of the original thirteen colonies, would you consider moving to the Northwest Territory? Working with a partner, discuss the pros and cons of settling in the territory.

Find Details As you read, add additional information to the graphic organizer on page 217 in your Inquiry Journal.

A Call for Stronger Government

The Articles of Confederation eventually proved to be weak in governing the United States as a single nation. Without the backing of a strong national government, American banks often found it difficult to make sure borrowers repaid their loans. In addition, each state maintained its own **currency**. Merchants and companies struggled to do business in more than one state. Doing so involved understanding highly complicated state laws as well as confusing differences in the value of states' money.

The national government, meanwhile, did not collect taxes. Instead, Congress asked for money from state governments. After the Revolutionary War, Congress needed $15.7 million to pay its debts. The states agreed to pay the national government only $2.4 million.

The United States could not afford to pay money owed to some of the military officials and leaders who had fought in the Revolutionary War. These people became increasingly frustrated with the government's lack of power over the states.

Did You Know?

The U.S. government first issued print money during the Revolutionary War. These bills, called Continental Currency, helped pay for the war against the British. Realizing this, the British government printed counterfeit bills and passed them out in the United States. They succeeded in weakening the U.S. government by lowering the worth of the Continental Currency. This was the first example of paper-money counterfeiting as a form of economic warfare.

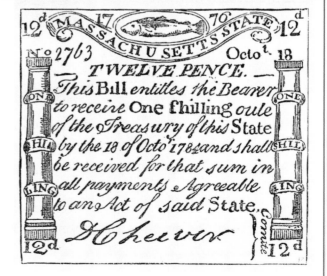

Paper money issued by the state of Massachusetts

In the 1780s, the national government's money problems led to violent conflict. Merchants in Boston decided to require that their bills be paid in gold and silver. They thought that the Massachusetts currency was too unstable. When farmers in western Massachusetts could not produce the necessary gold and silver coins to pay off their debts, they were jailed in large numbers.

The imprisoned farmers appealed to the Massachusetts legislature to help them pay their debts. The members of the legislature, however, were mostly lawyers and merchants who paid little attention to the farmers' requests. The legislators voted to raise taxes. This decision further burdened poor farmers.

The angry farmers had just recently experienced the power of revolt in the Revolutionary War. In 1786, they blocked the entrances of several county courthouses to stop the legal processes required to take the indebted farmers' land. Rebels attacked jails and released farmers who had been imprisoned. Daniel Shays, a Revolutionary War captain who was now a struggling farmer, led the rebels.

Daniel Shays and his supporters protested high taxes.

A group of Shays's men attacked a state arsenal—a building where weapons are stored—in 1787. A local militia defeated Shays's forces as they attempted to seize the weapons. Four men died and 20 more were wounded. Shays's Rebellion persisted nonetheless.

As the rebels continued to cause havoc in the state, the governor of Massachusetts, John Hancock, sent more than 4,000 troops to stop the rebellion. Badly outnumbered, most of Shays's men fled. The Massachusetts government captured and sentenced fifteen rebels to death. Two of the accused were executed, while Hancock pardoned the rest. Daniel Shays left Massachusetts for New York, where he returned to farming.

In the end, the Massachusetts government easily stopped Shays's Rebellion. The event nonetheless cast doubt over the Articles of Confederation. Wealthy Americans wanted a government that could protect their property against rebellions. Farmers needed a government that could print money and make laws on trade. The writers of the Articles had tried to avoid creating another overbearing national government, such as the British Parliament, which had passed laws without consulting with the American colonies. As a result, the states did not always think of themselves as a united country.

The nation's early leaders began to make plans to change. They wanted to act fast to avoid more rebellions. Members of Congress met to discuss how best to strengthen the Articles of Confederation. Eventually, they decided to hold a conference to change the document by which the nation was governed. Henry Lee, Jr., a friend of George Washington, explained the need for a change.

PRIMARY SOURCE

In Their Words ... Henry Lee, Jr.

The period seems to be fast approaching when the people of these United States must determine to establish a permanent capable government or submit to the horrors of anarchy …. The decay of their commerce leaves the lower order unemployed, idleness in this body, and the intriguing exertions of another class whose desperate fortunes are remediable only by the ruin of society.

—from a letter to George Washington, September 8, 1786

✓ Stop and Check   COLLABORATE

Talk How did the weaknesses of the Articles of Confederation lead to Shays's Rebellion?

Henry Lee, Jr. to George Washington, 8 September 1786. Founders Online, National Archives.

Views on Rebellion

Thomas Jefferson and Samuel Adams—two of the signers of the Declaration of Independence—had widely different opinions regarding Shays's Rebellion. Read the following quotations from both men and consider their views in the context of what you have just read.

Thomas Jefferson

"I hold it that a little rebellion now and then is a good thing, and as necessary in the political world as storms in the **physical**. . . ."

Samuel Adams

"The man who dares to rebel against the laws of a republic ought to suffer death."

✓ Stop and Check
COLLABORATE

You Decide Working with a partner, choose to support either Adams or Jefferson in the debate over rebellion. Then partner with another pair of students who chose to support the opposite position. Take turns arguing each side, making sure to use specific details from the lesson to support your position.

What Do You Think? Why would Adams, who rebelled against Britain, oppose a rebellion against the U.S. government?

TEXT: (l)Thomas Jefferson to James Madison, Paris, January 30, 1787. The Thomas Jefferson Papers Series 1. General Correspondence. 1651-1827. Library of Congress.; (r)Adams, Samuel. 1787. Quoted in Republic: A Monthly Magazine, Devoted to the Dissemination of Political Information, Vol. 4 (Washington, D.C.: The Republic Publishing Company, 1875), 185.; PHOTO: (t)McGraw-Hill Education; (l)Stocktrek Images/Getty Images; (r)Library of Congress Prints & Photographs Division [LC-US262-102271]

How Does the Constitution Set Up Our Government Framework?

The Constitutional Convention

Shays's Rebellion showed that there was much dissatisfaction with the Articles of Confederation. On February 21, 1787, the Confederation Congress decided to gather **delegates** to discuss changing the Articles. This convention of delegates would take place at the Pennsylvania State House in Philadelphia. Invitations were sent to the states. All but Rhode Island sent delegates to the Constitutional Convention. Members of the Continental Congress were not the only delegates at the convention. The delegates also included Revolutionary War veterans, governors, lawyers, plantation owners, merchants, and other influential people. In total, fifty-five men took part in the convention, which began on May 25, 1787. They met in secret so that the delegates could speak freely and suggest ideas that might have hurt their reputations if the ideas became known. The doors were locked and the windows were covered. Although the convention's purpose was to fix the Articles of Confederation, the delegates soon began to write a new constitution for a new government.

HSS 5.4.6, HSS 5.7.2, HSS 5.7.3, HSS.5.7.4, HAS.HI.3

McGraw-Hill Education

February 1787
Confederation Congress calls for the rewriting of the Articles of Confederation.

July 1787
The Great Compromise is made.

June 1788
New Hampshire ratifies the Constitution, making it the law of the land.

1787   1788   1789   1790

May 1787
Constitutional Convention begins.

December 1787
Delaware is the first state to ratify the Constitution.

May 1790
Rhode Island becomes the last of the original 13 colonies to ratify the Constitution.

CONSTITUTION
OF THE
UNITED STATES OF AMERICA

The U.S. Constitution on display at the National Archives

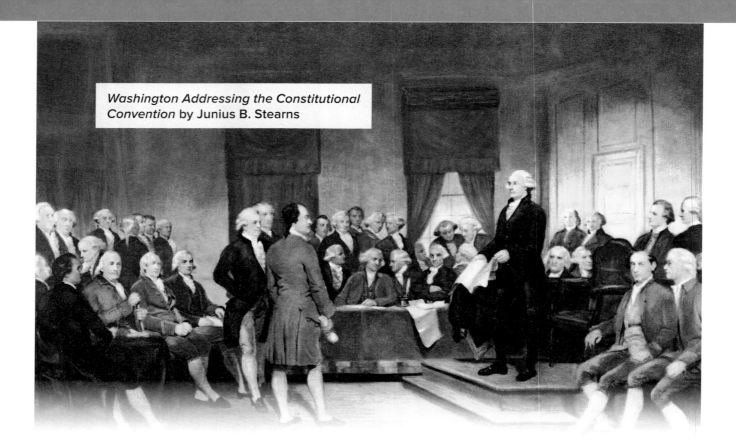

Washington Addressing the Constitutional Convention by Junius B. Stearns

Conflicts and Compromises

George Washington was elected to lead the convention, but James Madison of Virginia did most of the work on the actual writing of the Constitution. Madison was largely responsible for convincing the other delegates to abandon the idea of fixing the Articles of Confederation. Madison wanted to start over and create a stronger national government. He gave strong support to the Virginia Plan, a plan conceived by Virginia governor Edmund Randolph.

The Virginia Plan called for a two-part legislature to make the laws. The members of the first part, or lower house, were to be elected by voters. The members of the second part, or upper house, were to be chosen by the members of the lower house. The lower house would also select a president as well as judges for a national court. In the Virginia Plan, Congress had the ability to veto state laws and even take over a state's government. The number of legislators in the houses would be calculated based on the number of people in each state.

James Madison championed the Virginia Plan.

Some delegates had problems with the Virginia Plan. Under it, Congress would consist mainly of delegates from the states with the most people. These states would have more say in making laws and choosing officials. They could even take control of the governments of the smaller states. New Jersey delegate William Paterson offered an alternative. His New Jersey Plan also had a legislature to write laws. Its legislature would have only one house, and each state would have only one delegate. This way, every state would have an equal say.

This plan was opposed by the larger states. They asked why a small state should have the same power as a large state. If the government of a nation was not controlled by the majority of its people, then how could the government be a democracy? Furthermore, these delegates saw the plan as being too similar to the Articles of Confederation.

The New Jersey Plan did answer some of the problems in the Articles, however. The national government would have some control over trade and would be able to raise money through import and stamp duties. There would also be an executive position created to control the military. Nonetheless, these measures weren't enough to convince the other delegates. They believed the New Jersey Plan would fail just as the Articles of Confederation had.

William Paterson created the New Jersey Plan.

InfoGraphic

A Comparison of the Three Plans

New Jersey Plan

- Appealed to smaller states
- Had a one-part legislature
- Each state would get one representative in the legislature.

Virginia Plan

- Appealed to larger states
- Had a two-part legislature – a lower house would be elected by voters; an upper house would be elected by the lower house
- The number of representatives in the houses would be based on the number of people in each state.

Great Compromise

- Has a two-part legislature
- The House of Representatives' number of representatives would be determined by the population of each state.
- The Senate would have two delegates from each state.
- A law would not be approved until it passed through both the House of Representatives and the Senate.

So who was right? Both sides had fair points. *Democracy* means that laws should be agreed on by the majority of people, not by a small group of rulers. But states with small populations shouldn't be powerless against larger states. The argument continued for a month before Connecticut delegate Roger Sherman proposed the Great Compromise.

The Great Compromise combined the two plans. It called for a legislature with two houses. In one house, the House of Representatives, the population of a state would determine how many delegates the state would get. Here, the larger states had more power. In the other house, the Senate, each state would have two delegates. This would give the smaller states protection from the larger states. In order for a law to be approved, it would have to pass through both the House of Representatives and the Senate. In other words, a law would have to be supported by both a majority of the people and a majority of the states. The Great Compromise was adopted on July 16, 1787.

In addition to the Great Compromise, there was the Three-Fifths Compromise. Many of the delegates at the Constitutional Convention owned plantations with slaves. Should these people be counted as part of the population? Counting them would give states with slavery more representatives. Since the slaves didn't have any political power of their own, those extra votes would go to their masters. Without those extra votes, there was a good chance that Congress would outlaw slavery. The Southern states refused to join the new government unless they could be sure that Congress couldn't end slavery. Thus, the delegates decided that slaves would be counted, but for less than free persons. For every five slaves counted, three people would be added to the population count when determining representatives. The Southern states also agreed to stop future trading with other countries for slaves in 1808. However, people already enslaved, and their children, were to remain enslaved.

✅ Stop and Check

Think Which parts of the Great Compromise came from the Virginia Plan? Which part came from the New Jersey Plan?

Find Details As you read, add additional information to the graphic organizer on page 225 in your Inquiry Journal.

What Do You Think? Do you think the plan outlined in the Great Compromise was the best choice? Why or why not?

McGraw-Hill Education

The New Government

After nearly four months of work, the delegates of the Constitutional Convention completed and signed the new U.S. Constitution. The document begins with a one-sentence Preamble, or introduction, that explains the purpose of the Constitution. The Preamble reflects the primary belief of the founders of this country: A government is meant to serve its people. The government has to be effective enough to help people but organized in a way to prevent it from oppressing them. The delegates believed that a national government should have only as much power as the people allow it to have. To prevent the government from becoming too strong, the Constitution created a federal system in which the powers of government are divided. There is division of powers between state and national government, and there is also division of powers among the three branches of the national government.

The thirteen colonies rebelled against Great Britain because the British government had too much power and the colonies had too little. The Articles of Confederation failed because the states had too much power and the national government had too little. This time, the framers of the Constitution wanted to get the balance of power just right.

The Pennsylvania State House, now known as Independence Hall, where the U.S. Constitution was signed on September 17, 1787

Comstock/Getty Images

Both the state and the national governments can make laws and collect taxes. State governments, however, determine matters such as marriage age, driving age, and much of what is taught in public schools. State and local governments are also in charge of services like most police and fire protection, public libraries, and public transportation. What people need or want from a government can vary from person to person, city to city, and state to state. The founders thought it best to have many everyday duties handled by state and local governments. The average person can access these government bodies more easily. They also can shift more easily to suit the unique needs of their area.

Meanwhile, the national government is divided into three branches: the legislative branch, the executive branch, and the judicial branch. Each branch has its own set of powers and duties, and no branch can do the job of another. Not only that, each branch has powers and weaknesses compared with the other branches. This system of checks and balances ensures that no individual or group becomes too powerful.

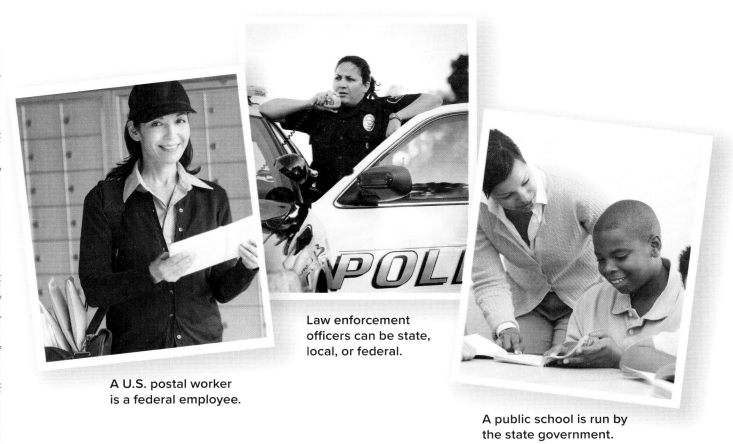

A U.S. postal worker is a federal employee.

Law enforcement officers can be state, local, or federal.

A public school is run by the state government.

The legislative branch is in charge of making laws. It consists of Congress, which has two houses. In the House of Representatives, each state has a number of representatives depending on how many people live in the state. The representatives serve for two-year **terms**, and then they have to be re-elected if they want to stay. The other house, the Senate, has two senators for every state. Senators serve six-year terms, and they also can be re-elected. The members of Congress write **bills**, and a bill must be approved by both houses to be passed. The bills passed by Congress must be approved by the executive branch to become laws. If a bill is not approved by the executive branch, it can still become a law if a large majority of Congress approves it. Laws can be ruled unconstitutional by the judicial branch.

The executive branch carries out the law. The highest position is the President of the United States, but the executive branch also includes the vice president and the cabinet, which is composed of the leaders of various government departments. These departments include the Department of State, the Department of Defense, and the Department of Justice. The department heads are chosen by the president. Through these departments, the executive branch enforces the law. The president also commands the military and has the ability to sign treaties. The president also chooses justices for the Supreme Court. If the president fails to do the job properly, the legislative branch can impeach him or her. The judicial branch can rule presidential actions as unconstitutional.

The judicial branch makes decisions on how laws are interpreted. It consists of the Supreme Court, a group of nine justices who make decisions about whether laws are fair and how they should be applied. Unlike the legislative and executive branches, most justices of the judicial branch serve for life. Each federal justice is selected by the president and must be approved by the Senate.

 Stop and Check

Think Why did the founders want the government's powers and duties separated?

Checks and Balances

Executive Branch

President (elected)

- Enforces laws
- Is Commander-in-Chief
- Signs or vetoes laws
- Nominates judges

Legislative Branch

Congress (elected)

- Can override veto
- Passes laws
- Approves spending and taxes
- Can charge judges with wrongdoing
- Approves treaties

Judicial Branch

Supreme Court and other federal courts (appointed)

- Interpret laws
- Can rule whether actions or laws passed are constitutional

 Stop and Check

Think Give two examples of checks by the legislative branch.

Economic Aspects of the Constitution

One of the weaknesses of the national government under the Articles of Confederation was its lack of power in economic matters. An important part of the new constitution was granting additional powers to Congress so that it could have some control of the U.S. economy. Under the Constitution, Congress could create and collect taxes and similar fees and borrow money if needed. This way, the government was finally able to pay some of its outstanding debts from the Revolutionary War.

On another economic matter, states would no longer be able to make their own currency. Congress now had the power to coin, or create, money. The whole nation would now use a single currency. This made it much easier for people from different states to do business across state lines. Congress also became responsible for overseeing trade with other nations, including American Indian groups.

Congress did not have total control of the economy, though. It wasn't allowed to pass certain types of taxes. Nor could it tax trade between states or do anything else that would favor one state over another. Any money that Congress received had to be appropriated, or set aside for a specific purpose. That money could not be spent on anything else. These rules were intended to ensure the fairness of the U.S. economy so that many people had a chance to prosper.

In Their Words... The Constitution

Article I Section 8. Powers Granted to Congress

1. The Congress shall have power to lay and collect taxes, duties, imposts and excises, to pay the debts and provide for the common defense and general welfare of the United States; but all duties, imposts, and excises shall be uniform throughout the United States;

2. To borrow money on the credit of the United States;

3. To regulate commerce with foreign nations, and among the several states, and with the Indian tribes;

4. To establish a uniform rule of naturalization, and uniform laws on the subject of bankruptcies throughout the United States;

5. To coin money, regulate the value thereof, and of foreign coin, and fix the standard of weights and measures;

6. To provide for the punishment of counterfeiting the securities and current coin of the United States;

7. To establish post offices and post roads . . .

What Do You Think? Reread the excerpt of the Constitution above. Why is it important that these duties are performed at the national level rather than at the state level?

✓ Stop and Check

COLLABORATE

Talk What was the most important improvement the Constitution had over the Articles of Confederation? Debate your opinion with a partner.

Find Details Complete the graphic organizer on page 225 in your Inquiry Journal using information you have gathered.

Lesson 3

How Do the Constitution and Bill of Rights Impact Citizens?

The Debate over Ratification

The states had to ratify, or officially approve, the Constitution for it to become law. The two sides of the constitutional debate went to work to earn the support of the people of the United States. The Federalists defended the Constitution. Their ranks included George Washington, James Madison, and Alexander Hamilton. The Antifederalists opposed the Constitution. Antifederalists such as Samuel Adams, George Mason, and Patrick Henry preferred the Articles of Confederation. Both the Federalists and Antifederalists wrote papers in defense of their positions.

The Federalists insisted that the Constitution would unify the states. They wanted to divide power between different parts of the federal government. They hoped to avoid giving too much power to any one person. James Madison, Alexander Hamilton, and John Jay made the case for Federalism in a series of 85 essays called *The Federalist Papers*. They wrote anonymously under the pen name "Publius." From 1787 to 1788, the essays appeared in several New York newspapers. Their authors reasoned that the Constitution would maintain order in the nation. "If men were angels," Madison wrote, "no government would be necessary."

HSS.5.7.2, HSS.5.7.3, HSS.5.7.4, HSS.5.7.5, HAS.CS.1, HAS.CS.3, HAS.HR.1, HAS.HR.2, HAS.HI.1, HAS.HI.3

McGraw-Hill Education

Time Line

1791
Bill of Rights
ratified

1865
Thirteenth
Amendment
ratified

1870
Fifteenth
Amendment
ratified

1961
Twenty-Third
Amendment
ratified

1971
Twenty-Sixth
Amendment
ratified

| 1750 | 1800 | 1850 | 1900 | 1950 | 2000 |

1868
Fourteenth
Amendment
ratified

1920
Nineteenth
Amendment
ratified

1964
Twenty-Fourth
Amendment
ratified

Women did not receive the constitutional
right to vote in national elections until 1920.

Tetra Images/Shutterstock.com

Antifederalists objected to the Constitution by pointing to its limited ability to protect Americans' liberties. In his essay "Objections to This Constitution of Government," George Mason attacked the document. He argued, "There is no declaration of any kind, for preserving the liberty of the **press**, or the trial by **jury** in civil cases; nor against the danger of standing armies in time of peace."

Nine out of thirteen states' votes were required to pass the Constitution. Delaware, New Jersey, and Pennsylvania first ratified the Constitution in December of 1787. New Hampshire gave the decisive ninth vote to accept the Constitution in 1788.

Some worried that the remaining states would prevent the Constitution from being enforced. New York and Virginia were the two largest states in the country. Many of their leaders refused to support the Constitution as written. In Massachusetts, Elbridge Gerry had argued against the Constitution. He felt that "a free people," not the government, "are the proper guardians of their rights and liberties." Massachusetts Antifederalists demanded that the Constitution be revised to clearly indicate the rights of citizens.

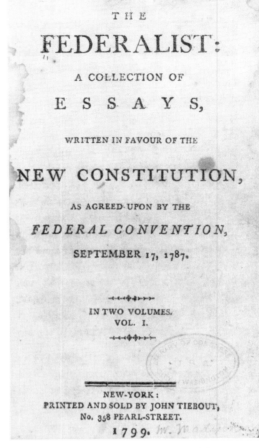

The Federalist Papers appeared in New York newspapers from 1787 to 1788.

PRIMARY SOURCE

In Their Words... Patrick Henry

Show me that age and country where the rights and liberties of the people were placed on the sole chance of their rulers being good men without a consequent loss of liberty! I say that the loss of that dearest privilege has ever followed, with absolute certainty, every such mad attempt.

—from a speech at the Virginia Constitution Ratifying Convention, 1788

TEXT: Patrick Henry, speaking before the Virginia Ratifying Convention, June 1788; PHOTO: Library of Congress, Prints & Photographs Division, LC-US262-70508

James Madison, a Federalist, agreed to propose a Bill of Rights to Congress. The Bill of Rights included liberties that the Antifederalists believed the Constitution would not guarantee Americans. Madison promised to argue on behalf of the bill if the Antifederalists ratified the Constitution.

The agreement worked. Virginia and New York ratified the Constitution in 1788. The House of Representatives received the Bill of Rights in June 1789. North Carolina and Rhode Island then became the final states to ratify the Constitution.

Many Antifederalists would not support the Constitution without a Bill of Rights.

✔ Stop and Check

Perspectives Why did the Federalists continue to seek approval from all remaining states after the Constitution was ratified?

Find Details As you read, add additional information to the graphic organizer on page 233 in your Inquiry Journal.

The Bill of Rights

In 1789, James Madison approached Congress with the first draft of a list of constitutional **amendments**. Congress chose 12 of these amendments to send to the states for approval. State leaders picked 10 of the amendments to ratify. Congress added the amendments, called the Bill of Rights, to the Constitution in December 1791.

Previously, government leaders had written documents defining the rights of their citizens. The British government signed a bill of rights in 1689. Several American states already had their own bills of rights by 1790. James Madison based his amendments partly on Virginia's bill of rights. Madison's Antifederalist rival, George Mason, had written this document in 1776.

The Bill of Rights was ratified after the main text of the Constitution, but that does not make the section any less important. The rights outlined in the Bill of Rights define many aspects of life in the United States. The Bill of Rights sets limits on the U.S. government and protects the basic rights of all U.S. citizens.

Included in the Bill of Rights is freedom of speech, which includes the right to protest.

The first part of the Bill of Rights secures the individual rights of the citizens of the United States. The First Amendment protects five freedoms: freedom of religion, freedom of speech, freedom of the press, freedom of assembly, and freedom to petition.

The Second Amendment protects the right of U.S. citizens "to keep and bear arms." The Supreme Court's interpretation of the amendment sets two constitutional rules. First, states can maintain militias. And second, the government may pass laws to control, but not prevent, the use of firearms by citizens. The Third Amendment makes it unconstitutional for the government to force people to house soldiers.

The Fourth through Eighth Amendments guarantee the right to "due process." Due process of the law requires the government to follow a set of procedures when taking legal action against citizens. Due process is important in limiting the power of government. The amendments name specific actions that the government cannot take against its people.

The Ninth Amendment states that the rights of Americans extend beyond what is recorded in the Constitution. In the Tenth Amendment, the Constitution reserves all rights not provided to the federal government to be left for the states and the people.

Due process includes the right to trial by jury.

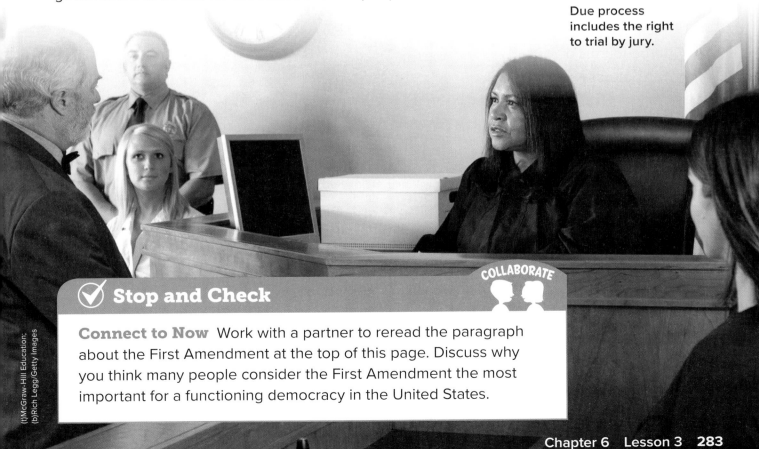

(t)McGraw-Hill Education; (b)Rich Legg/Getty Images

✓ Stop and Check

COLLABORATE

Connect to Now Work with a partner to reread the paragraph about the First Amendment at the top of this page. Discuss why you think many people consider the First Amendment the most important for a functioning democracy in the United States.

Amendments and Expanding Rights

The Bill of Rights introduced the first ten amendments to the Constitution. Seventeen more amendments have since been added. The Constitution's writers knew that the constitutional system needed flexibility. They wrote Article Five of the Constitution to define a process for amending the Constitution.

To become a part of the Constitution, an amendment must go through proposal and ratification. There are two ways to propose an amendment and two ways to ratify it.

Amendments may be proposed with the support of two-thirds of Congress. Alternatively, an amendment can be proposed if two-thirds of state legislatures call for a national convention. The amendment can then be ratified through approval by three-fourths of state legislatures.

Only white males had a voice in colonial governments.

Many of the seventeen amendments outside of the Bill of Rights expanded voting rights. In 1870, ratification of the Fifteenth Amendment allowed formerly enslaved African American men to vote. The Fifteenth Amendment would not be possible without the Thirteenth and Fourteenth Amendments. These amendments are sometimes called the Civil War amendments. The Thirteenth Amendment made slavery illegal. The Fourteenth Amendment guaranteed African Americans U.S. citizenship and the same legal rights as whites.

North Wind Picture Archives

Then and Now

Voting Then

Until 1870, only white men could vote. Even after several amendments guaranteed voting rights for other groups such as women, nonwhite citizens were often discriminated against. In many cases, the government has tried to enforce the amendments by passing voter protection laws. For example, the Voting Rights Act of 1965 put into place specific rules that helped enforce the Fifteenth Amendment.

Voting Now

Today, most United States citizens who are 18 years or older can vote. U.S. citizens living in other countries can submit their ballots by mail. Different states have different laws about whether people who have been convicted of certain crimes can vote. States also require varying types of registration and identification to vote on Election Day.

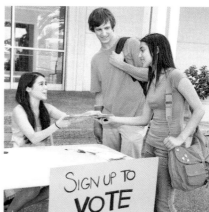

Protests for voting rights for women led to the ratification of the Nineteenth Amendment in 1920. The Twenty-Third Amendment gave residents of Washington, D.C., voting rights in 1961. Three years later, the practice of poll taxes was made illegal in the Twenty-Fourth Amendment. Poll taxes, or fees citizens had to pay to vote, had prevented many people from voting, especially African Americans in the South.

Until 1971, only citizens 21 and older could vote. Some Americans argued that if 18-year-olds could fight in wars, they should be allowed to vote. The Twenty-Sixth Amendment set the new voting age at 18.

Stop and Check

Connect to Now Choose one of the amendments mentioned in the section. Write a law that would help enforce the amendment. How does your law help guarantee the liberties protected by the amendment?

Civic Responsibilities

Citizens of the United States are responsible for participating in certain aspects of the government. William Tyler Page expressed these responsibilities in his 1917 patriotic statement "The American's Creed." He wrote that Americans had a duty "to love it, to support its Constitution, to obey its laws, to respect its flag, and to defend it against all enemies."

Obeying the law is a civic responsibility because it contributes to the safety of U.S. citizens. The government can also call on citizens to defend the nation. People can sometimes be required to join the military if the country is at war. U.S. citizens have a civic responsibility to pay taxes. State and federal governments use taxes for programs and projects that better the country. Roads, government buildings, and public schools rely on tax money for maintenance and improvements.

As a part of due process, the Sixth Amendment guarantees the right to a trial by jury. Americans must judge court cases as part of a jury. In many cases, the jury makes the final decision about whether someone is guilty or innocent. Without citizens' participation in juries, Americans could not be guaranteed their right to due process.

Citizens can help their government by exercising their voting rights.

(b)McGraw-Hill Education

One important way citizens can participate in politics is by expressing their opinions at local-government meetings.

Participating in Politics

U.S. citizens have the right to vote. Participating in elections is not required, though. Our government depends on people exercising their right to vote. Citizens of the United States are responsible for guiding the direction of the country. Responsible citizens stay informed about the issues and candidates. Each person's vote influences the direction of government. Voting is one of the ways citizens make their voices heard.

Citizens participate in United States politics in other ways. Government leaders use information from citizens to act in the public interest. People can write, email, or call their elected officials. They can sign petitions to argue for change in government. Protesting and marching are other direct ways for citizens to express their support or opposition to a political position.

Citizens can also contribute to the nation by volunteering. Volunteers often respond to civic issues that affect the health, safety, and liberties of people in the United States. Political campaigns also depend on volunteers to reach voters.

Finally, citizens may serve as public officials. Any citizen who fulfills basic requirements is eligible to run for office. Public officials help determine the course of the country.

✓ Stop and Check

Perspectives Work with a partner to reread the section on civic responsibilities. Talk about the quotation from "The American's Creed." What do you think about the duties mentioned in the Creed? What other responsibilities do you think are important for citizens in a country?

What Do You Think? Should Americans be required to vote?

Connections in Action!

Back to the EQ

Think about the Chapter EQ, **"How Does the Constitution Help Us Understand What It Means to Be an American?"**

- **Talk** with a partner about what you learned about in the chapter. Discuss what it means to be an American. Then identify how the Constitution supports that definition.

- Consider the Bill of Rights as well as later amendments that expanded rights to all citizens. Come to an agreement about which amendments were most important and take notes about your conclusions.

- **Share** your ideas with the class. Then have a class discussion about how the Constitution helps us understand what it means to be an American.

More to Explore
How Can You Make an IMPACT?

Act Out Amendments

Choose an amendment to the Constitution. Identify the purpose of the amendment, the year it was ratified, and three to five details about its history. Present the amendment to your class and listen as others present the amendments they have chosen. Discuss as a group how each amendment works together to create a unified Constitution.

Letter to a Friend

Imagine you are one of the delegates at the Constitutional Convention. Write a letter to a friend from the delegate's point of view. The letter should be about an issue that was important to the delegate, such as the Bill of Rights, strong state governments, a strong national government, and so on. Use evidence from the text in your letter.

Word Play

Choose three words from the chapter Word Bank. Define each word by drawing a picture that explains what the word is, describes it in context, or shows it in action.

Chapter 7

Life in the Young Republic

ESSENTIAL EQ QUESTION

How Were the Early Years of the United States Transformative for the Nation?

In this chapter, you'll read about how early leaders, the first conflicts, and a growing population led to major changes within the new United States. You'll also read about how important inventions changed the way of life for many Americans and allowed them to expand their own horizons by traveling west.

Step into the Time Chronological Thinking

Look at the timeline. What was happening in other parts of the world while the United States was growing and changing?

Americas

1788
The U.S.
Constitution
becomes law.

1789
George
Washington
becomes the
first president.

1793
Eli Whitney
invents the
cotton gin.

1803
President
Thomas
Jefferson makes
Louisiana
Purchase.

1804
Lewis and
Clark
expedition
begins.

1780   1790   1800   1810

World Events

1796
English physician
Edward Jenner
develops smallpox
vaccine.

1798
French general
Napoleon Bonaparte
conquers Egypt.

1800
Alessandro Volta
creates the first
electric battery.

HSS.5.7.6, HSS.5.8.1, HSS.5.8.3, HAS.CS.1

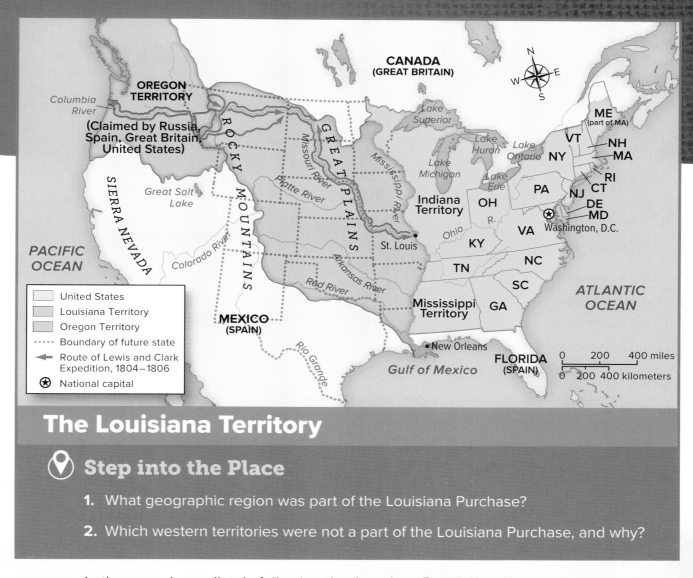

The Louisiana Territory

Step into the Place

1. What geographic region was part of the Louisiana Purchase?

2. Which western territories were not a part of the Louisiana Purchase, and why?

In the years immediately following the American Revolution, the new nation added several new states, including Vermont, Kentucky, and Tennessee. The biggest addition to the nation's territory came in 1803, however, with the purchase of the Louisiana Territory from France by President Thomas Jefferson.

1811–1813
Tecumseh's War

1812–1815
War of 1812

1819
Simón Bolívar liberates New Granada in South America.

1823
President James Monroe issues Monroe Doctrine.

1844
First U.S. telegraph lines begin operating.

10   1820   1830   1840   1850

1815
Napoleon is defeated at Battle of Waterloo.

1824
Beethoven writes his Ninth Symphony.

1839
First Opium War occurs between Great Britain and China.

1845
The Great Famine (Irish Potato Famine) begins.

Connect Through Literature

The Petticoat Skipper

by Josephine Rascoe Keenan

Illustrated by Sue Todd

Mary grew up working in a store, but always dreamed of captaining a steamboat. However, Mary was discouraged from her dream when her mother told her, "Steamboat captains don't wear petticoats." Mary got her chance to live on a steamboat after marrying a steamboat captain, but would she ever be captain of her own ship?

On November 18, 1890, when I was twenty-two and he was twenty-eight, I married Captain Gordon Greene. I loved the dusky smells of river warehouses and the sight of goods on the wharves ready to be loaded. My blood ran faster when the showboat steamed by with its calliope piping bright tunes. A nip of excitement filled the air when the steamboat whistle blew. Folks rushed to the riverbanks to see her tall stacks puffing smoke billows and the paddle wheel splashing through the water.

Serving as a lifeline to folks living on the river, we transported all kinds of supplies on the steamboat. The big pine packing boxes held yard goods. (That's fabrics sold by the yard, not flower seeds!) We hauled all kinds of things—shoes, dresses, and overalls for dry-goods merchants like my father. We brought machinery and sugar, salt and flour. Folks came into town from their farms to trade eggs, butter, apples, and meat for "store-boughten" goods from the steamboat.

Hard as we tried to stick to a schedule, the river current dictated how fast we moved. If the river was high, boats could go fifteen miles an hour in midstream! But in the hot summer the current slowed, and so did we. We completely stopped whenever we saw produce or livestock waiting on the riverbank to be picked up. Once we stopped to let a woman get off the boat for a minute to gossip with another on the riverbank.

The passengers slept in staterooms, so called because the suites were named after states. A whole deck was named for our biggest state in those days, Texas, and that's where Gordon's and my stateroom was. I loved steamboat life, except for one thing— I still wanted to be a riverboat captain.

One day Gordon said, "I dream about steamboats. Someday I want to own a whole fleet of 'em. But right now, I want to buy just one, and I don't have the money to pay another captain."

"I know someone you wouldn't have to pay."

"I can tell by your conniving look that you're up to something, Mary."

"Let me be the captain of the new boat! I can do it, Gordon! Give me a chance."

"All right, see that sand bar in the river? You have to memorize where it is, so you don't run the boat aground."

That night in the pilothouse, after we'd unloaded and turned around to head back the way we came, Gordon said, "Mary, remember that sand bar I pointed out this afternoon? I'm relying on you to tell me where it is."

"But, Gordon, it's dark!"

"So it is! I told you being a captain isn't easy. A journey's success and the lives of the passengers depend on the pilot's accurate reading of the river. And the river is fickle. As soon as you think you know the location of sand bars and snags, the depth of the water and the current, it'll all change. You've got to know what's coming ahead from the feel of the boat and the way the water looks, its swirls and ripples, day and night, in all kinds of weather."

It wasn't easy, but I memorized every turn and twist of the river, every foot of it. I learned to navigate around shifting sand bars, snags, rocks, and fluctuating river depths. When it came to steering the steamboat, sometimes I had to put both feet on the spokes of the pilot wheel to hold her steady. But in 1896 I got my pilot's license, and in 1897, a master's credential, making me a captain, the first woman in the history of the river to accomplish both feats.

Gordon bought that second steamboat, the *Argand*, and he gave it to me. I started with the West Virginia run, from Parkersburg to Wheeling, and I was determined to be a good captain. I had my deck hands unload the minute we pulled into port, and right away we bested the time of the Lexington, our biggest competitor.

Once, near Steubenville, Ohio, a gigantic explosion rocked the boat. Every window blew out. Folks onshore said the steamboat lifted clean out of the water! At first I thought the boilers had blown, but that was wrong—the engines kept running. Turned out, the wake of our steamboat had set off forty quarts of nitro-glycerin sitting in a nearby rowboat.

My worst scare came in 1899 when I was lounging in my cabin and the wind slammed my door shut so hard the crew had to break it down. By the time I got below to the second deck, the pounding rain had soaked through the old calico wrapper I had on. The passengers, who'd been dancing, were down on their knees praying. I kept my head and acted like I wasn't scared, when all the time I was praying as hard as they were.

"Hear that noise, like a train coming through?" I yelled. "It's a cyclone! Don't panic, folks. Captain Mary won't let you drown. Lie down on the floor, quick, and hold on to something secure!"

The ship ran aground on a sand bar. We had some broken furniture and some bruised and scared people, but I saved every single one. The secret I never told them was I couldn't swim a lick.

Gordon's dream of having a fleet came true. My dream came true, too, of a grand steamboat flying the Greene Line flag as she graced the sparkling waters like a great swan. Her home was in Cincinnati, Ohio, and she reigned over the mighty rivers from Pittsburgh to Cairo, and Saint Paul to New Orleans. And when folks saw her steaming by, they said, "There goes the great Delta Queen, piloted by Captain Mary, the Petticoat Skipper."

Think About It

1. What does Mary's mother mean when she tells her, "Steamboat captains don't wear petticoats"?

2. Why does Mary have to put both feet on the steering wheel to hold the ship steady?

3. What are three things Mary does to prove she is a good captain?

People You Should Know

Alexander Hamilton

After serving as George Washington's aide during the Revolutionary War, Alexander Hamilton was chosen as a delegate to the Constitutional Convention. He argued for a strong central government, which put him at odds with some other founders. The essays he wrote in *The Federalist Papers* argued for specific elements of the Constitution in an effort to convince the states to ratify the document. He served as Washington's Secretary of the Treasury and developed much of the plan for the United States financial system. Hamilton died in a duel with Vice President Aaron Burr in 1804.

Dolley Madison

First Lady Dolley Madison is best remembered for her actions during the War of 1812. As the British neared Washington D.C., Madison realized that the brand new White House would be a tempting target. She managed to find a wagon, had it loaded with fine china and other valuable objects, and sent it off for safekeeping at the Bank of Maryland. Just before she was forced to leave, she convinced her staff to break the frame on the famous portrait of George Washington by Gilbert Stuart so that the painting could be removed. Her quick thinking saved important pieces of U.S. history and culture from the fire that later burned down the mansion.

(l)Library of Congress, Prints and Photographs Division [LC-USZC4-6423]; (r)Niday Picture Library/Alamy

Sacagawea

Tecumseh

When she was about 12 years old, Sacagawea (also spelled Sacajawea and Sakakawea) was kidnapped by the Hidatsa people from her Shoshone family. A few years later, a French Canadian fur trader named Toussaint Charbonneau purchased her. She later became his wife. Soon after, Lewis and Clark hired Charbonneau as a guide and interpreter for their expedition to explore the Louisiana Purchase. However, when they realized they would need someone who also spoke Shoshone, they agreed to bring Sacagawea along. She was pregnant at the time, and she gave birth on the trail to a son, Jean Baptiste. She lent her knowledge of languages and landmarks to the expedition, helping to make it a success.

Shawnee chief Tecumseh was a respected leader in the Ohio River Valley. A gifted and inspiring orator, he crafted an alliance between several groups of American Indians to try to stop white expansion. He used this alliance to help the British fight the Americans during the War of 1812. Tecumseh helped the British win several important battles before the Americans defeated him in Canada. Tecumseh's death at the Battle of the Thames in 1813 signaled the end of American Indian resistance to U.S. settlement of the Ohio River Valley.

How Did Early Decisions Shape the Nation?

A New Government Is Launched

In 1789, George Washington became the first President of the United States sworn in under the new Constitution. The Constitution had merely outlined how the new government would operate. Now the new President and Congress would have to fill in all the details.

Congress created three departments to help President Washington govern and set **policy**. The Department of Treasury managed the nation's finances. The Department of State dealt with foreign relations. The Department of War (now called the Department of Defense) handled military matters. To head these departments, President Washington appointed three talented people: Alexander Hamilton as Secretary of the Treasury, Thomas Jefferson as Secretary of State, and Henry Knox as Secretary of War. Washington also appointed Edmund Randolph as Attorney General, or the main lawyer for the federal government. Randolph would join Hamilton, Jefferson, and Knox in the nation's first Cabinet, or group of top presidential advisers.

McGraw-Hill Education

HSS.5.3.4, HSS 5.3.6, HSS.5.6.6, HSS.5.7.3, HSS.5.7.4, HSS.5.7.6, HSS.5.8.3, HAS.CS.1, HAS.CS.4, HAS.CS.5, HAS.HR.1, HAS.HR.2, HAS.HI.1, HAS.HI.3

1800 U.S. capital moves to Washington, D.C.

1803 President Thomas Jefferson makes Louisiana Purchase.

1804 Lewis and Clark Expedition begins.

1814 British burn Washington, D.C., during War of 1812.

1823 President James Monroe issues Monroe Doctrine.

'90 | 1800 | 1810 | 1820 |

1789 George Washington becomes president.

Library of Congress, Prints and Photographs Division (LC-USZC4-1201)

George Washington at his second inauguration at Congress Hall in Philadelphia, March 4, 1793

All of these changes to help the government work also made it bigger. So in 1790, President Washington signed a law to establish a new national capital called the District of Columbia. The President hired Pierre L'Enfant, a French engineer, to design the city and later replaced him with Andrew Ellicott, who kept much of L'Enfant's grand plan. Working with Ellicott was Benjamin Banneker, a free-born African American, who helped lay out the city. Banneker was one of the first African Americans appointed by a President to work for the federal government.

The years of George Washington's presidency saw a rise in political tension. Washington had chosen his Cabinet to provide a variety of opinions. Alexander Hamilton and Thomas Jefferson had very different views of what the new nation should be like. Hamilton thought the United States should have a strong central government and an economy that emphasized commerce and industry. Jefferson thought a strong central government would lead to **corruption**. He preferred a more agricultural nation with a weak federal government and more political power for the states. In general, President Washington agreed with Hamilton's economic proposals. He believed they were vital to the foundation of the new nation's economy.

Benjamin Banneker

MPVHistory/Alamy

After two terms in office, George Washington decided to leave the presidency. He wished to retire from public life and establish that the president was not a monarch. By then, the division in his Cabinet had led to the beginning of the nation's first political parties. John Adams, Washington's vice president, shared Hamilton's views, and they helped to form what became known as the Federalist Party. James Madison and many other Southern politicians shared Jefferson's views in what became known as the Democratic-Republican Party. In the election of 1796 to succeed Washington, John Adams ran against Thomas Jefferson and won. Four years later, Adams ran against Jefferson again and lost.

John Marshall

Just before leaving office, President Adams appointed a judge named William Marbury. Then James Madison, Secretary of State for President Jefferson, refused to give Marbury his official papers, even though a section of the Judiciary Act of 1789 passed by Congress said he should. At a famous hearing of the U.S. Supreme Court, Chief Justice John Marshall ruled that this section of the Judiciary Act was **unconstitutional**, or against the guidelines included in the U.S. Constitution. The case, *Marbury* v. *Madison*, is very important. It established the principle that the Supreme Court can review laws passed by Congress and, if necessary, declare them unconstitutional.

✓ Stop and Check

COLLABORATE

Talk What government divisions, positions, and other "firsts" were established during George Washington's presidency?

Find Details As you read, add additional information to the graphic organizer on page 247 in your Inquiry Journal.

A Nation Expands

In 1789, George Washington signed a new Northwest Ordinance. It made clear that the rules for settling territory, established in the previous ordinance, were still in effect under the new Constitution. One part of the ordinance banned slavery north of the Ohio River. However, settlers from the South brought slaves into Kentucky and Tennessee. Even in the northern territories, African Americans had a difficult time. Laws were passed to keep African Americans out of some states. These same states forced free African Americans already there to show papers proving they were free.

American Indians did not recognize the right of U.S. citizens to purchase land in the new territories. As newcomers poured in, tensions mounted. Violence between native peoples and new settlers led President Washington to send the army to Ohio three times during his presidency. The American Indians would eventually be forced to give up most of Ohio.

✓ Stop and Check

COLLABORATE

Talk Why do you think settlers were able to bring slaves into the new territory even though it was against the law?"

General Harmar defeated by Miamis, 1790

The Louisiana Purchase

During the 1790s, control of the port of New Orleans had passed from France to Spain, and back to France again. While the United States had a deal with Spain to use the river and port, Jefferson was worried that the French could close the river and port to U.S. commerce. So he sent Robert Livingston, U.S. Minister to France, and future President James Monroe, a special ambassador, to meet with the French and offer to buy New Orleans.

France and Great Britain were involved in a series of conflicts. France needed money for its military. The French also realized that they could not protect Louisiana if the British attacked from Canada. So the French government made a surprising offer: France would sell not just New Orleans but the entire Louisiana colony to the United States.

The American flag is raised in New Orleans after the city became part of the United States as a result of the Louisiana Purchase.

The deal was an excellent one for Jefferson—530 million acres of land for 15 million dollars. That's about 3.5 cents an acre. Still, making the purchase was a hard decision for the president. For years, he had argued for a federal government with limited power. Having the federal government buy new territory was not a power spelled out in the Constitution. Nevertheless, Jefferson decided that he could not pass up such a good opportunity for the nation.

President Jefferson officially announced the Louisiana Purchase on July 4, 1803. The Louisiana Territory became part of the United States, doubling the size of the nation. As in the past, these land exchanges involved European nations, and the United States would mostly ignore the claims of American Indians already living on the land. This would bring conflict in future decades, when more and more settlers came west to mine and farm the land.

Meanwhile, to most U.S. citizens living east of the Mississippi River, the land that the nation had purchased was largely unknown territory. Jefferson himself had been fascinated by the West and its potential for some time. Even before the Louisiana Purchase, Jefferson had asked Congress for money to fund an expedition to explore the western part of the continent and seek a route to the Pacific Ocean. Those plans took on new significance after the Louisiana Purchase.

To lead the expedition, Jefferson chose his personal secretary, Meriwether Lewis, an army captain with experience on the frontier. Lewis then asked William Clark, an army friend, to share his command. Calling their group the Corps of Discovery, Lewis, Clark, and more than thirty others set out from a camp near St. Louis on May 14, 1804. Among them were John Ordway, a New Hampshire soldier who kept a daily log of the journey, and a slave named York.

> **PRIMARY SOURCE**

In Their Words... The Louisiana Purchase

The inhabitants of the ceded territory shall be incorporated in the Union of the United States and admitted as soon as possible according to the principles of the federal Constitution to the enjoyment of all these rights, advantages and immunities of citizens of the United States, and in the mean time they shall be maintained and protected in the free enjoyment of their liberty, property and the Religion which they profess.

—from the Louisiana Purchase, Article III

Louisiana Purchase: Treaty between the United States of America and the French Republic, art. 3. April 30, 1803. National Archives and Records Administration.

The Louisiana Territory, 1806

Map Skills Identify four rivers that go through the Louisiana Territory. On which of these did Lewis and Clark mostly travel?

The Corps traveled west on the Missouri River, meeting with many native tribes, including the Oto, the Missouri, and the Teton and Yankton Sioux. In late October of 1804, near Mandan and Hidatsa villages in what is now North Dakota, the explorers established a winter camp that they called Fort Mandan. Not long afterward, Lewis and Clark hired a French-Canadian fur trapper named Toussaint Charbonneau and his American Indian wife, Sacajawea, to serve as interpreters and guides for the rest of the trip.

Sacajawea, traveling with a newborn baby, proved enormously helpful to the expedition. As a member of the Shoshone people from what is now Idaho, she was familiar with some of the area the Corps would cross. Her presence made other American Indians friendlier, and she could learn from them the best trails to use. In a famous incident, she even saved important supplies and papers when one of the expedition's boats overturned on the Missouri River.

Traveling on water when possible and land when necessary, the expedition crossed the Rocky Mountains, continued to the Columbia River, and then went down it to the Pacific Ocean. There the Corps camped for another winter before traveling back east, reaching St. Louis on September 23, 1806. Having completed a journey of about 8,000 miles, Lewis and Clark were treated as national heroes.

Sacajawea, shown in the statue with her newborn baby, is also honored on a one-dollar coin.

Lewis and Clark's Corps of Discovery was not the only group to explore the Louisiana Territory. In 1805, President Jefferson sent army lieutenant Zebulon Pike to search for the source of the Mississippi River. He did not find it. A year later, Pike was sent to explore the southwestern portion of the Louisiana Purchase. There he tried and failed to climb the mountain peak now named in his honor.

✓ Stop and Check

Talk Why did Jefferson purchase the Louisiana Territory? What role did Sacajawea play in helping to explore it?

The War of 1812

Britain and France were at war when James Madison was elected president in 1808. The United States tried to stay neutral and trade with both sides. Neither side liked that policy. Each kept trying to block the United States from trading with its enemy. British actions, however, made that nation very unpopular with the United States.

The British stopped U.S. ships, claiming they were searching for British sailors who had deserted. Then they took American sailors off the ships, claiming they were British, and forced them to serve in the British navy. This policy, called impressment, made people in the United States furious. Many also thought the British in Canada were purposely causing American Indian unrest in the Northwest Territories with the hope of getting back land they had lost to the United States. In Congress, pro-war politicians, or "war hawks," demanded U.S. action. President Madison came to agree with them. And so, with Congress eager for war and the president in agreement, the War of 1812 began.

U.S. attacks on Canada were unsuccessful, although one attack resulted in the burning of legislative buildings in the town of York. A British attack from Canada was also repelled in the Battle of Lake Erie in 1813. The next year, British troops landed in Maryland and successfully attacked Washington, D.C. The entire government had to flee the capital. Evacuating the White House, First Lady Dolley Madison managed to save important government papers. White House employees saved a famous portrait of George Washington. The British destroyed the White House and badly damaged the Capitol, which had been under construction.

PRIMARY SOURCE

In Their Words... Dolley Madison

I have pressed as many Cabinet papers into trunks as to fill one carriage; our private property must be sacrificed, as it is impossible to procure [get] wagons for its transportation. I am determined not to go myself until I see Mr. Madison safe.

—from Dolley Madison's Letter to Her Sister, August 23, 1814

TEXT: Dolley Madison to her sister, Anna Cutts, August 23, 1814. In Dolley Madison, by Maud Wilder Goodwin, pp. 173.–175. New York: C. Scribner's Sons, 1896.; PHOTO: McGraw-Hill Education

This print gives a British artist's impression of what the 1814 burning of Washington, D.C., might have looked like.

Library of Congress Prints and Photographs Division [LC-DIG-ppmsca-31113]

The British attempt to attack Baltimore was less successful. Francis Scott Key, an American lawyer and poet held captive on a British ship in Baltimore Harbor, watched the British attack Fort McHenry there. The next morning, the American flag was still flying over the fort. Key was so moved that he wrote a poem that later became the words to the U.S. national anthem, "The Star-Spangled Banner."

Finally, British and U.S. diplomats met in Europe and signed the Treaty of Ghent to end the war. Neither side won or lost, but Britain abandoned its efforts to establish an Indian state in the Northwest. American Indians in the Northwest Territory suffered the most losses in the War of 1812. The United States defeated them and forced them to sign away lands with no interference from the British.

The Federalist Party, which had opposed the war, now nearly vanished from the political scene. With just one effective political party and a strong sense of national unity and purpose, the period following the War of 1812 is often called the Era of Good Feeling. The president most associated with this era is James Monroe, who won the election of 1816 with the support of retiring President Madison and was reelected with little opposition four years later.

 Stop and Check

Think What were the causes of the War of 1812?

The Monroe Doctrine

Starting in 1810, many colonies in Latin America began declaring their independence from the European countries that had colonized them. The United States generally supported these efforts and worried that European nations would try to reestablish colonial rule. In an 1823 speech to Congress, President Monroe laid out U.S. policy on such behavior. That policy came to be called the Monroe Doctrine. It would become the single most influential piece of foreign policy in U.S. history. The doctrine had these main points:

- The United States would not involve itself in European politics.
- The United States recognized current European colonies in the Americas.
- Except for the colonies existing at the time, the United States expected Europe to stay out of North and South America and would regard any interference there as a hostile act—an act that could lead to warfare.

James Monroe

Read the two different points of view about the Monroe Doctrine. Then answer the questions that follow.

Pro-Monroe Doctrine View	Anti-Monroe Doctrine View
The Monroe Doctrine shows that the United States wanted to protect its neighbors in the Americas and wanted them to be free and independent nations.	The Monroe Doctrine shows that the United States thought of itself as the main power in the Americas and wanted to control its neighbors without any competition.

Think About It

1. Think about the conflicts that led up to the Monroe Doctrine. What earlier events or conflicts might have caused the United States to be wary of European powers in North America?

2. Research times when the United States has used the Monroe Doctrine, such as the Spanish American War or the Cuban Missile Crisis. Was the United States justified in its actions?

3. Do you agree with either of the points of view above? Why or why not? Can you think of a point of view different from both of these?

How Did Advancements in Technology and Transportation Shape the Nation?

New Technology Paves the Way

In the years after the American Revolution, another revolution was taking place. It wasn't a revolution in government or politics, but it did greatly change the way people lived. Before, almost everything was made by hand. But beginning in the late 1700s, machines were invented that could more quickly do the same work that people were doing. New technology also changed how people traveled and how they sent messages over long distances. This great shift to a society that relied on machines to make and do things is known as the Industrial Revolution.

PETER COOPER'S "TOM THUMB" 1829~30 BALT

HSS 5.8.1, HAS.CS.5, HAS.HI.1, HAS.HI.2, HAS.HI.3

310 Lesson 2 How Did Advancements in Technology and Transportation Shape the Nation?

Time Line

1790	1793	1807	1811	1825	1844
Samuel Slater builds the first factory in the U.S.	Eli Whitney invents the cotton gin.	Robert Fulton builds a practical steamboat.	Construction begins on the National Road.	The Erie Canal opens.	The first U.S. telegraph lines begin operating.

| 1790 | 1800 | 1810 | 1820 | 1830 | 1840 |

The Industrial Revolution began in Britain. For years, the British tried to keep secret how they used moving water in streams and rivers to power machines. Then a man named Samuel Slater, who had worked in a British factory with water-powered machines, moved to the United States and brought those secrets with him. Slater built the first factory on U.S. soil in Pawtucket, Rhode Island, in 1790. Like most other early factories, Slater's was a textile mill, a factory producing cloth or other woven fabrics.

1830 B & O Railroad begins using *Tom Thumb*, the first U.S. steam locomotive.

The *Tom Thumb* was the first American-built steam locomotive to travel by railroad.

Vintage Images/Alamy

Twenty years later, a Boston merchant named Francis Cabot Lowell went to Britain to learn about new developments in its factories. In 1813, he built his own factory on the Charles River in Waltham, Massachusetts. It had a large power **loom** for weaving and all the equipment for making cloth under one roof. Lowell died soon after starting the factory. But his partners decided to expand. They built several mills on the Merrimack River and a town for their workers, which they called Lowell. Many of those workers were **immigrants** from other nations. They also hired young women from farms all over New England; these women became known as the Lowell Mill Girls.

Cotton mill workers spun cotton into thread and wove thread into cloth.

Lowell, Massachusetts, was the first of many U.S. mill towns. These towns needed to be on rivers or streams with moving water to power the machinery. The towns were especially common in New England. The region had many rapidly flowing rivers. Its rocky soil and short growing season made it hard to earn a lot of money from farming. This is why farmers were glad to have their daughters working in the mills. The chief products of the mills were cotton cloth and woolen fabric. Wool came from sheep. Cotton came from plants that needed a warm climate to grow. In the United States, it was grown mainly in the South.

While visiting a cotton plantation, a New Englander named Eli Whitney saw that common green-seed cotton was very hard to clean because the seeds stuck to the fiber. He began working on a machine to separate the seeds from the fiber. That machine, the cotton gin, revolutionized Southern agriculture. It made growing cotton so profitable that most plantation owners made it their main crop. Growing cotton still required much labor, however. As cotton plantations grew larger, more and more slaves were put to work in the cotton fields. By 1850, there were five times as many slaves in the United States as there had been in 1790.

The use of the cotton gin was not the only big change in agriculture. For thousands of years, farmers had cut down their crops using a hand-held tool called a scythe. The slow process limited the number of crops farmers could harvest. Then, in 1831, a farmer's son named Cyrus McCormick invented a horse-drawn **reaping** machine that could harvest crops much faster. Farmers using the McCormick reaper could plant many more acres of crops. Planting itself was made easier by another invention, the mechanical plow. This device dug up the soil so seeds could be planted. Charles Newbold, a New Jersey blacksmith, invented the first cast iron plow in 1797. Another blacksmith, John Deere, improved the plow in 1837 by using steel blades. Steel was stronger than the iron previously used.

Many other inventions changed the way people made or did things. In 1845, Elias Howe, who had once worked in a machine shop in Lowell, created the first practical sewing machine. Also in the 1840s, Charles Goodyear developed a way to make rubber withstand heat and cold without cracking. The process, called vulcanization, made rubber the useful material it is today.

In 1803, Eli Whitney, inventor of the cotton gin, was hired to make 10,000 guns for the U.S. Army. Whitney realized that the job would go much faster if he could produce, for all guns, large quantities of parts that were exactly the same. This would allow the parts to be assembled more quickly. Whitney's idea of **interchangeable** parts affected far more industries than just the one that made guns. Clocks, furniture—in fact, just about anything built in factories—could be made more quickly and cheaply by using interchangeable parts.

The cotton gin, invented by Eli Whitney, separated seeds from cotton fiber much more quickly and easily than could be done by hand.

✓ Stop and Check

COLLABORATE

Talk What effects, both good and bad, did the cotton gin have on the Southern economy? Why was Eli Whitney's development of interchangeable parts so important?

Find Details As you read, add additional information to the graphic organizer on page 255 in your Inquiry Journal.

New Forms of Transportation

In 1800, there were four main ways to travel: on foot, on horseback, by water, or in horse-drawn vehicles such as stagecoaches. All were very slow. Private roads, which charged tolls, were better maintained than public roads. Both types of roads, however, grew muddy when it rained, and they developed potholes. Yet roads were needed to unify the expanding nation. In 1806, Congress voted to fund a road connecting the East and the Midwest. By the early 1830s, the National Road carried many carts and stagecoaches along a route that extended from Maryland to Illinois. Parts of the road were among the first U.S. roadways made of macadam, a newly developed paving material using crushed gravel.

In 1800, the easiest way to ship goods was by water, but waterways did not always connect. One way to solve this problem was to build artificial waterways called canals to make the connections. In 1817, New York Governor DeWitt Clinton began a project to build a canal connecting the Hudson River in the eastern part of the state with Lake Erie on New York's western border. Critics called the expensive project Clinton's Ditch. It was complicated because the land was higher at one end than the other. Engineers solved this problem by building locks, which worked like elevators to lift and lower boats in the water. When the Erie Canal finally opened in 1825, Clinton's critics were proved wrong. An instant success, the canal let people ship goods much more quickly and cheaply. Soon people in the United States began building other canals.

Steamboats on the
Hudson River

ISAAC NEWTON

FRANCIS SKIDDY.

Yale University Art Gallery

The steam engine, one of the most important inventions of the Industrial Revolution, could be used to run many kinds of equipment. In 1807, Robert Fulton showed the world that a steam engine could be used to run a boat. His steamboat took about a day and a half to travel up the Hudson River from New York City to Albany, New York—a distance of about 150 miles. Before the steamboat, the same trip took much longer. Fulton's steamboat was not the first one ever invented, but it was the first to prove successful. Soon many different kinds of steamboats were traveling the nation's waterways. They were especially important for quickly moving goods against the direction of a river's current—for example, north on the Mississippi River.

Steam power was also the source of another form of transportation, the train. For centuries, people had recognized that running carts on rails instead of bumpy dirt roads made the ride smoother. However, early vehicles on rails were pulled by animals. Now engineers began experimenting with iron locomotives, engines that ran on rails and were powered by steam. The first locomotives were built in Britain. As the design improved, the locomotive was used to pull cars behind it in a new form of transportation—the train. It was nicknamed the Iron Horse. The rails on which trains ran were called railroads, and so were the companies that ran them. In 1828, the first U.S. railroad company, the Baltimore & Ohio (B & O) Railroad, was formed. Many more would follow.

Trains were much faster than other types of transportation at the time. Even the earliest trains cut down on travel time by about half. Trains made it possible to go from one region to another in a reasonable time. This meant that trains helped unite the large, spread-out nation that the United States was becoming.

✓ Stop and Check

Talk Why were trains particularly helpful in uniting the nation?

McGraw-Hill Education

Advancements in Communication

When George Washington became President in 1789, the United States had about 75 post offices. That number grew as the nation grew. Mail traveled by horse, stagecoach, boat, and eventually train. As transportation improved, so did communication, since messages could be carried more quickly. Nevertheless, the messages still had to be carried.

An important new invention changed the way Americans communicated. In the 1830s, a group of inventors including Samuel F. B. Morse developed a device called a telegraph that could send messages by using electrical signals over a wire. Morse and his fellow inventor Alfred Vail also developed a code—called Morse Code—to give meaning to the electrical signals. The code used different sequences of short and long signals to represent letters. Workers used the coded letters to spell out the words of a message. Morse demonstrated the telegraph to members of Congress, who awarded him $30,000 to set up a telegraph line between Baltimore, Maryland, and Washington, D.C. On May 24, 1844, Morse tapped out his first long-distance message on the telegraph, "What hath God wrought?"

By pressing down on a key, the telegraph operator could send electrical messages in Morse code.

Over the next few years, telegraph poles went up across the United States, with telegraph wires strung between them. A person would go to a telegraph office and pay to send a message to another office in a distant location. The message would usually move across the wires and reach its destination in minutes. Like the new forms of transportation, this rapid new form of communication helped tie the nation together.

✓ Stop and Check

COLLABORATE

Talk How was the telegraph different from the type of long-distance communication people had used before?

©Comstock Images/Alamy

The Growth of Cities

The Industrial Revolution turned towns into cities and made existing cities much larger. Factory jobs paid better than farm labor did. So factories lured people away from farms to cities and towns. They also drew immigrants to the United States, mostly from Canada and Europe. In 1820, only about 700,000 people lived in all the cities of the United States. By 1840, the population of cities was nearly 1.8 million.

New forms of transportation also led to the growth of cities. Steamboat traffic helped make river ports, like Cincinnati and St. Louis, much busier. The Erie Canal in upstate New York spurred the growth of Albany at its eastern end, Buffalo at its western end, and Syracuse and Rochester in between. It also made New York City an even greater center of shipping and trade.

Like boat traffic, the growth of railroads also led to the growth of cities. Atlanta, Georgia, began its existence as the junction, or meeting point, between the Georgia Railroad and the Western & Atlantic Railroad. Indianapolis, Indiana, had fewer than 8,000 residents in 1847. Then the Indianapolis & Madison Railroad came to town. The city's population quickly doubled. As the railroads moved farther west, Chicago, Illinois, emerged as the great railroad center of the nation. Chicago had fewer than 5,000 residents in 1840. Twenty years later, it had well over 100,000.

In the 1800s, many immigrants lived in large cities such as New York City.

✓ Stop and Check

COLLABORATE

Talk What were two reasons for the growth of cities?

The First Pioneers

The American Revolution had created a new nation, but there were still many Americans without land. About one out of five Americans lived in poverty, or without enough money for proper food or supplies. Without land, people were unlikely to improve their lives.

Between 1790 and 1820, the population of the United States grew, from about 4 million to nearly 10 million. Most Americans were farmers. They needed large families to do the many chores a farm required. When farmers died, their land was divided among their children. Even a large farm might not provide enough land for all of the children. Some people moved to cities, but others looked to the lands in the West. For poor people, these lands offered a chance to build a new life.

After the British gave up its western lands in 1783, settlers rushed into western Georgia, Pennsylvania, New York, and beyond. Some of this area later became the states of Kentucky, Tennessee, and Ohio. A person who is the first to enter a new land or region is called a pioneer. Even though we call the white settlers who moved into the area west of the Appalachians "pioneers," they were not the first people in these lands. This area had been inhabited by American Indians for centuries.

HSS.5.3.4, HSS.5.3.6, HSS.5.6.6, HSS.5.8.1, HAS.CS.5

Mc-Graw-Hill Education

Time Line

1794
Battle of Fallen Timbers

1795
Treaty of Greenville

1811–1813
Tecumseh's War

1812–1815
War of 1812

1845–1849
The Great Famine (Irish Potato Famine)

70 | ★ | |1780| | | |1790| | | |1800| | | |1810| | | |1820| | | |1830| | | |1840| | | |1850| | |

1775 Daniel Boone travels through the Cumberland Gap.

Settlers often passed through the Cumberland Gap (above).

In 1769, a trader named John Findley chose an experienced explorer, Daniel Boone, to help him find an **inland** trail from North Carolina to Kentucky. They found a natural passage through the Appalachian Mountains, which they called the Cumberland Gap. When they crossed the Cumberland Gap into Kentucky, they found a land of rich soil. Boone and his friends wanted to make money from this new land. In 1775, Boone and 30 other pioneers began to improve the trails between the Carolinas and the West.

David Sanger/Photodisc/Getty Images

Daniel Boone leading settlers through the Cumberland Gap in 1775

Daniel Boone was the most famous of the American pioneers of this era. His father had come from Great Britain and settled in Pennsylvania. Boone was born in 1734. Young Boone learned to survive on the unsettled lands around his home. When Boone was 16, his family moved to North Carolina. Boone married Rebecca Bryan in 1756 and tried farming, but he preferred life on the frontier.

Boone had a sense of humor. He is believed to have once said, "I have never been lost, but I will admit to being confused for several weeks."

In 1775, Boone founded Boonesborough, Kentucky. In 1776, during the Revolutionary War, he and his men were captured by Shawnee people and taken to a British military post. Boone gained the trust of the Shawnee and learned of a British plan to attack Boonesborough. He escaped in time to save the town. After exploring Tennessee and Kentucky in the early 1770s, Boone and his family moved to what is now Missouri in 1799. Daniel Boone died in 1820.

 COLLABORATE

✓ Stop and Check

Talk What were some of the reasons people in the early United States moved farther west?

American Indians in the Early Republic

TEXT: A Treaty of Peace between the United States of America and the Tribes of Indians..., art. 3." In The Public Statutes at Large of the United States of America, Vol. 7, edited by Richard Peters, 49. Boston: Charles C. Little and James Brown, 1848.; PHOTO: McGraw-Hill Education

The greatest threat to American Indians during this period was white settlers. For more than 150 years, American Indians had seen settlers stream west and into their territory. This threatened their land and their way of life.

In 1787, Congress passed the Northwest Ordinance. The law was intended to outline how the western territories should be governed and the rules for becoming a state. It did, however, include a promise that Indian lands and territories would never be taken away from them. But that promise was not kept.

In 1794, eight American Indian groups joined together to drive invading settlers out of their land in what is today Ohio. They were defeated by the United States Army at the Battle of Fallen Timbers in northwestern Ohio.

The next year, these American Indians had to accept the Treaty of Greenville. The treaty forced them to give up most of their land in the Ohio Territory. However, some American Indians would continue to resist the settlers.

PRIMARY SOURCE

In Their Words... The Treaty of Greenville

And in consideration of the peace now established . . . the said Indian tribes do hereby cede and relinquish forever, all their claims to the lands lying eastwardly and southwardly of the general boundary line now described: and these lands, or any part of them, shall never hereafter be made a cause or pretense, on the part of said tribes, or any of them, of war or injury to the United States, or any people thereof.

—from The Treaty of Greenville, August 3, 1795

One of the American Indians who remained in Ohio and had not signed the Treaty of Greenville was Tecumseh of the Shawnee people. Tecumseh spoke to his people of native pride and hoped that native peoples could reclaim some of their lost territory in what are now Ohio and Indiana. Tecumseh founded his own community in Indiana. Tecumseh tried to unite all western native peoples to fight against invading settlers. William Henry Harrison, who was the governor of the Indiana Territory, became alarmed at Tecumseh's growing power. In 1811, Harrison attacked and destroyed Tecumseh's community. Tecumseh and the Shawnees were among the American Indian groups who sided with the British in the War of 1812. Native peoples hoped that a British victory would stop the invasion of U.S. settlers into their territories. Tecumseh was eventually killed in 1813 while fighting for the British.

PRIMARY SOURCE

In Their Words... Tecumseh

You ought to know what you are doing to the Indians. . . . It is a very bad thing and we do not like it. . . . No groups among us have the right to sell, even to one another, and surely not to outsiders who want it all, and will not do with less. . . . Sell a country! Why not sell the air, the clouds, and the Great Sea, as well as the earth? Did not the Great Spirit make them all for the use of his children?

—a passage from Tecumseh's speech to Governor William Harrison, Indiana Territory, 1810

TECUMSEH.

Stop and Check

Talk What about Tecumseh made William Henry Harrison alarmed?

Find Details As you read, add additional information to the graphic organizer on page 263 in your Inquiry Journal.

African Americans in the Early United States

In the late 1700s, feelings about slavery began to change in the United States. The economies, cultures, and attitudes of the North and South grew increasingly different.

Large cities and new factories were growing quickly in the North. Immigrants flooded the United States to fill factory jobs. By 1804 all northern states had outlawed slavery. Slavery may have been illegal north of the Ohio River, but free African Americans faced discrimination there. Ohio, Indiana, and Illinois passed laws requiring African Americans to show papers proving they were free.

In the South, the economy had not changed much. The plantation was still the main way of life. On large farms, hundreds of slaves worked without pay. There were very few free African Americans in the region. Some white Southerners worked on small farms, and not all had slaves. However, the plantation owners were the wealthiest and had the most political power.

As the United States expanded west, many wondered if slavery would expand as well. In 1819 Missouri applied for statehood as a slave state, a state in which slavery is allowed. At the time, the nation had a balance of 11 slave states and 11 free states in which slavery was not allowed. Letting Missouri enter the Union as a slave state would give slave states more votes in the U.S. Senate.

An antique sketch of slaves laboring in a cotton field

(t)McGraw-Hill Education; (b)ilbusca/iStock/Getty Images

The Missouri Compromise, 1820

Map Skills Working with a partner, use the information provided in the key to determine which states made up the larger area of the United States—slave states or free states.

Congress argued over Missouri for a year. In 1820, Senator Henry Clay from Kentucky came up with the Missouri Compromise. Under this plan, Missouri was added as a slave state. Maine, which had been part of Massachusetts, became a free state. The compromise stated that, in the future, slavery would not be allowed in any states north of Missouri's southern border.

This compromise was only a temporary solution. As the United States continued to expand, new compromises and decisions had to be made.

✓ Stop and Check

Write How was life for African Americans in the South different from those in the North?

A Nation of Immigrants

In the mid-1800s, the **composition** of the U.S. population began to change dramatically. More immigrants came to the United States between 1845 and 1860 than ever before. Many Europeans came to find work. Some Chinese came in the 1840s to seek fortunes. Later, they worked on the railroads. The Irish, however, left their homeland for a very different reason.

In the mid-1800s, many people in Ireland were forced by British property owners to plant and eat potatoes, and little else. Most of the livestock and food the Irish raised went to England or was sold to pay high rents. Depending on only one crop proved disastrous. Starting in 1846, potatoes throughout Ireland did not grow because of a plant disease involving a fungus. The results were devastating. About 2.5 million people starved to death. Between 1846 and 1861, a million Irish people immigrated to the United States to escape starvation.

Immigrants often found work at docks along the East Coast.

The 1820s and 1830s is often called the Canal Age. It was during this period that the construction of several major canals filled the transportation needs of the young country. One of the largest such projects was the construction of the Erie Canal. Irish, German, and English immigrants did most of the backbreaking work required to build these canals. The work was difficult and often dangerous. Many of the workers died from accidents and disease. Later, when the canal work was done, some immigrants settled in towns and cities along the canal. Others decided to seek their fortunes by traveling west.

Around the World

Irish Potato Famine Causes

- British control of Ireland results in poor Irish farmers giving or selling to Britain most of their crops.
- As a result, most of Ireland's poor depended almost exclusively on the potato for food.
- In 1846, a blight—a destructive disease caused by a fungus—attacked Ireland's potatoes, and most of the crop was ruined.
- Ireland's poor lacked the money to purchase the food their farms produced.

A disease that destroyed potato crops in Ireland in 1846 would have a massive impact on the United States

Irish Potato Famine Effects

- Famine occurred among Ireland's poor.
- About 2.5 million people starved to death.
- Between 1846 and 1861, a million Irish people immigrated to the United States.

 Stop and Check COLLABORATE

Talk What was difficult about working on the Erie Canal?

Fighting for Women's Education

Benjamin Rush (1746–1813) is perhaps best known for his political activities during the American Revolution, which included signing the Declaration of Independence. He is also known for his career as a doctor, a professor of chemistry, and a political leader. Somewhat overlooked, however, are the various causes to which he devoted himself. One of these causes was the education of women.

Colonial America did not offer many educational opportunities to women. It was widely believed that there was no need to educate women beyond the very basics of reading, writing, and math. The Young Ladies' Academy of Philadelphia was founded in 1787 and sponsored and supervised by many of Philadelphia's male religious and political leaders, including Benjamin Rush. The academy offered its female students a wide variety of courses, including writing, English grammar, mathematics, geography, chemistry, and natural philosophy.

Benjamin Rush led the way in educational reform for women because he believed that such reform was good for the country. Rush gave many speeches on the importance of women's education. Rush believed that all children, including girls, should be rigorously educated. Rush believed that people who did not support the education of women had "little minds." His hope was that education would help students become good citizens, create national character, and unite the country.

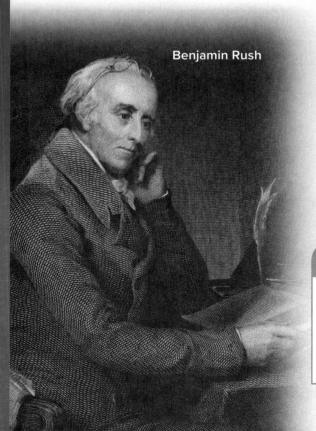

Benjamin Rush

(t)McGraw-Hill Education; (b)The Miriam and Ira D. Wallach Division of Art, Prints and Photographs: Print Collection, Emmet Collection of Manuscripts Etc. Relating to American History. The New York Public Library

✓ Think About It

Imagine you are in a position to devote yourself to a cause, as Benjamin Rush did. What would the cause be? What would you do to benefit the cause?

Map and Globe Skills

The United States, 1821

By the time of the Missouri Compromise, the United States had changed significantly. A nation that had begun with thirteen states now had twenty-four. The United States had covered about 860,000 square miles in 1790. By the 1820 census, the area was roughly 1.7 million square miles, about double its original size. The population had grown from about 3.9 million people to about 9.6 million.

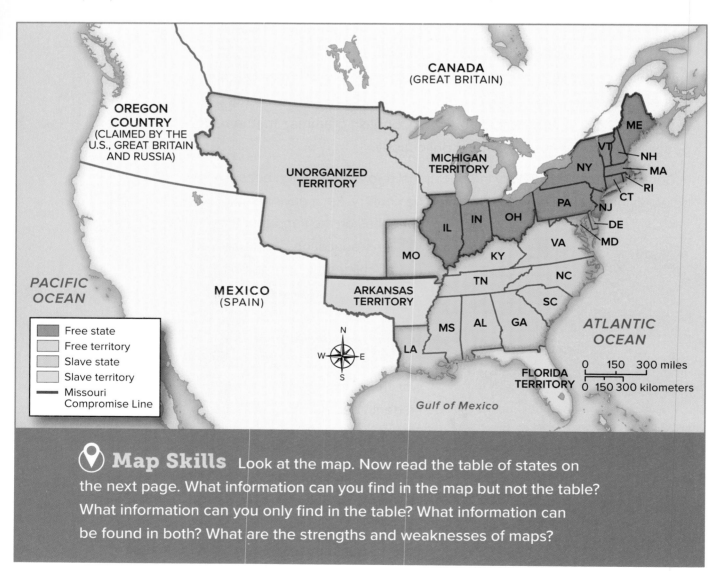

CANADA
(GREAT BRITAIN)

OREGON
COUNTRY
(CLAIMED BY THE
U.S., GREAT BRITAIN
AND RUSSIA)

UNORGANIZED
TERRITORY

MICHIGAN
TERRITORY

ME
VT
NH
NY
MA
RI
CT
PA
NJ
IL   IN   OH
DE
VA
MD
MO
KY
PACIFIC
OCEAN

MEXICO
(SPAIN)

ARKANSAS
TERRITORY

TN
NC
SC
MS   AL   GA
ATLANTIC
OCEAN

LA

N
W   E
S

FLORIDA
TERRITORY

0   150   300 miles
0 150 300 kilometers

Gulf of Mexico

Free state
Free territory
Slave state
Slave territory
Missouri
Compromise Line

Map Skills Look at the map. Now read the table of states on the next page. What information can you find in the map but not the table? What information can you only find in the table? What information can be found in both? What are the strengths and weaknesses of maps?

Alabama
1820 Population: 127,901
2015 Population: 4,858,979
★ **Capital:** Montgomery

Illinois
1820 Population: 55,211
2015 Population: 12,859,995
★ **Capital:** Springfield

Indiana
1820 Population: 147,178
2015 Population: 6,619,680
★ **Capital:** Indianapolis

Kentucky
1820 Population: 564,317
2015 Population: 4,425,092
★ **Capital:** Frankfort

Louisiana
1820 Population: 153,407
2015 Population: 4,670,724
★ **Capital:** Baton Rouge

Maine
1820 Population: 298,335
2015 Population: 1,329,328
★ **Capital:** Augusta

Mississippi
1820 Population: 75,448
2015 Population: 2,992,333
★ **Capital:** Jackson

Missouri
1820 Population: 66,586
2015 Population: 6,083,672
★ **Capital:** Jefferson City

Ohio
1820 Population: 581,434
2015 Population: 11,613,423
★ **Capital:** Columbus

Tennessee
1820 Population: 422,813
2015 Population: 6,600,299
★ **Capital:** Nashville

Vermont
1820 Population: 235,764
2015 Population: 626,042
★ **Capital:** Montpelier

Connections in Action!

Back to the EQ

Think about the Chapter EQ, **"How Were the Early Years of the United States Transformative for the Nation?"**

- **Talk** with a partner about what you learned from the chapter. Discuss what happened during the early years of the United States. What does it mean when something is "transformative"?

- **Think** about how the nation changed in terms of its structure, its territory, and its relationships with American Indians and with other nations around the world. What were the most important changes? Why?

- **Share** your ideas with the class. Then have a class discussion about how the early years of the United States were transformative for the nation and its people.

(bkgd)Yale University Art Gallery; (l)North Wind Picture Archives; (r)Library of Congress Prints and Photographs Division [LC-DIG-ppmsca-31113]

More to Explore

How Can You Make an IMPACT?

Write a Skit for Reader's Theater

As a class, create a skit that discusses the major events of the War of 1812. There should be enough parts for each student and a narrator, but you can write from the point of view of the Americans, the British, the American Indians, or any combination of the groups.

Perform Your Skit

Perform the skit you wrote for Reader's Theater. Work as a class to distribute copies of the script you wrote together. Read your lines slowly and clearly, keeping in mind the perspective of the character you are playing.

Crossword Puzzle

Create a crossword puzzle and write clues for each word in the chapter Word Bank. Exchange puzzles with a partner. Solve your partner's puzzle.

McGraw-Hill Education

Chapter 8

The Westward Expansion

Lesson 1
Stories of the Settlers

Lesson 2
Hard Times for American Indians

Lesson 3
California and Texas Join the Union

ESSENTIAL EQ QUESTION

What Does the Westward Expansion Reveal about the Character of Our Nation?

In this chapter, you'll read about why settlers decided to brave dangerous trails to start new lives in the western territories. You'll learn more about how Westward Expansion impacted American Indians, and you'll examine the events that resulted in statehood for California and Texas.

Step into the Time Chronological Thinking

Look at the timeline. What was happening in other parts of the world while the United States was expanding west?

Americas

1821 Mexico wins independence from Spain.

1830 Indian Removal Act is passed.

1835 Second Seminole War begins.

1838 Cherokee are forced to relocate on Trail of Tears.

1820   1830   1840

World Events

1825 First railroad carries passengers in England.

1826 The first photograph is taken.

1829 Greece becomes independent from Turkey.

1837 Victoria becomes queen of England.

HSS.5.8.4, HSS.5.8.5, HSS.5.8.6, HAS.CS.1

The United States and Territories, 1850

Step into the Place

1. Which state shared no boundaries with other states in 1850?

2. Compare this map with the map on page 291. What new states were added to the United States after the Louisiana Purchase in 1803?

After the Louisiana Purchase was completed, the people and policies of the United States began to support expanding the nation all the way to the Pacific Ocean. However, territories controlled by Mexico (which had recently won its independence from Spain) were in the way. Through war and diplomacy, the United States slowly began chipping away at those territories to become the nation it is today.

1841
First wagon train on the Oregon Trail

1846–1847
Mexican War

1848–1849
California Gold Rush

1850
California becomes a state.

1840

1850

1847
In England, Emily Brontë writes *Wuthering Heights* and Charlotte Brontë writes *Jane Eyre*.

1848
Revolution of 1848 in France removes King Louis-Philippe.

A Time of TROUBLES

by Ruth Spencer Johnson

A 13-year-old Sioux girl might have described what life was like for her family on a reservation in 1880 in this way:

No longer do the men of my tribe mount their horses and ride out on great bison hunts. The women do not prepare feasts of fresh bison meat roasted over the fire. The enormous herds are gone, and so are the days when we traveled freely, setting up our tepee camps wherever the bison led us. The white men say we must learn to farm instead of hunt. They insist we become "civilized" and adopt their ways. Our tribe must stay on this reservation, which is a small part of the land we used to roam.

Before the reservation, my people rose with the sun, ready to use the gifts of nature to meet our needs. Each day was a challenge, but we were free. Now we must depend on the white man's promise to feed and clothe us, but the government has not kept its word.

The Great Father pledged to give us cattle, tools, and seeds for farming, as well as blankets and cloth. While we learn to grow our own food, the government promises us beef, flour, beans, coffee, and other supplies. We line up to receive our rations, but there is never enough. The food is often not fit to eat. My father says dishonest agents steal provisions meant for us and sell them for a profit.

Like my father, the men of our tribe were once proud hunters providing us with meat and skins from bison, elk, and other animals. They were warriors, ready to protect their families at a moment's notice. When we moved to the reservation, they had to give up their weapons and learn to plow. But farming takes fertile land and good weather, and we have neither. Settlers take the best land, and drought and hot summer winds kill many of the crops. We have not been able to raise enough food, and now we are starving.

As always, my mother and the other women cook, clean, and raise children. The home is a woman's responsibility, but without fresh bison hides, Mother cannot repair our tepee or make a new one. Government officials insist we dress like white settlers, so we must now sew our garments from thin cloth instead of animal skins. Without our warm bison robes and deerskin clothing, we are always cold in the winter winds.

Sioux (Lakota) Indians resting at camp

As if cold and hunger aren't enough to deal with, our people have been sick. We have little resistance to white men's diseases, and many people die—especially children. Officials have forbidden our medicine men from using traditional ways to treat the sick, so they must act in secret. We children are busy doing chores and helping our parents, but we try to find a little time to play so we can forget our troubles for a while. Boys pretend to be warriors and hunters. Girls play with their dolls, and we all like to play ball and stick games. In the evening, we gather around our grandparents to hear them tell stories about their youth. They have so much wisdom to pass on to us!

Churches have set up schools on the reservation to teach us English and try to turn us into Christians. The teachers cut our hair short and give us new names. They want us to learn to live like them and hope we will help our parents give up the ancient ceremonies and customs. But when we go home after school, most of us still speak our own language and follow our traditional ways.

Some of my friends have been sent to boarding schools where they must live year-round. The white men think children are more likely to change if they are separated from their families for long periods. Students who return to their families after years at boarding school often feel like they no longer belong with their own people. This is a sad thing because we place a high value on family. My tribe has struggled since we were forced onto the reservation. Some of our people want to learn the white man's ways, thinking that's the only path to survival. A few men have even become policemen and help enforce the reservation laws. But many people cling to tradition, and this has created conflict. The reservation officials do not allow us to mourn our dead or celebrate the seasons in the traditional ways.

Flandreau Indian School choir, South Dakota, early 1900s

Still, some things have not changed. The Sioux will always love the earth and all its creatures. We treasure our children and respect our elders. We try to follow the right path in life, and we ask the Great Spirit to give us strength and wisdom.

Many of us long for the old days and desperately hope for a way off the reservation. You can hear our yearning in the songs we sing around the fire on cold nights. Oh, Great Spirit, please hear our cries!

Think About It

1. What has changed for the Sioux girl and her family?

2. How does life on the reservation compare with the life the Sioux led before?

3. How do the Sioux maintain their way of life despite the hardships of the reservation?

People You Should Know

Antonio López de Santa Anna

Osceola

In 1833, after assuming the presidency of the independent nation of Mexico, Antonio López de Santa Anna established a strong national government. In 1836, Texas declared its independence from Mexico and its desire to join the United States. Santa Anna tried to bring Texas back into Mexico. He had a small victory when he trapped Texas forces at the Alamo, but he lost to Sam Houston at the Battle of San Jacinto. Later, he overthrew the Mexican government to become president a second time. He fought the United States again from 1846–1848 in the Mexican-American War. After Mexico lost, he fled to Jamaica.

As a leader during the Second Seminole War (1835–1842), Osceola used guerilla warfare against U.S. troops. In guerilla warfare, one side uses the landscape to hide and attack the other side by surprise. Osceola and the Seminoles used the swamps of southern Florida to fight the Americans who wanted to move the Seminole away from their ancestral lands. The Seminole had success until they went to St. Augustine to try to come to an agreement with U.S. military leaders. The soldiers captured and imprisoned Osceola and his men. Osceola later died in prison, and the Second Seminole War came to an end.

Laura Ingalls Wilder

Cesar Chavez

In 1932, Laura Ingalls Wilder published her first children's book, *Little House in the Big Woods*. The book told stories about her own childhood on the prairie in the late 1800s. Wilder's father had taken his family in a covered wagon across the northern plains states before settling in Missouri, where Laura also raised her own family. She worked as an editor and writer for many newspapers and magazines, but it is her books, often called the "Little House" series, that won her lasting fame as an American writer.

Born into a family of migrant farm workers, Cesar Chavez devoted his life to making sure farm laborers in the United States were treated fairly. In 1962, he founded the NFWA, the National Farm Workers Association. This union of farm workers conducted strikes and boycotts of large farms that refused to provide good wages and benefits to their workers. This brought national attention to the issue and economic pressure on the farm owners. After about five years, the farms gave in and signed agreements with the NFWA.

(t)McGraw-Hill Education; (bl)Heritage Images/Hulton Archive/ Getty Images; (r)Frank Hurley/New York Daily News/Getty Images

What Did Settlers Experience in Their Movement Westward?

Trails to the West

The first European settlers to travel west were fur traders who used American Indian trails and lived in the wilderness. The American Indians in the area often helped these "mountain men" survive. By the 1830s, there was less demand for furs, and the number of traders declined. New settlers consisted mainly of families who traveled in groups of wagons led by experienced guides. Their destination was the rich farmland of the Oregon Territory. It was said that these settlers had "Oregon Fever," because of their desire to start new lives in the far West.

Since 1818, Great Britain and the United States had shared a claim to the Oregon Territory. After 1840, however, U.S. citizens began to believe their country should extend all the way from the Atlantic Ocean to the Pacific Ocean. This idea, called **Manifest Destiny**, led U.S. President James K. Polk to negotiate the Oregon Treaty with Great Britain. The two nations agreed to extend the United States-Canada border at the 49th parallel of latitude all the way to the Pacific Ocean.

(t)McGraw-Hill Education

HSS.5.8.2, HSS.5.8.4, HAS.CS.4, HAS.HR.2

340 Lesson 1 What Did Settlers Experience in Their Movement Westward?

1820s
Mountain men appear in Rockies.

1841
First wagon train on Oregon Trail

1847
Mormons settle Utah.

|1820| |1830| |1840| |1850

1846
Oregon Treaty divides United States and Canada at the 49th parallel.

Settlers on a trail, traveling westward

Everett Collection/Shutterstock.com

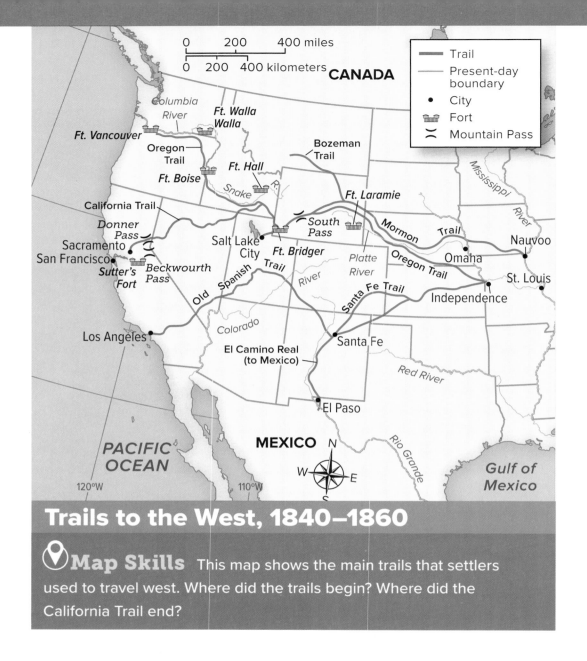

Trails to the West, 1840–1860

 Map Skills This map shows the main trails that settlers used to travel west. Where did the trails begin? Where did the California Trail end?

✓ Stop and Check

COLLABORATE

Talk Why did "Oregon Fever" cause settlers to move west?

Find Details As you read, add new information to the graphic organizer on page 277 in your Inquiry Journal.

What Do You Think? Would you have been willing to leave your livelihood in the East to stake your claim to land in the West? Why?

Life on the Wagon Train

Life on the trails was challenging but exciting. On the Oregon Trail, settlers had to travel for six months across about 2,000 miles of wilderness. Many families traveled in groups of wagons called wagon trains. These families were able to provide protection for one another.

Most wagon trains consisted of wagons called "prairie schooners" because their white covers looked like a ship's sails from a distance. This type of wagon was usually pulled by a team of **oxen**. The wagon had to carry everything the family would need for the journey and for its new home. The supplies included tools, weapons, food, seeds for planting, books, cooking utensils, spare wagon parts, medicine, and clothes.

Each member of the family had jobs to do on the journey. Men drove the wagon and were responsible for repairing it. They also hunted for food and protected their families. Women cooked and cleaned, set up camp, and were responsible for managing their families' supplies. They also cared for and taught their children. Children helped out where they could, and collected "buffalo chips," manure that was used as fuel for campfires.

A wagon train traveling west with the Rocky Mountains in the background

In Their Words... Sarah Byrd

We came from I-O-WAY in 1848. That's a long time ago, ain't it? Joe Watt was captain of our train. Bein' so little, I don't remember how many was in the train, but I've heard 'em say it was a big one. Every night when we camped the wagons was pulled in a circle an' hooked together with chains an' oxen yokes. The folks camped inside that circle, an' close along-side was the [livestock], an' a guard was set up for the night.

Yes, it must have ban an awful job cookin'. I was too little to do anything. 'Course they had to cook on the open fire, an' on the plains, most o' the time there was nothin' to burn but buffalo chips. I guess they got use to it, but I wouldn't like to.

—from an interview of Byrd recalling her journey to Oregon, February 28, 1939

Along the trail, conditions could be difficult. The settlers had to face dangerous thunderstorms, floods, snow and ice, rocky terrain, and deep rivers. Disease was also a danger, as settlers lacked access to good medical care. Each obstacle put the people and their precious supplies in danger.

The dangers didn't stop people from using the trails, however. By 1861, about 300,000 people had traveled the Oregon Trail to the West.

 Stop and Check

Talk What were the benefits and drawbacks of moving west?

Sarah L. Byrd, interview by Sara B. Wrenn, March 1, 1939, Portland, Oregon. Library of Congress, Manuscript Division, WPA Federal Writers' Project Collection, Folklore Project, Life Histories, 1936–39, MSS55715: BOX A729.

An early engraving of Salt Lake City, Utah

Mormons Head West

While some people wanted to journey west to find land and a fresh start in life, others traveled to find religious freedom. The members of the Church of Jesus Christ of Latter-Day Saints, also known as Mormons, left New York when their beliefs caused difficulties with their neighbors. They moved to Illinois but again experienced **hostility** from neighbors. After their leader, Joseph Smith, was shot and killed by a mob in 1844, they decided to move farther west.

In 1845, led by Brigham Young, the Mormons set out on a route near the Oregon Trail. They turned southwest at Fort Bridger, in what is now Wyoming. They decided to settle in present-day Utah at the Great Salt Lake. Soon there were about 2,000 people in the settlement, which they named Salt Lake City. While the area around the lake was dry and difficult to farm, the Mormon settlers were able to use irrigation to grow crops.

Other religious movements also thrived on the trails to the West. One popular style of worship, called "camp meetings," was the result of the Second Great Awakening. At these meetings, pioneers attended services in tents.

✓ Stop and Check

Talk Why did the Mormons leave New York and Illinois? Is their relocation similar to any earlier migrations of people you have read about?

How Did Westward Expansion Impact American Indians?

The Age of Jackson

As the United States expanded westward, the government began to include members of Congress who gave a voice to the needs and opinions of western settlers. In 1824, only about 360,000 American citizens voted. Then new laws allowed all white men age 21 or older to vote. Before then, only wealthy male landowners could vote. Four years later, the number of voters increased more than 200 percent to about 1.2 million. This **surge** of new voters—farmers, frontier settlers, and city workers—helped elect a "common man," Andrew Jackson, as president in 1828. Born on the frontier, Jackson was a farmer-politician with no college education or public-speaking skills. He had fought in the Revolutionary War at the age of 13 and later became a popular general during the War of 1812. This "man of the people" went on to become one of the most powerful and controversial presidents in U.S. history.

Jackson's actions as president ignited much conflict. Opponents accused Jackson of trying to take away Congress's power. He **vetoed** much legislation, preventing Congress from passing the laws it wanted.

One major conflict arose in South Carolina. When Congress passed a new federal tax on imported goods in 1832, South Carolina politicians threatened to leave the Union. Because Southern states had few local industries, they relied on imported products. The new tax would make these products very expensive. Jackson responded to South Carolina's threat by sending troops and warships to force the state to pay the tax. The action enraged citizens, who compared the move to Britain's attempts to enforce new taxes on colonists in the 1700s.

HSS.5.3.4, HSS.5.3.5, HSS.5.3.6, HAS.CS.1, HAS.CS.3, HAS.CS.4, HAS.HR.1, HAS.HR.2, HAS.HI.1

346 Lesson 2 How Did Westward Expansion Impact American Indians?

McGraw-Hill Education

1817
First
Seminole War

1830
Indian Removal
Act

1835
Second
Seminole War

1838
Cherokee
forced to
relocate

1855
Third
Seminole War

|1820| |1830| |1840| |1850|

1829
Andrew Jackson
takes office as
President.

Chief Justice John Marshall swears
in Andrew Jackson as president.

Everett Historical/Shutterstock.com

InfoGraphic

Political Cartoons

Through political cartoons, artists express their opinions on current news, people, and events. Cartoons usually exaggerate details in a humorous or ridiculous way to make a statement. To identify the artist's opinion, look closely at the title, labels, and details of the cartoon. How do you think this artist felt about Jackson's actions as president?

King Andrew the First (artist unknown)

Subject
Andrew Jackson

Symbol
King's clothing stands for Jackson's power

Detail
Jackson holds the veto in his hand

Detail
Jackson tramples on the Constitution

Title

BORN TO COMMAND.

OF VETO MEMORY.

HAD I BEEN CONSULTED.

KING ANDREW THE FIRST.

Another controversial action by Jackson concerned the Second Bank of the United States, which helped to manage the nation's money supply. Convinced that the **charter** of the Bank of the United States was unconstitutional, Jackson removed all of the federal government's money from the bank in 1836. He ordered that the money be transferred to state and local banks. There were no regulations in place to monitor these banks, however. Many of them made unwise investments in land. When the economy weakened in 1837, the invested money could not be recovered.

The "man of the people" had caused a major economic crisis, putting many working people he claimed to represent in difficult times.

> ## ✓ Stop and Check
>
> **Think** How was Jackson's leadership different from that of the presidents before him?
>
> **Find Details** As you read, add additional information to the graphic organizer on page 285 in your Inquiry Journal.

Lands and Routes of
Native American Relocation

← Cherokee
← Chickasaw
← Choctaw
← Seminole
← Muscogee
— Present-day boundary
• City

The Indian Removal Act

In the early 1800s, American Indians in the Southeast were protected by the treaties signed with the U.S. government. The treaties guaranteed their right to their homeland and protection from settlers. American Indian communities flourished with their own schools and local governments. Life alongside settlers was peaceful until settlers began demanding more land. Settlers' demands for land increased when gold was discovered on Cherokee lands in Georgia. Conflict grew worse.

As a general, Andrew Jackson had fought several campaigns against American Indians. He believed that American Indians threatened the expansion of the United States. He supported violating the treaties to free up more land for white settlers. He believed that moving American Indians to land west of the Mississippi would end the threat.

In 1830, Congress passed the Indian Removal Act and Andrew Jackson signed it into law. This law forced American Indians to leave their homelands so settlers could live there. The act allowed the U.S. government to relocate American Indians to "Indian Territory," in parts of what is now Oklahoma.

Stop and Check

Discuss Why did Andrew Jackson want to relocate American Indians?

The Trail of Tears

The Cherokee fought against the Indian Removal Act. Led by Chief John Ross, they took their case to court and sued the state of Georgia. Eventually, the U.S. Supreme Court, the highest court in the land, ruled in favor of the Cherokee, determining that "the laws of Georgia can have no force" on American Indian lands. President Jackson ignored that ruling, however. He ordered soldiers to force the Cherokee off the lands they legally owned.

In 1838, General Winfield Scott led about 7,000 federal troops onto Cherokee lands in northwest Georgia and neighboring areas. He told the Cherokee that they were surrounded, escape was impossible, and force would be used if they did not comply. The soldiers then burned the Cherokee's homes and forced them to travel 800 miles into Indian Territory.

PRIMARY SOURCE

In Their Words... Chief John Ross

We are overwhelmed! Our hearts are sickened, our utterance is paralyzed, when we reflect on the condition in which we are placed, by the audacious practices of unprincipled men. . . . In truth, our cause is your own; it is the cause of liberty and of justice; it is based upon your own principles, which we have learned from yourselves; for we have gloried to count your Washington and your Jefferson our great teachers . . .

—from a letter to the U.S. Congress, 1836

TEXT: The Papers of Chief John Ross, vol 1, 1807-1839. Translated by Gary E. Moulton Norman OK: University of Oklahoma Press, 1985.; PHOTO: Library of Congress, Prints & Photographs Division [LC-DIG-pga-07513]

In Their Words... Chief Justice John Marshall

Treaties have been duly ratified by the Senate of the United States of America, and by which treaties the United States of America acknowledge the said Cherokee Nation to be a sovereign nation, authorized to govern themselves, and all persons who have settled within their territory, free from any right of legislative interference by the several states composing the United States of America in reference to acts done within their own territory, and by which treaties the whole of the territory now occupied by the Cherokee Nation on the east of the Mississippi has been solemnly guarantied to them, all of which treaties are existing treaties at this day, and in full force . . .

—from *Worcester* v. *Georgia* ruling, 1831

Of the approximately 15,000 Cherokee forced to leave their homes, about 2,000 died in camps waiting for the move to begin. During the one-year march, another 2,000 Cherokee died from disease, starvation, and severe weather conditions. The Cherokee called this forced march "the place where they cried." In English, it became known as the Trail of Tears.

Stop and Check

Think What illegal actions did President Jackson and Congress take to force the removal of the Cherokee from their own land?

Sequoyah

A Cherokee silversmith named Sequoyah developed the first written American Indian alphabet. Borrowing letters from Greek, Hebrew, and English, Sequoyah created 85 symbols, each of which represented a Cherokee sound. It took him 12 years to create the alphabet. He compared the difficult task to "catching a wild animal and taming it."

In 1824, Sequoyah began using this new writing system to send printed messages from Arkansas to Cherokee people living farther east. Since the symbols were based on the way the spoken language sounded, Cherokee learned the alphabet quickly. Within a few months, thousands of Cherokee had learned the new alphabet. They called it "talking leaves," since it was printed on paper that resembled tree leaves and allowed them to talk with others over long distances.

In 1828, Sequoyah's alphabet was used in the first American Indian newspaper, the *Cherokee Phoenix*. The paper focused on issues affecting American Indian communities. A version of it still exists today.

Sequoyah became a respected leader for his contribution to American Indian culture. The California giant redwood tree is named *sequoia* in his honor.

Sequoyah with his Cherokee alphabet, called "talking leaves"

(bkgd)McGraw-Hill Education; (c) Library of Congress, Prints & Photographs Division [LC-DIG-pga-07569]

The Seminole Wars

Andrew Jackson had a long history of interfering with the rights of American Indians, starting when he was a general in the U.S. military. It was then that he first became involved in wars between the U.S. military and the Seminole people of Florida.

In the first Seminole War in 1817, General Jackson led forces in an invasion of Seminole land to recapture runaway slaves that the Seminole had welcomed. U.S. soldiers burned down the towns in this region.

When Jackson became president, he again attempted to relocate the Seminole in Florida and take over their land. Settlers and Jackson sought to enforce the Indian Removal Act in Florida. Some of the Seminole formed an army under the leadership of Chief Osceola and fought against U.S. troops. When the U.S. Army approached Osceola, claiming to come in peace, they took him prisoner. He later died in prison. Even so, the Seminole continued fighting to remain in Florida. By the end of the Seminole Wars, U.S. soldiers had removed 3,000 Seminole from their Florida homes and killed 1,500 more.

Chief Osceola

Stop and Check

Talk What similarities were there between the Trail of Tears and the Seminole Wars?

How Did California and Texas Become Part of the United States?

Americans in Texas

In 1821, Mexico won its independence from Spain. At that time, Mexico was a much larger country than it is today. Mexican **territories** also included land that stretches from present-day Texas to California. Despite covering a large land area, the northern provinces of Mexico had small populations. In the early 1820s, for example, there were only about 2,500 Mexicans living throughout Texas.

The Mexican government came up with a plan to draw new groups of settlers to the area. It offered land to U.S. citizens almost free of charge, but there were some conditions. The new residents had to become Mexican citizens, and they had to convert to Catholicism, which was the main religion of Mexico. They also had to follow laws that made slavery illegal in Mexico and its territories.

Because of this plan, Americans began to move to Texas. Among them were Moses Austin and his son Stephen. In 1821, Moses Austin received almost 18,000 acres of land from the Mexican government to sell to other Americans. By 1835, more than 25,000 Americans had moved to Texas, including about 2,000 people who were enslaved, despite Mexican law.

McGraw-Hill Education

HSS.5.8.5, HSS.5.8.6, HAS.CS.4, HAS.HI.3, EEI.PV

354 Lesson 3 How Did California and Texas Become Part of the United States?

Time Line

1821
Mexico wins independence from Spain.

1836
The Republic of Texas declares independence from Mexico.

1846–1847
Mexican-American War

1845
Texas joins the Union.

1848 The Treaty of Guadalupe Hidalgo is signed.

1850
California becomes a state.

| | 1820 | | | | | 1830 | | | | 1840 | | | | | 1850 | | | | |

1848–1849
The Gold Rush begins.

Today, the Alamo is the most visited historical landmark in the state of Texas.

©McGraw-Hill Education

The Settlers Rebel

Many Americans resisted Mexico's conditions. They did not want to become Mexican citizens or convert to Catholicism. They also complained about Mexican laws, especially those regarding slavery.

In December 1835, 500 Texans, including Stephen Austin, attacked San Antonio. They took control of the Alamo, a Spanish mission that the Mexican Army had turned into a fort. On March 2, 1836, Texas declared its independence. Four days later, Mexican General Antonio López de Santa Anna recaptured the Alamo, killing every American inside. Consequently, Texas General Sam Houston attacked a large Mexican force at San Jacinto a month later. The battle cry "Remember the Alamo!" inspired Texas troops, who defeated Santa Anna in less than 20 minutes.

Texans voted to join the United States. They adopted a constitution and legalized slavery. The U.S. government did not want to admit a slave state and feared war with Mexico, so it did not let Texas join the Union in 1835. Texas became an independent country, the Republic of Texas. Its flag had a single star, so it was also known as the Lone Star **Republic**.

Then and Now

The first official flag of the Republic of Texas

The current state flag of Texas

The current state flag of Texas was not always the official flag. In addition to the first official flag, shown above, another design was recognized by the Congress of Texas. That flag had a blue star along with thirteen red and white stripes. In time, the elements of these flags were combined to create the state flag that Texas flies today.

The Mexican-American War

The Lone Star Republic came to an end in 1845. American ideas about Texas had changed. U.S. President James K. Polk did not fear a war with Mexico. Congress voted to accept Texas into the Union. Along with statehood came a disagreement over Texas's **boundaries**. The United States believed the Rio Grande was the border between Texas and Mexico, but Mexico claimed it was the Nueces River, 130 miles to the north. President Polk's interest in California and other Mexican territories

The Battle of Resaca de la Palma in Texas
during the Mexican-American War

also caused tension. He tried to buy the land for $30 million, but his offer was rejected. In 1846, Polk ordered General Zachary Taylor to march through Texas to the Rio Grande. As a result, fighting broke out between the U.S. and Mexican armies, and Congress declared war on Mexico.

Meanwhile, few Americans living in California were loyal to Mexico. In 1846, a group including John C. Frémont raised a flag with a bear on it and declared the area to be a free republic. The republic lasted only a month. When Polk heard about the Bear Flag Republic, he sent troops to claim California for the United States.

In 1847, U.S. troops attacked Mexico City, the Mexican capital. The Mexican government agreed to end the war. Both nations signed the Treaty of Guadalupe Hidalgo in 1848. According to the terms of the treaty, Mexico would sell a total of 320 million acres of land—55 percent of its territory—to the United States for $15 million. As a result, the Rio Grande was recognized as Texas's southern border. The future states of California, Nevada, and Utah, and parts of Arizona, New Mexico, Colorado, and Wyoming were also part of the deal.

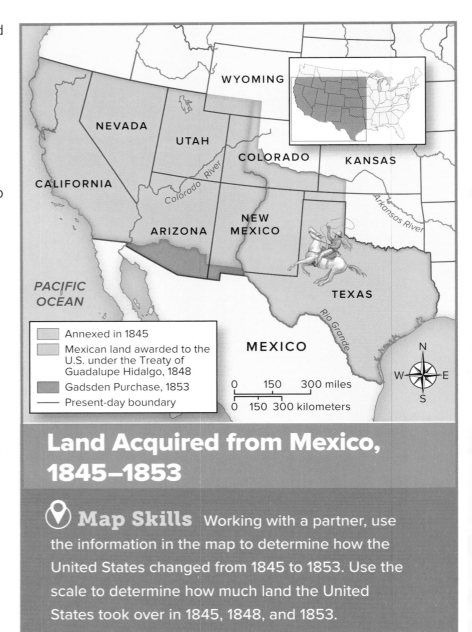

Annexed in 1845
Mexican land awarded to the U.S. under the Treaty of Guadalupe Hidalgo, 1848
Gadsden Purchase, 1853
Present-day boundary

0   150   300 miles
0   150 300 kilometers

Land Acquired from Mexico, 1845–1853

Map Skills Working with a partner, use the information in the map to determine how the United States changed from 1845 to 1853. Use the scale to determine how much land the United States took over in 1845, 1848, and 1853.

COLLABORATE

✓ Stop and Check

Talk What factors contributed to the Mexican-American War?

Find Details As you read, add additional information to the graphic organizer on page 293 in you Inquiry Journal.

What Do You Think? Of the many factors that led to the war, which do you think had the biggest impact? Why?

John C. Frémont

Born in Savannah, Georgia, in 1813, John C. Frémont spent many years exploring the United States. In 1838, the U.S. Secretary of War chose Frémont to assist Joseph Nicolas Nicollet, a French scientist, on a three-year mission to **survey** and map the Mississippi and Missouri Rivers. From there, Frémont went on to explore much of the land between the Mississippi River and the Pacific Ocean.

In 1843, Frémont traveled through the least-known parts of the American West. His route covered the present-day states of Oregon, Idaho, Wyoming, Colorado, Utah, Nevada, and California. His reports on what he saw in these areas led many Americans to move westward.

When the Mexican-American War began, Frémont joined a group of Americans near Sonoma in Mexico's California Territory. The group created the Bear Flag Republic. Then Frémont was made a major in the U.S. Army and fought to seize California for the United States.

After the war, Frémont served as governor of California for two months before moving to Washington, D.C., but he returned to his home on the West Coast in time for the Gold Rush. Gold was found on his property, and he soon became a multimillionaire. He also was elected one of the state's first senators in 1850, and he was nominated as the first Republican candidate for the presidency in 1856. He lost to James Buchanan.

John C. Frémont in about 1850

✓ Stop and Check

Talk How do you think Fremont's early years surveying rivers influenced his later life?

The Gold Rush

The Mexican-American War was not the only major event that transformed California and the United States in the 1840s and 1850s. In January 1848, a worker named James Marshall saw something glittering in the water at Sutter's Mill, a sawmill near Sacramento in the California Territory. It was gold. As news of his find spread by the end of 1848, about 6,000 miners soon flooded the area. The Gold Rush had begun.

Prospecting, or searching for gold, was time-consuming, but all it required was a few tools and dedication. Thousands of people swarmed the West Coast in the following year. By May 1849, more than 10,000 wagons had crossed the Missouri River heading for California. That year, a total of 80,000 people came from all over the world to seek a fortune. They were known as forty-niners, a term that reflected the year of their journey to the American West. The majority of the fortune hunters were young, unmarried men. There were also some women among the forty-niners, however. Many sought to benefit from the Gold Rush in a different way. Instead of joining miners at the edges of rivers and streams, they made money by cooking, cleaning houses, running boardinghouses and taverns, and washing laundry.

Miners used flat, shallow dishes to pan for gold.

Americans were not the only ones who traveled to California seeking gold. A quarter of the forty-niners came from places outside of the United States, including China, Latin America, Australia, and Europe. Journeys to California could take between three and six months. Travelers coming from Europe or the East Coast of the United States could sail around South America. They could also dock in Panama, cross the thin strip of land, and sail to California from the other side. Forty-niners coming from Asia faced a lengthy sea voyage. Those who chose to make the trip on land made a difficult, dangerous, and emotionally challenging journey. One traveler wrote, "The trip is a sort of magic mirror and exposes every man's qualities of heart connected with it, vicious or amiable."

Despite the difficulty and length of the journey, about 100,000 people made their way to California. Among them there were about 2,000 African Americans and 20,000 Chinese. For these groups, getting to California was only part of the challenge. Discrimination was common against nonwhite people in California. California Indians, Chinese, Latin Americans, and African Americans were often prevented from staking claims on land. In 1850, the state of California passed a law that made it illegal for nonwhite people to speak under oath in court cases involving white people. The law remained in place until 1872.

"Gold fever" drew people to California.

At first, mining for gold was simple. All a miner had to do was pan for it. That meant uncovering gold nuggets by washing dirt in a flat, shallow strainer. By 1853, however, most of the easy-to-find gold had already been collected. Miners formed companies to pay for machinery that could be used to dig deeper. With hydraulic mining, companies used powerful streams of water to blast gold-bearing gravel directly from the sides of mountains. However, hydraulic mining was very hard on the land. It washed away millions of tons of soil, destroying thousands of acres of land in California.

Nonetheless, California thrived during the Gold Rush. In particular, the city of San Francisco benefited from the steady stream of travelers. Located along the Pacific Ocean, San Francisco's harbor helped the city become the center of trade for the region. The people of San Francisco made money by feeding, clothing, housing, supplying, and entertaining the miners who settled in the city.

✓ Stop and Check

COLLABORATE

Talk How did the discovery of gold in California change the nation?

San Francisco grew rapidly beginning in 1849.

Library of Congress, Prints & Photographs Division [LC-DIG-pga-01463]

The Golden State

Due to the Gold Rush, California's population boomed. By 1849, California had enough people to form a state. Californians wanted the benefits of government services, including a court system, land and water laws, and mail delivery. A group of delegates formed to draft a state constitution. It was made up of men who had moved to California during the Gold Rush as well as eight

Although the Bear Flag Republic did not last, a bear still appears on the California state flag.

Californios, or people of Mexican or Spanish descent who had lived on the land since the time it had been a Mexican territory. The constitution they drafted gave the vote to white males only, whom it defined as including Latinos, but it allowed married women to hold property. It also outlawed slavery.

Congress was hesitant to admit California to the Union. The Senate was equally divided between slave states and free states. Senators from slave states did not want to give free states more power in Congress. The Compromise of 1850 solved this problem. California would enter the Union as a free state, and in return, the territories of Utah and New Mexico could decide whether or not to allow slavery.

When California became the thirty-first state, less than one percent of the population was made up of Californios. Even though Californios had lived in California for generations, most Americans treated them as if they had no right to the land. Settlers moved onto Californios' ranches without permission and used the courts to make unfair claims on their property.

☑ Stop and Check

COLLABORATE

Perspectives What similarities are there between the way settlers treated the Californios and how settlers treated American Indians elsewhere?

Map and Globe Skills

The States and Territories, 1850

Throughout the 1800s, the United States continued to grow and change. As the nation's population grew, so did the number of states and territories. The Treaty of Guadalupe Hidalgo greatly expanded the nation's boundaries. Furthermore, between the years of 1821 and 1850, Arkansas, California, Michigan, Florida, Iowa, Texas, and Wisconsin were welcomed to the Union.

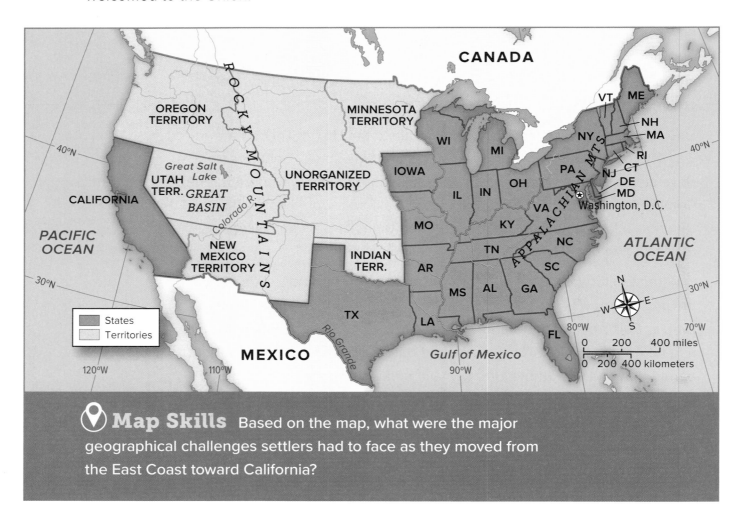

Map Skills Based on the map, what were the major geographical challenges settlers had to face as they moved from the East Coast toward California?

Arkansas
Population in 1850: 209,897
Population in 2015: 2,978,204
★ **Capital:** Little Rock

California
Population in 1850: 92,597
Population in 2015: 39,144,818
★ **Capital:** Sacramento

Florida
Population in 1850: 87,445
Population in 2015: 20,271,272
★ **Capital:** Tallahassee

Iowa
Population in 1850: 192,214
Population in 2015: 3,123,899
★ **Capital:** Des Moines

Michigan
Population in 1850: 397,654
Population in 2015: 9,922,576
★ **Capital:** Lansing

Texas
Population in 1850: 212,592
Population in 2015: 27,469,114
★ **Capital:** Austin

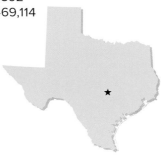

Wisconsin
Population in 1850: 305,391
Population in 2015: 5,771,337
★ **Capital:** Madison

The States Adopted after 1850

Since 1850, nineteen more states have joined the United States. The most recent additions, Alaska and Hawaii, achieved statehood in 1959. This means that no new state has joined the Union in nearly 60 years. However, citizens have begun statehood movements in Washington, D.C., and Puerto Rico.

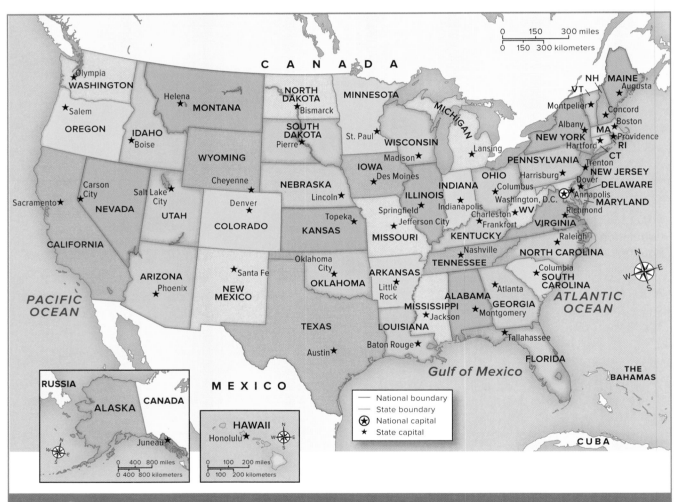

Map Skills Compare this map to the one on page 364. Which part of the country gained the most states after 1850? Which two new states share no borders with the other 48?

Alaska
Population in 1900: 63,592
Population in 2015: 738,432
★ Capital: Juneau

Arizona
Population in 1900: 122,931
Population in 2015: 6,828,065
★ Capital: Phoenix

Colorado
Population in 1900: 539,700
Population in 2015: 5,456,574
★ Capital: Denver

Hawaii
Population in 1900: 154,001
Population in 2015: 1,431,603
★ Capital: Honolulu

Idaho
Population in 1900: 161,772
Population in 2015: 1,654,930
★ Capital: Boise

Kansas
Population in 1900: 1,470,495
Population in 2015: 2,911,641
★ Capital: Topeka

Minnesota
Population in 1900: 1,751,394
Population in 2015: 5,489,594
★ Capital: St. Paul

Montana
Population in 1900: 243,329
Population in 2015: 1,032,949
★ Capital: Helena

Nebraska
Population in 1900: 1,066,300
Population in 2015: 1,896,190
★ Capital: Lincoln

Nevada
Population in 1900: 42,335
Population in 2015: 2,890,845
★ Capital: Carson City

New Mexico
Population in 1900: 195,310
Population in 2015: 2,085,109
★ Capital: Santa Fe

North Dakota
Population in 1900: 319,146
Population in 2015: 756,927
★ Capital: Bismark

Oklahoma
Population in 1900: 790,391
Population in 2015: 3,911,338
★ Capital: Oklahoma City

Oregon
Population in 1900: 413,536
Population in 2015: 4,028,977
★ Capital: Salem

South Dakota
Population in 1900: 401,570
Population in 2015: 858,469
★ Capital: Pierre

Utah
Population in 1900: 276,749
Population in 2015: 2,995,919
★ Capital: Salt Lake City

Washington
Population in 1900: 518,103
Population in 2015: 7,170,351
★ Capital: Olympia

West Virginia
Population in 1900: 958,800
Population in 2015: 1,844,128
★ Capital: Charleston

Wyoming
Population in 1900: 92,531
Population in 2015: 586,107
★ Capital: Cheyenne

Connections in Action!

Back to the EQ

Think about the Chapter EQ, **"What Does the Westward Expansion Reveal about the Character of Our Nation?"**

- **Talk** with a partner about what you learned from the chapter. Discuss what the desire to move west says about the character of the United States.

- **Think** about how the nation changed. What was it like to travel there? Why were people interested in taking risks to establish new lives there? Who benefited from expansion? Who suffered from it? Does this suffering reflect poorly on the character of our nation?

- **Share** your ideas; then have a discussion about the positive and negative characteristics that Westward Expansion reveals about our nation.

More to Explore
How Can You Make an IMPACT?

Write a Song

Work with a partner or small group to write a song that captures the spirit of Westward Expansion. You can write any kind of song, even a kind that wasn't invented at the time, such as rap, hip-hop, or Broadway musical.

Perform Your Song

Perform your song by presenting it to your class or recording it and posting it to your class website or blog. Work together to practice it before performing it. Listen respectfully to other groups' songs.

Word Play

Choose five words from the chapter Word Bank. Make a list of words in the same family by adding prefixes and suffixes or by changing the tense or part of speech of the word; for example: *surge, surged, surging, resurgent, upsurge, insurgency.* Use a dictionary to confirm whether the words you are creating are actual words.

Reference Sources

The Reference Section has many parts, each with a different type of information. Use this section to explore people, places, and events as you investigate and take action.

Presidents of the United States

1. George Washington (1732-1799)
Years in Office: 1789-1797
Vice President: John Adams
Home State: Virginia
Political Party: Federalist
First Lady: Martha Dandridge Washington

2. John Adams (1735-1826)
Years in Office: 1797-1801
Vice President: Thomas Jefferson
Home State: Massachusetts
Political Party: Federalist
First Lady: Abigail Smith Adams

3. Thomas Jefferson (1743-1826)
Years in Office: 1801-1809
Vice President: Aaron Burr 1801-1805;
George Clinton 1805-1809
Home State: Virginia
Political Party: Democratic-Republican
First Lady: (none)

4. James Madison (1751-1836)
Years in Office: 1809-1817
Vice President: George Clinton 1809-1812,
died; Elbridge Gerry 1813-1814, died
Home State: Virginia
Political Party: Democratic-Republican
First Lady: Dolley Payne Madison

5. James Monroe (1758-1831)
Years in Office: 1817-1825
Vice President: Daniel D. Tompkins
Home State: Virginia
Political Party: Democratic-Republican
First Lady: Elizabeth Kortright Monroe

6. John Quincy Adams (1767-1848)
Years in Office: 1825-1829
Vice President: John C. Calhoun
Home State: Massachusetts
Political Party: Democratic-Republican
First Lady: Louisa Johnson Adams

7. Andrew Jackson (1767-1845)
Years in Office: 1829-1837
Vice President: John C. Calhoun 1829-1832
resigned; Martin Van Buren 1833-1837
Home State: Tennessee
Political Party: Democrat
First Lady: (none)

8. Martin Van Buren (1782-1862)
Years in Office: 1837-1841
Vice President: Richard M. Johnson
Howme State: New York
Political Party: Democrat
First Lady: (none)

9. William Henry Harrison (1773-1841)
Years in Office: 1841 (one month);
died in office
Vice President: John Tyler
Home State: Ohio
Political Party: Whig
First Lady: Anna Symmes Harrison

10. John Tyler (1790-1862)
Years in Office: 1841-1845
Vice President: (none)
Home State: Virginia
Political Party: Whig
First Lady: Letitia Christian Tyler, died 1842; Julia Gardiner Tyler

16. Abraham Lincoln (1809-1865)
Years in Office: 1861-1865 (assassinated)
Vice President: Hannibal Hamlin (1861-1865); Andrew Johnson 1865
Home State: Illinois
Political Party: Republican
First Lady: Mary Todd Lincoln

11. James K. Polk (1795-1849)
Years in Office: 1845-1849
Vice President: George M. Dallas
Home State: Tennessee
Political Party: Democrat
First Lady: Sarah Childress Polk

17. Andrew Johnson (1808-1875)
Years in Office: 1865-1869
Vice President: (none)
Home State: Tennessee
Political Party: Democrat
First Lady: Eliza McCardle Johnson

12. Zachary Taylor (1784-1850)
Years in Office: 1849-1850 (died in office)
Vice President: Millard Fillmore
Home State: Kentucky
Political Party: Whig
First Lady: Margaret Smith Taylor

18. Ulysses S. Grant (1822-1885)
Years in Office: 1869-1877
Vice President: Schuyler Colfax 1869-1873; Henry Wilson 1873-1875, died
Home State: Illinois
Political Party: Republican
First Lady: Julia Dent Grant

13. Millard Fillmore (1800-1874)
Years in Office: 1850-1853
Vice President: (none)
Home State: New York
Political Party: Whig
First Lady: Abigail Powers Fillmore

19. Rutherford B. Hayes (1822-1893)
Years in Office: 1877-1881
Vice President: William A. Wheeler
Home State: Ohio
Political Party: Republican
First Lady: Lucy Webb Hayes

14. Franklin Pierce (1804-1869)
Years in Office: 1853-1857
Vice President: William R. King, died 1853
Home State: New Hampshire
Political Party: Democrat
First Lady: Jane Appleton Pierce

20. James A. Garfield (1831-1881)
Years in Office: 1881 (assassinated)
Vice President: Chester A. Arthur
Home State: Ohio
Political Party: Republican
First Lady: Lucretia Rudolph Garfield

15. James Buchanan (1791-1868)
Years in Office: 1857-1861
Vice President: John C. Breckinridge
Home State: Pennsylvania
Political Party: Democrat
First Lady: (none)

21. Chester A. Arthur (1829-1886)
Years in Office: 1881-1885
Vice President: (none)
Home State: New York
Political Party: Republican
First Lady: (none)

22. Grover Cleveland (1837-1908)
Years in Office: 1885-1889
Vice President: Thomas A. Hendricks
Home State: New York
Political Party: Democrat
First Lady: Frances Folsom Cleveland

23. Benjamin Harrison (1833-1901)
Years in Office: 1889-1893
Vice President: Levi P. Morton
Home State: Indiana
Political Party: Republican
First Lady: Caroline Scott Harrison, died 1892

24. Grover Cleveland (1837-1908)
Years in Office: 1893-1897
Vice President: Adlai E. Stevenson
Home State: New York
Political Party: Democrat
First Lady: Frances Folsom Cleveland

25. William McKinley (1843-1901)
Years in Office: 1897-1901 (assassinated)
Vice President: Garret A. Hobart 1897-1899, died; Theodore Roosevelt 1901
Home State: Ohio
Political Party: Republican
First Lady: Ida Saxton McKinley

26. Theodore Roosevelt (1858-1919)
Years in Office: 1901-1909
Vice President: Charles W. Fairbanks 1905-1909
Home State: New York
Political: Republican
First Lady: Edith Carow Roosevelt

27. William Howard Taft (1857-1930)
Years in Office: 1909-1913
Vice President: James S. Sherman 1909-1912, died
Home State: Ohio
Political Party: Republican
First Lady: Helen Herron Taft

28. Woodrow Wilson (1856-1924)
Years in Office: 1913-1921
Vice President: Thomas R. Marshall
Home State: New Jersey
Political Party: Democrat
First Lady: Ellen Louise Axson Wilson, died 1914; Edith Bolling Galt Wilson

29. Warren G. Harding (1865-1923)
Years in Office: 1921-1923 (died in office)
Vice President: Calvin Coolidge
Home State: Ohio
Political Party: Republican
First Lady: Florence King Harding

30. Calvin Coolidge (1872-1933)
Years in Office: 1923-1929
Vice President: Charles G. Dawes 1925-1929
Home State: Massachusetts
Political Party: Republican
First Lady: Grace Goodhue Coolidge

31. Herbert C. Hoover (1874-1964)
Years in Office: 1929-1933
Vice President: Charles Curtis
Home State: California
Political Party: Republican
First Lady: Lou Henry Hoover

32. Franklin D. Roosevelt (1882-1945)
Years in Office: 1933-1945 (died in office)
Vice President: John Nance Garner 1933-1941; Henry Wallace 1941-1945; Harry S. Truman 1945
Home State: New York
Political Party: Democrat
First Lady: Anna Eleanor Roosevelt

33. Harry S. Truman (1884-1972)
Years in Office: 1945-1953
Vice President: Alben W. Barkley (1949-1953)
Home State: Missouri
Political Party: Democrat
First Lady: Elizabeth (Bess) Wallace Truman

34. Dwight D. Eisenhower (1890-1969)
Years in Office: 1953-1961
Vice President: Richard M. Nixon
Home State: Kansas
Political Party: Republican
First Lady: Marie (Mamie) Doud
Eisenhower

35. John F. Kennedy (1917-1963)
Years in Office: 1961-1963 (assassinated)
Vice President: Lyndon B. Johnson
Home State: Massachusetts
Political Party: Democrat
First Lady: Jacqueline Bouvier Kennedy

36. Lyndon Baines Johnson (1908-1973)
Years in Office: 1963-1969
Vice President: Hubert H. Humphrey
Home State: Texas
Political Party: Democrat
First Lady: Claudia (Lady Bird) Taylor
Johnson

37. Richard M. Nixon (1913-1994)
Years in Office: 1969-1974 (resigned)
Vice President Spiro T. Agnew 1969-1973,
resigned; Gerald R. Ford 1973-1974
Home State: California
Political Party: Republican
First Lady: Patricia (Pat) Ryan Nixon

38. Gerald R. Ford (1913-2006)
Years in Office: 1974-1977
Vice President: Nelson A. Rockefeller
Home State: Michigan
Political Party: Republican
First Lady: Elizabeth (Betty) Bloomer Ford

39. James (Jimmy) Carter (1924-)
Years in Office: 1977-1981
Vice President: Walter F. Mondale
Home State: Georgia
Political Party: Democrat
First Lady: Rosalynn Smith Carter

40. Ronald W. Reagan (1911-2004)
Years in Office: 1981-1989
Vice President: George Bush
Home State: California
Political Party: Republican
First Lady: Nancy Davis Reagan

41. George H. W. Bush (1924-)
Years in Office: 1989-1993
Vice President: J. Danforth (Dan) Quayle
Home State: Texas
Political Party: Republican
First Lady: Barbara Pierce Bush

42. William Jefferson Clinton (1946-)
Years in Office: 1993-2001
Vice President: Albert Gore, Jr.
Home State: Arkansas
Political Party: Democrat
First Lady: Hillary Rodham Clinton

43. George W. Bush (1946-)
Years in Office: 2001-2009
Vice President: Richard Cheney
Home State: Texas
Political Party: Republican
First Lady: Laura Welch Bush

44. Barack H. Obama (1961-)
Years in Office: 2009-2017
Vice President: Joseph (Joe) Biden
Home State: Illinois
Political Party: Democrat
First Lady : Michelle LaVaughn Robinson
Obama

45. Donald John Trump (1946-)
Years in: Office 2017 –
Vice President: Michael Richard (Mike) Pence
Home State: New York
Political Party: Republican
First Lady: Melania Trump

The Themes of Geography

To understand how our world is connected, some geographers have divided the study of geography into five different themes. The themes are location, place, region, movement, and human interaction. Understanding these themes of geography will help you understand historical events.

Location

In geography, location means a place on Earth's surface. A location can be defined in different ways. One way is by street name and number. You write a location when you address a letter. Places can also be located by a set of numbers. These numbers refer to a geographical grid system called latitude and longitude.

Place

Each place on Earth has physical features such as rivers, mountains, or valleys. Its different features make each place unique. A mountain peak, for example, has very different features from an ocean beach. Most places also have human characteristics. These include population densities, major cities, or languages and religions. Descriptions of most places are combinations of both their human and physical features.

Region

A region is bigger than a place or a location. Regions cover large areas of land that share physical or human characteristics. The Mountain States of America, for example, share a cool climate and high mountains. The Middle West is known for its farms.

Movement

Throughout history, wars, economic troubles, or climate changes have caused people to move from one place to another. As people moved, they often made changes to a place. Geographers study why these movements occurred. They also look at how movement changed the culture and physical landscape of an area.

Human Interaction

Geographers are interested in how the environment influences people. Hot areas, for example, draw people to the beach. Cold areas draw people to the ski slopes. Geographers also study how people interact with, or affect, their environment. This human interaction determines how land is used for recreation, housing, and industry.

Dictionary of Geographic Words

1 CANAL A channel built to carry water for irrigation or transportation

2 CANYON A deep, narrow valley with steep sides

3 COAST The land along an ocean

4 DAM A wall built across a river, creating a lake that stores water

5 DELTA Land made of soil left behind as a river drains into a larger body of water

6 DESERT A dry environment with few plants and animals

7 GLACIER A huge sheet of ice that moves slowly across the land

8 GULF Part of an ocean that extends into the land; larger than a bay

9 HARBOR A sheltered place along a coast where boats dock safely

10 HILL A rounded, raised landform; not as high as a mountain

11 ISLAND A body of land completely surrounded by water

12 LAKE A body of water completely surrounded by land

13 MOUNTAIN A high landform with steep sides; higher than a hill

14 MOUNTAIN PASS A narrow gap through a mountain range

15 MOUNTAIN RANGE A row or chain of mountains

McGrow-Hill Education

16 MOUTH The place where a river empties into a larger body of water

17 OASIS A fertile area in a desert that is watered by a spring

18 OCEAN A large body of salt water; oceans cover much of Earth's surface

19 PEAK The top of a mountain

20 PENINSULA A body of land nearly surrounded by water

21 PLAIN A large area of nearly flat land

22 PLATEAU A high, flat area that rises steeply above the surrounding land

23 PORT A city where ships load and unload goods

24 RESERVOIR A natural or artificial lake used to store water

25 RIVER A stream of water that flows across the land and empties into another body of water

26 RIVER BASIN All the land that is drained by a river and its tributaries

27 SOURCE The starting point of a river

28 TRIBUTARY A smaller river that flows into a larger river

29 VALLEY An area of low land between hills or mountains

30 VOLCANO An opening in Earth's surface through which hot rock and ash are forced out

United States: Political

PACIFIC OCEAN

WASHINGTON
- Seattle
- Olympia ★
- Spokane
- River
- Columbia

OREGON
- Portland
- Salem ★
- Eugene

IDAHO
- Boise ★
- Pocatello
- Snake River

MONTANA
- Great Falls
- Helena ★
- Billings
- Missouri River

WYOMING
- Casper
- Cheyenne ★

CALIFORNIA
- Eureka
- Redding
- San Francisco
- Oakland
- San José
- Sacramento ★
- Carson City ★
- Reno
- Fresno
- Bakersfield
- Los Angeles
- Long Beach
- San Diego
- Sacramento River

NEVADA
- Las Vegas

UTAH
- Great Salt Lake
- Ogden
- Salt Lake City
- Provo
- Colorado River

COLORADO
- Denver ★
- Colorado Springs
- Pueblo

ARIZONA
- Phoenix ★
- Tucson

NEW MEXICO
- Santa Fe ★
- Albuquerque
- El Paso
- Rio Grande

MEXICO

Gulf of California

40°N
130°W
120°W
110°W

ARCTIC OCEAN
RUSSIA
180°W
70°N
120°W
ARCTIC CIRCLE
CANADA
ALASKA
- Nome
- Yukon R.
- Fairbanks
- Anchorage
- Juneau ★
60°N
130°W
170°W   160°W   150°W   140°W

0   200   400 miles
0   200   400 kilometers

N
W   E
S

HAWAII
160°W   155°W
- Kauai
- Oahu
- Niihau
- Honolulu ★
- Molokai
- Lanai
- Kahoolawe
- Maui
- Hilo
- Hawaii
PACIFIC OCEAN
20°N
N
W   E
S

0   100   200 miles
0   100   200 kilometers

Legend:
- ⊛ National capital
- ★ State capital
- ● Other city

CANADA

Lake Superior

NORTH DAKOTA
Grand Forks
Fargo
Bismarck

SOUTH DAKOTA
Pierre
Sioux Falls

MINNESOTA
Duluth
St. Paul
Minneapolis

WISCONSIN
Green Bay
Milwaukee
Madison

MICHIGAN
Grand Rapids
Lansing
Detroit

Lake Michigan
Lake Huron
Lake Ontario
Lake Erie

NEBRASKA
Omaha
Lincoln

IOWA
Cedar Rapids
Des Moines
Davenport

ILLINOIS
Chicago
Gary
Springfield

INDIANA
Indianapolis

OHIO
Toledo
Cleveland
Columbus
Cincinnati

Pittsburgh

NEW YORK
Buffalo
Albany

NEW HAMPSHIRE
VERMONT
Montpelier
Concord

MAINE
Augusta
Portland

Boston
MASSACHUSETTS
Providence
RHODE ISLAND
Hartford
CONNECTICUT

PENNSYLVANIA
Harrisburg
Newark
New York
Trenton
NEW JERSEY
Philadelphia
Dover
DELAWARE
Baltimore
Annapolis
MARYLAND

Washington, D.C.

WEST VIRGINIA
Charleston

Platte River
Missouri River

KANSAS
Kansas City
Kansas City
Topeka
Wichita

MISSOURI
St. Louis
Jefferson City

Springfield
Evansville

KENTUCKY
Frankfort
Louisville

Ohio River

VIRGINIA
Richmond
Norfolk

70°W

NORTH CAROLINA
Raleigh
Charlotte

OKLAHOMA
Oklahoma City
Tulsa

Arkansas River

ARKANSAS
Fort Smith
Little Rock

Red River

TENNESSEE
Nashville
Knoxville
Memphis

Tennessee River

Mississippi River

SOUTH CAROLINA
Columbia
Charleston

TEXAS
Fort Worth
Dallas
Austin
San Antonio
Laredo
Houston
Corpus Christi

Brazos River
Colorado River

MISSISSIPPI
Jackson

ALABAMA
Birmingham
Montgomery

GEORGIA
Atlanta
Columbus
Savannah

LOUISIANA
Shreveport
Baton Rouge
New Orleans
Mobile
Biloxi

Jacksonville
Tallahassee

FLORIDA
Orlando
Tampa
Miami

ATLANTIC OCEAN

THE BAHAMAS

Gulf of Mexico

50°N
40°N
30°N

90°W
80°W

N
W E
S

0   200   400 miles
0   200   400 kilometers

United States: Physical

Puget
Sound
Mt. Rainier
14,410 ft. (4,392 m) ▲
Mt. St. Helens
8,363 ft. (2,549 m) ▲
Columbia R.
Mt. Hood
11,239 ft.
(3,426 m) ▲
Mt. Shasta
14,162 ft.
(4,317 m) ▲
Cape
Mendocino
San Francisco
Bay
Sacramento R.
San Joaquin R.
COAST RANGES
CASCADE RANGE
SIERRA NEVADA
CENTRAL VALLEY
Lake
Tahoe
Mt. Whitney
14,495 ft.
(4,418 m) ▲
Death Valley
-282 ft. ▼
(-86 m)
MOJAVE
DESERT
Channel
Islands
Salton
Sea
SONORAN
DESERT
COLUMBIA PLATEAU
Snake River
GREAT
BASIN
Great Salt
Lake
GREAT
SALT LAKE
DESERT
WASATCH RANGE
Lake
Mead
Colorado
River
Gila River
COLORADO
PLATEAU
Humphreys Peak
12,633 ft.
(3,851 m) ▲
Missouri River
ROCKY
Granite Peak
12,799 ft.
(3,901 m) ▲
BLACK
HILLS
Kings Peak
13,528 ft.
(4,123 m) ▲
Mt. Elbert
14,433 ft.
(4,399 m) ▲
Pikes
Peak
14,110 ft.
(4,301 m) ▲
Wheeler
Peak
13,161 ft.
(4,011 m) ▲
MOUNTAINS
Guadalupe Peak
8,749 ft.
(2,667 m) ▲
Pecos River
Rio Grande
MEXICO
Gulf of California

Alaska inset
ARCTIC OCEAN
70°N
RUSSIA
BROOKS RANGE
ALASKA
Bering Strait
Denali
20,310 ft.
(6,190 m) △
ALASKA RANGE
CANADA
Yukon River
60°N
Bering
Sea
Gulf of
Alaska
Aleutian Islands
170°W 160°W 150°W 140°W
0   200   400 miles
0 200 400 kilometers

Hawaii inset
160°W   155°W
Kauai
Niihau
Oahu
HAWAII
Molokai
PACIFIC
OCEAN
Lanai Maui
Kahoolawe
Hawaii
20°N
Mauna Kea
13,796 ft.
(4,205 m) ▲
0   100   200 miles
0 100 200 kilometers

Legend
— National boundary
— State boundary
▲ Mountain peak
△ Highest point
▼ Lowest point
━ Continental Divide

40°N   130°W

120°W   110°W

CANADA

MESABI RANGE

GREAT LAKES

Lake Superior

Lake Michigan

Lake Huron

Lake Ontario

Lake Erie

St. Lawrence River

WHITE MTS.

Mt. Washington
6,288 ft.
(1,917 m)

ADIRONDACK MTS.

GREEN MTS.

Cape Cod

G R E A T   P L A I N S

Mississippi River

Missouri River

Platte River

CENTRAL PLAINS

River

Wabash

Ohio

River

ALLEGHENY PLATEAU

ALLEGHENY MTS.

Hudson R.

Susquehanna R.

Long Island

40°N

Delaware Bay

Potomac River

PIEDMONT

Chesapeake Bay

Arkansas River

INTERIOR PLAINS

OZARK PLATEAU

OUACHITA MOUNTAINS

Red River

Brazos River

Colorado River

DWARDS LATEAU

Tennessee River

Mississippi

River

Alabama River

Mt. Mitchell
6,684 ft.
(2,037 m)

A P P A L A C H I A N   M O U N T A I N S

Savannah River

Chattahoochee River

A T L A N T I C   C O A S T A L   P L A I N

Cape Hatteras

ATLANTIC OCEAN

30°N

GULF COASTAL PLAIN

Mobile Bay

Galveston Bay

Mississippi River Delta

Lake Okeechobee

T H E   B A H A M A S

Gulf of Mexico

Florida Keys

Straits of Florida

N
W   E
S

90°W

80°W

McGraw-Hill Education

0   200   400 miles
0   200   400 kilometers

World: Political

160°W 120°W
80°N

ALASKA
(U.S.)
60°N

CANADA

**NORTH
AMERICA**
40°N

UNITED STATES

BERMUDA
(U.K.)

ATLANTIC
OCEAN

MIDWAY ISLANDS
(U.S.)

TROPIC OF CANCER

See inset below

HAWAII
(U.S.)
20°N

MEXICO

Caribbean Sea

GUYANA
VENEZUELA SURINAME

PACIFIC OCEAN

GALAPAGOS ISLANDS
(Ecuador)

COLOMBIA
ECUADOR FRENCH GUIANA
(France)

0° EQUATOR

PERU

**SOUTH
AMERICA**

AMERICAN
SAMOA
(U.S.)
SAMOA

COOK
ISLANDS
(N.Z.)
FRENCH POLYNESIA
(France)

BOLIVIA

BRAZIL

TONGA

20°S
TROPIC OF CAPRICORN

PITCAIRN
ISLAND
(U.K.)

PARAGUAY

URUGUAY
CHILE
ARGENTINA

40°S

FALKLA
ISLANDS

SOUTH GEORG
SOUTH SANDW
ISLANDS (

60°S

ANTARCTIC CIRCLE
80°W

60°W
160°W

120°W

Inset map

90°W   80°W   70°W

Gulf of Mexico
FLORIDA
(U.S.)

0   200   400 miles

0   200 400 kilometers

THE
BAHAMAS

ATLANTIC
OCEAN

TROPIC OF CANCER

20°N

TURKS &
CAICOS
ISLANDS (U.K.)

20°N

CUBA

PUERTO RICO VIRGIN IS.
(U.S.)   (U.K.) ST. KITTS & NEVIS

MEXICO

CAYMAN IS.
(U.K.)

HAITI
DOMINICAN
REPUBLIC

ANTIGUA &
BARBUDA

BELIZE

JAMAICA

VIRGIN IS. (U.S.)
MONTSERRAT (U.K.)

GUADELOUPE
(France)

GUATEMALA

HONDURAS

N Caribbean Sea

DOMINICA MARTINIQUE
(France)

EL
SALVADOR

CURAÇAO
(Netherlands)

BONAIRE
(Netherlands)

ST. LUCIA

W   E

NICARAGUA

ARUBA (Netherlands)

ST. VINCENT &
THE GRENADINES

BARBADOS

S

GRENADA

TRINIDAD
AND
TOBAGO

10°N

PACIFIC
OCEAN

COSTA
RICA

PANAMA

VENEZUELA

90°W

COLOMBIA
80°W

70°W

60°W

GUYANA

ARCTIC OCEAN

REENLAND
(Denmark)

SVALBARD
(Norway)

ARCTIC CIRCLE

ICELAND

See inset below

EUROPE

ES
(gal)

RUSSIA

KAZAKHSTAN

MONGOLIA

ASIA

GEORGIA

UZBEKISTAN

KYRGYZSTAN

NORTH
KOREA

JAPAN

PACIFIC
OCEAN

ARMENIA
TURKEY

TURKMENISTAN

TAJIKISTAN

SOUTH
KOREA

TUNISIA

LEBANON

SYRIA
IRAQ

AZERBAIJAN

AFGHANISTAN

CHINA

TROPIC OF CANCER

MOROCCO

ISRAEL

IRAN
KUWAIT

PAKISTAN

BHUTAN
NEPAL

TAIWAN

WAKE
ISLAND
(U.S.)

ALGERIA

LIBYA

JORDAN
QATAR

BANGLADESH

20°N

estern
ahara
OCCO)

EGYPT

SAUDI
ARABIA

UNITED ARAB EMIRATES

OMAN

INDIA

MYANMAR
(BURMA)

LAOS

NORTHERN
MARIANA
ISLANDS (U.S.)

GUAM (U.S.)

MARSHALL
ISLANDS

E

MAURITANIA

MALI

NIGER

CHAD

ERITREA
SUDAN

YEMEN

DJIBOUTI

THAILAND

VIETNAM

PHILIPPINES

FEDERATED STATES
OF MICRONESIA

EGAL

BURKINA
FASO

BENIN

AFRICA

CAMBODIA

PALAU

EA
SAU

GUINEA

GHANA

NIGERIA

CENTRAL
AFRICAN
REPUBLIC

SOUTH
SUDAN

ETHIOPIA

SRI
LANKA

BRUNEI
MALAYSIA

EQUATOR

KIRIBATI

0°

ERRA
EONE

LIBERIA

TOGO

CAMEROON

UGANDA

KENYA

MALDIVES

COTE D'IVOIRE

GABON

RWANDA
DEM.
REPUBLIC
OF THE
CONGO

BURUNDI

INDONESIA

PAPUA
NEW
GUINEA

SOLOMON
ISLANDS

SAO TOMÉ AND
PRINCIPE

EQUATORIAL
GUINEA

TANZANIA

SEYCHELLES

EAST
TIMOR

ATLANTIC
OCEAN

CONGO

ANGOLA

MALAWI

COMOROS

INDIAN
OCEAN

TUVALU

ZAMBIA

NAMIBIA

ZIMBABWE

MADAGASCAR

VANUATU

FIJI

BOTSWANA

MAURITIUS

TROPIC OF CAPRICORN

20°S

REUNION
(France)

NEW
CALEDONIA
(France)

N

W   E

S

SOUTH
AFRICA

MOZAMBIQUE
SWAZILAND

LESOTHO

AUSTRALIA

FRENCH SOUTHERN &
ANTARCTIC LANDS
(France)

NEW
ZEALAND

40°S

0   1,000   2,000 miles

0   1,000 2,000 kilometers

40°E

80°E

120°E

160°E

60°S

ANTARCTIC CIRCLE

ANTARCTICA

80°S

0°

RUSSIA

NORWAY

FINLAND

60°N

SWEDEN

0   200   400 miles

North
Sea

DENMARK

ESTONIA

Baltic Sea

LATVIA

0   200 400 kilometers

IRELAND

UNITED
KINGDOM

LITHUANIA

RUSSIA

N

50°N

NETHERLANDS

BELARUS

W   E

BELGIUM

GERMANY

POLAND

S

ATLANTIC
OCEAN

LUXEMBOURG

LIECHTENSTEIN

CZECH
REPUBLIC

UKRAINE

50°N

FRANCE

SWITZERLAND

AUSTRIA

SLOVAKIA

HUNGARY

MOLDOVA

RUSSIA

SLOVENIA

ROMANIA

MONACO

CROATIA

Black Sea

GEORGIA

ANDORRA

CORSICA
(France)

BOSNIA AND
HERZEGOVINA

SERBIA

40°N

PORTUGAL

SPAIN

MONTENEGRO

KOSOVO

BULGARIA

SARDINIA
(Italy)

ITALY

MACEDONIA

TURKEY

BALEARIC IS.
(Spain)

ALBANIA

40°N

SICILY
(Italy)

GREECE

GIBRALTAR (U.K.)

10°E

CYPRUS

SYRIA

MOROCCO

ALGERIA

TUNISIA

MALTA

CRETE (Gr.)

LEBANON

20°E

Mediterranean Sea

30°E

0°

World: Physical

Beaufort Sea

60°N

ALASKA RANGE
▲
Denali
20,310ft
(6,190m)

NORTH AMERICA

CANADIAN SHIELD

CASCADE RANGE

ROCKY MOUNTAINS

Missouri River

GREAT PLAINS

Mississippi River

APPALACHIAN MTS.

ATLANTIC OCEAN

30°N

Rio Grande

TROPIC OF CANCER

PACIFIC OCEAN

Caribbean Sea

0° EQUATOR

Amazon River

SOUTH AMERICA

0   1,000   2,000 miles

0   1,000 2,000 kilometers

ANDES MOUNTAINS

PAMPAS

TROPIC OF CAPRICORN

Mt. Aconcagua ▲
22,834ft. (6,960m)

30°S

PACIFIC OCEAN

PATAGONIA

ATLANTIC OCEAN

— National boundary
▲ Mountain peak

Cape Horn

60°W   30°W

60°S

120°W   90°W

150°W   ANTARCTIC CIRCLE

Weddell Sea

Vinson Massif ▲
16,067 ft. (4,897 m)

ARCTIC OCEAN

CENTRAL SIBERIAN PLATEAU

Ob River

Sea of Okhotsk

60°N

NORTHERN EUROPEAN PLAIN

URAL MTS.

Volga River

ALPS **EUROPE**

Mt. Elbrus 18,510 ft. (5,642 m)

▲Mont Blanc 15,711 ft. (4,807 m)

Black Sea

Caspian Sea

ASIA

GOBI

NORTH CHINA PLAIN

Mediterranean Sea

HINDU KUSH

Indus River

HIMALAYA MTS.

Chang River

30°N

ATLAS MOUNTAINS

SYRIAN DESERT

Ganges River

▲ Mt. Everest 29,035 ft. (8,850 m)

TROPIC OF CANCER

SAHARA

Red Sea

Nile River

DECCAN PLATEAU

South China Sea

PACIFIC OCEAN

SAHEL

Arabian Sea

Bay of Bengal

Philippine Sea

AFRICA

Congo River

CONGO BASIN

▲ Mt. Kilimanjaro 19,340 ft. (5,895 m)

EQUATOR 0°

INDIAN

OCEAN

Coral Sea

NAMIB DESERT

KALAHARI DESERT

TROPIC OF CAPRICORN

GREAT SANDY DESERT

GREAT DIVIDING RANGE

Cape of Good Hope

AUSTRALIA

Darling River

30°S

N

W   E

S

▲ Mt. Kosciusko 7,310 ft (2,228 m)

McGraw-Hill Education

30°E   60°E   90°E   120°E

ANTARCTIC CIRCLE

150°E

60°S

ANTARCTICA

California: Physical

OREGON

IDAHO

Goose Lake

LAVA BEDS
NATIONAL
MONUMENT

WARNER MTS.

UTAH

REDWOOD
NATIONAL
PARK

Klamath R.

CASCADE RANGE

KLAMATH
MTS.

Shasta
Lake

Pit R.

0   50   100 miles
0   50   100 kilometers

N
W   E
S

Trinity R.

LASSEN VOLCANIC
NATIONAL PARK

Eagle
Lake

WHISKEYTOWN-SHASTA-
TRINITY NATIONAL
RECREATION AREA

SACRAMENTO VALLEY

Lake
Almanor

NEVADA

Eel R.

Lake
Oroville

Sacramento R.

Feather R.

Yuba R.

SIERRA NEVADA

Lake
Tahoe

C O A S T

Clear
Lake

American R.

Folsom
Lake

Russian R.

POINT REYES
NATIONAL
SEASHORE

Lake
Berryessa

Mokelumne R.

R

San Pablo Bay

Stanislaus R.

Hetch Hetchy
Aqueduct

Mono Lake

San Francisco
Bay

A

YOSEMITE
NATIONAL
PARK

KINGS
CANYON
NATIONAL
PARK

N

San Joaquin R.

Merced R.

DIABLO RANGE

SAN JOAQUIN

DEATH
VALLEY
NATIONAL
PARK

Badwater Basin
282 ft. (86 m)
below sea level

PANAMINT RANGE

DEATH VALLEY

Monterey Bay

G

San Luis
Reservoir

Kings R.

E

VALLEY

SEQUOIA
NATIONAL
PARK

S

ARIZONA

SANTA LUCIA RANGE

36°N

Salinas R.

Mt. Whitney
14,495 ft.
(4,418 m)

TEHACHAPI MTS.

Estero
Bay

Cuyama R.

TEMBLOR RANGE

Kern R.

Los Angeles Aqueduct

MOJAVE DESERT

PACIFIC
OCEAN

SAN
RAFAEL MTS.

Santa
Clara R.

Lake
Havasu

Colorado River

Santa Barbara Channel

JOSHUA TREE
NATIONAL PARK

34°N

CHANNEL ISLANDS
NATIONAL PARK

Colorado Aqueduct

San Diego Aqueduct

Salton
Sea

124°W   122°W

Gulf of
Santa
Catalina

COLORADO
DESERT

IMPERIAL
VALLEY

SONORAN
DESERT

— National boundary
▲ Highest point
▼ Lowest point
‧‧‧‧ Aqueduct
⬛ National Park

120°W   118°W

MEXICO

42°N
40°N
38°N

North America: Political

ARCTIC OCEAN

ASIA

Chukchi Sea

Bering Sea

Bering Strait

Beaufort Sea

Ellesmere Island

Queen Elizabeth Islands

Parry Islands

Banks Island

Greenland (Denmark)

ICELAND

Alaska (U.S.)

Yukon River

Fairbanks

Anchorage

Gulf of Alaska

Juneau

Victoria Island

Mackenzie River

Great Bear Lake

Yellowknife

Great Slave Lake

Lake Athabasca

Baffin Island

Baffin Bay

Davis Strait

Nuuk

Iqaluit

Labrador Sea

Hudson Bay

CANADA

Edmonton

Lake Winnipeg

Vancouver

Seattle

Portland

Columbia R.

Snake River

Missouri River

Winnipeg

Lake Superior

Island of Newfoundland

Quebec

Montreal

Ottawa

Lake Huron

Lake Michigan

Minneapolis

Lake Ontario

Toronto

Lake Erie

Detroit

Boston

New York

Philadelphia

San Francisco

Salt Lake City

Great Salt Lake

Colorado River

Denver

Chicago

St. Louis

Ohio R.

Tennessee River

Washington, D.C.

ATLANTIC OCEAN

UNITED STATES

Los Angeles

Phoenix

Arkansas River

Red River

Mississippi R.

Atlanta

Bermuda (U.K.)

Dallas

Ciudad Juarez

Rio Grande

Houston

New Orleans

PACIFIC OCEAN

Monterrey

Gulf of Mexico

Miami

Havana

THE BAHAMAS

Nassau

CUBA

Puerto Rico (U.S.)

ANTIGUA AND BARBUDA

ST. KITTS AND NEVIS

St. John's

MEXICO

Guadalajara

Mexico City

DOMINICAN REPUBLIC

HAITI

Port-au-Prince

Santo Domingo

Roseau

DOMINICA

ST. LUCIA

BELIZE

Belmopan

JAMAICA

Kingston

Caribbean Sea

ST. VINCENT & THE GRENADINES

GRENADA

GUATEMALA

Guatemala City

HONDURAS

Tegucigalpa

TRINIDAD AND TOBAGO

San Salvador

NICARAGUA

EL SALVADOR

Managua

COSTA RICA

San José

Panama City

PANAMA

SOUTH AMERICA

★ National capital

• Other city

McGraw-Hill Education

0   300   600 miles

0   300   600 kilometers

N
W   E
S

EQUATOR

R19

Europe: Political

Asia: Political

ARCTIC OCEAN

EUROPE

AFRICA

PACIFIC OCEAN

INDIAN OCEAN

RUSSIA

CHINA

INDIA

KAZAKHSTAN

MONGOLIA

JAPAN

INDONESIA

Bering Sea

Sea of Okhotsk

Sea of Japan

Kuril Islands

East China Sea

Ryukyu Islands (Japan)

South China Sea

Bay of Bengal

Arabian Sea

Red Sea

Black Sea

Caspian Sea

Aral Sea

Celebes (Sulawesi)

Borneo (Sulawesi)

Sumatra

Java

New Guinea

PAPUA NEW GUINEA

EAST TIMOR

Arafura Sea

EQUATOR

TROPIC OF CANCER

ARCTIC CIRCLE

Rivers and features

Lake Baikal
Lena River
Yenisey River
Ob River
Ural River
Syr Darya
Huang River
Yangtze River
Mekong River
Chengdu Zee
Indus River

Countries and cities

Moscow
Magadan
Yakutsk
Khabarovsk
Krasnoyarsk
Irkutsk
Chelyabinsk
Semey
Astana
Qaraghandy
Urumqi
Ulaanbaatar
MONGOLIA
Vladivostok
Sapporo
Tokyo
Kyoto
Nagasaki
Seoul
Pyongyang
NORTH KOREA
SOUTH KOREA
Harbin
Beijing
Jinan
Nanjing
Shanghai
Guangzhou
Hong Kong
Macau
Taipei
Taiwan
Quezon City
Manila
PHILIPPINES
Davao
Manado
Bandar Seri Begawan
BRUNEI
MALAYSIA
Kuala Lumpur
Singapore
Palembang
Jakarta
Yogyakarta
Dili
Lhasa
Thimphu
BHUTAN
NEPAL
Kathmandu
Dhaka
BANGLADESH
Mandalay
MYANMAR (BURMA)
Yangon (Rangoon)
Naypyidaw
LAOS
Vientiane
Hanoi
Hue
Ho Chi Minh City
VIETNAM
CAMBODIA
Phnom Penh
THAILAND
Bangkok
Chengdu
Kolkata (Calcutta)
Patna
Jabalpur
Hyderabad
New Delhi
Islamabad
PAKISTAN
Kabul
Kandahar
AFGHANISTAN
Karachi
Mumbai (Bombay)
Bangalore
Male
MALDIVES
Colombo
SRI LANKA
Andaman Islands (India)
Nicobar Islands (India)
Lakshadweep (India)
Chagos Archipelago (British Indian Ocean Territory)
Socotra (Yemen)
KAZAKHSTAN
KYRGYZSTAN
Bishkek
Tashkent
UZBEKISTAN
TAJIKISTAN
Dushanbe
TURKMENISTAN
Ashgabat
Baku
AZERBAIJAN
ARMENIA
Yerevan
GEORGIA
Tbilisi
Ankara
Istanbul
TURKEY
CYPRUS
Nicosia
Beirut
LEBANON
SYRIA
Damascus
ISRAEL
Jerusalem
JORDAN
Amman
IRAQ
Baghdad
Basra
KUWAIT
Kuwait
Tabriz
Tehran
Isfahan
IRAN
BAHRAIN
Manama
QATAR
Doha
Abu Dhabi
UNITED ARAB EMIRATES
Muscat
OMAN
Riyadh
SAUDI ARABIA
Medina
Mecca
YEMEN
San'a
Jabalpur

Legend

⊕ National capital
• Other city

1,000 miles
500
500 1,000 kilometers
0

McGraw-Hill Education

Africa: Political

EUROPE

ASIA

Mediterranean Sea

Madeira Islands (Portugal)

Tangier
Rabat • Fez
Casablanca
MOROCCO
Marrakech
Oran
Algiers
Tunis
TUNISIA
Tripoli
Benghazi
Alexandria
Cairo

Canary Islands (Spain)

Laayoune
Western Sahara (Morocco)

ALGERIA
LIBYA
EGYPT
Aswan
Lake Nasser
Nile R.
Red Sea
TROPIC OF CANCER

MAURITANIA
Nouakchott
MALI
NIGER
CHAD
Khartoum
Port Sudan
ERITREA
Asmara
DJIBOUTI
Gulf of Aden

Senegal R.
Dakar
SENEGAL
Banjul
GAMBIA
GUINEA-BISSAU
Bissau
GUINEA
Conakry
SIERRA LEONE
Freetown
Monrovia
LIBERIA
Niger River
Bamako
Ouagadougou
BURKINA FASO
Niamey
Kano
N'Djamena
SUDAN
Khartoum
SOUTH SUDAN
Addis Ababa
ETHIOPIA
Djibouti

BENIN
GHANA
CÔTE D'IVOIRE
TOGO
Accra
Yamoussoukro
Lomé
Porto-Novo
Lagos
NIGERIA
Abuja
Benue River
CENTRAL AFRICAN REPUBLIC
Juba
SOMALIA
Mogadishu

Gulf of Guinea
Malabo
EQUATORIAL GUINEA
SÃO TOMÉ AND PRÍNCIPE
São Tomé
Libreville
CAMEROON
Yaoundé
Bangui
Kisangani
Kampala
UGANDA
RWANDA
Kigali
Lake Victoria
KENYA
Nairobi
INDIAN OCEAN

GABON
CONGO
Brazzaville
DEMOCRATIC REPUBLIC OF THE CONGO
Kinshasa
Bujumbura
BURUNDI
Dodoma
Mombasa
Pemba Island
Zanzibar
Dar es Salaam

EQUATOR

Cabinda (Angola)
Kananga
Lake Tanganyika
TANZANIA
SEYCHELLES

ATLANTIC OCEAN
Luanda
ANGOLA
COMOROS
Moroni
Mayotte (France)

Lilongwe
MALAWI
Lake Malawi
MOZAMBIQUE
MADAGASCAR
Antananarivo

ZAMBIA
Lusaka
Zambezi River
Harare
ZIMBABWE

NAMIBIA
Windhoek
TROPIC OF CAPRICORN
BOTSWANA
Gaborone
Pretoria
Maputo
Johannesburg
Mbabane
SWAZILAND
Bloemfontein
Maseru
LESOTHO
Durban

Orange R.
SOUTH AFRICA

⊛ National capital
• Other city

N
W E
S

0   500   1,000 miles
0   500   1,000 kilometers

Cape Town
Cape of Good Hope
Port Elizabeth

R22

20°W   10°W   0°   10°E   20°E   30°E   40°E   50°E

40°N   30°N   20°N   10°N   0°   10°S   20°S   30°S

South America: Political

Caribbean Sea

15°N

CENTRAL AMERICA

Barranquilla
Maracaibo
Valencia
Caracas
Lake Maracaibo
Orinoco River
VENEZUELA
Georgetown
Paramaribo
Cayenne
GUYANA
SURINAME
FRENCH GUIANA (France)

ATLANTIC OCEAN

Medellín
Gulf of Panama
Bogotá
Cali
Magdalena River
COLOMBIA

Quito
EQUATOR
ECUADOR
Guayaquil
Iquitos

Negro River
Manaus
Belém
Amazon River
River
Tapajós River
Xingu River

Equator 0°

Trujillo
PERU
Callao Lima
Cuzco
Madeira River

BRAZIL
São Francisco River
Recife

Arequipa
Lake Titicaca
La Paz
BOLIVIA
Sucre

Brasília
River
Salvador (Bahía)

15°S

Paraguay River
Belo Horizonte

PARAGUAY
Paraná
Rio de Janeiro

Antofagasta
TROPIC OF CAPRICORN
Tucumán
Asunción
São Paulo
TROPIC OF CAPRICORN

CHILE
Paraná River
Uruguay River
Porto Alegre

Córdoba
Rosario
URUGUAY

Valparaíso
Santiago
ARGENTINA
Buenos Aires
Montevideo
Rio de la Plata

30°S

PACIFIC OCEAN
Concepción
Colorado River

ATLANTIC OCEAN

45°S

Falkland Islands
(Islas Malvinas)
(U.K.)

0   250   500 miles
0 250 500 kilometers

⊛ National capital
• Other city

Punta Arenas
Strait of Magellan

South Georgia (U.K.)

105°W   90°W   75°W   60°W   45°W   30°W

N
W E
S

McGraw-Hill Education

R23

Glossary

A

amendment an addition to the Constitution

article a paragraph in a legal document

assembly a government legislature that represents the people of a particular place

B

bill a suggestion for a new law

blockade an obstacle preventing the movement of people or goods

boundary a line that marks where one area ends and another begins

boycott to refuse to do business or have contact with a person, group, company, country, or product

C

cash crop a plant that is grown for making money

cede to give up something to someone else

charter a document granting someone special legal powers

claim to declare that a place belongs to one's country upon arrival at the place

colony a territory settled by people from another place, usually far away

commerce the buying and selling of goods

composition the way in which something is put together

conquest victories by invading armies

corruption the use of government money for personal gain

covenant a contract, an agreement

currency the type of money used in a particular place

D

delegate a person who represents other people

demand the level of need for something

dissension disagreement between members of a group over an important issue

diverse containing many types of people or things

E

encomiendas system of forced labor in Spanish colonies

endeavor try hard to achieve a goal

environment the setting in which something takes place

H

habitat an environment that is favorable to the survival of a species

harvest to take and gather such crops as wheat and corn for use

hieroglyph a type of ancient writing that uses pictures for words

hostility opposition; ill will

hunter-gatherer early humans who lived by gathering wild plants and hunting animals

I

immigrant a person who arrives in a new country after leaving his or her country of birth

imposing putting in place by a government order

inflation increase in the cost of goods and services

inland in an area that is away from oceans and coastal regions

interchangeable something that can be used in place of something else because it is identical

issue to give out or publish

J

jury a group of citizens that decides the outcome of a court case

L

loom a machine for making thread or yarn into cloth

M

manifest destiny the belief that it was divine will for the United States to expand westward to the Pacific Ocean

mercenary soldiers from a different country who are paid to fight in a war

merchants people who buy and sell goods

mesa a flat-topped hill with steep sides

militia a group of citizens organized for military service

missionary person on a religious mission, usually to convert others to Christianity

monarch a king and queen who rules nations

monopoly complete control of something

musket long guns similar to rifles

N

navigation the art of guiding a boat, plane, or other transportation vehicle

negotiate to discuss and bargain for a solution

oral history spoken records, including stories, that have been passed from one generation to the next

outpost a fort or other military structure established away from the main army to help guard against surprise attacks

oxen cattle that are used for doing work

physical relating to material objects; having actual form

policy an official position on an issue

potlatch a special feast given by American Indians of the Northwest Coast, in which the guests receive gifts

prairie flat or gently rolling land covered mostly with grasses and wildflowers

press the news media, including newspapers and magazines, websites, and TV and radio

profiteer people who take advantage of a poor economic situation, hoarding goods and selling them at high prices to make a large profit

proprietor the owners

R

reaping having to do with cutting down and gathering

rebel person who defies authority

recession a temporary downturn in business activity

reconcile to become friendly again after a disagreement; to make peace with

reconciliation returning to the previous friendly condition of a relationship after a disagreement

repeal cancelation or withdrawal

republic an area of land that has its own government and elected leaders

resistance defense to diseases developed by the immune system

settlement town created by people in an area previously uninhabited by that people

slash-and-burn a method of clearing land for farming by cutting and burning trees

sovereign having independent authority

surge sudden increase

survey to examine and measure

term the period of time during which an elected person is in office

territory an area of land that belongs to a government

totem pole a tall carved log used by American Indians of the Northwest Coast to honor an important person or to mark a special event

traitor someone who betrays his or her country

unconstitutional an action or policy that goes against the Constitution of the United States

vandalism destruction of property

veto to reject or prevent

warship ships mounted with cannons or other large guns

Index

This index lists many topics along with the pages in this book on which they are found. Page numbers after a *c* refer you to a chart or graph; after an *m,* a map; after a *p,* photographs; after a *ptg,* artwork; and after a *q,* a quotation.

McGraw-Hill Education

Grade Five
Historical and Social Sciences Content Standards and Analysis Skills

History-Social Sciences Content Standards

United States History and Geography: Making a New Nation

Students in grade five study the development of the nation up to 1850, with an emphasis on the people who were already here, when and from where others arrived, and why they came. Students learn about the colonial government founded on Judeo-Christian principles, the ideals of the Enlightenment, and the English traditions of self-government. They recognize that ours is a nation that has a constitution that derives its power from the people, that has gone through a revolution, that once sanctioned slavery, that experienced conflict over land with the original inhabitants, and that experienced a westward movement that took its people across the continent. Studying the cause, course, and consequences of the early explorations through the War for Independence and western expansion is central to students' fundamental understanding of how the principles of the American republic form the basis of a pluralistic society in which individual rights are secured.

5.1 Students describe the major pre-Columbian settlements, including the cliff dwellers and pueblo people of the desert Southwest, the American Indians of the Pacific Northwest, the nomadic nations of the Great Plains, and the woodland peoples east of the Mississippi River.

1. Describe how geography and climate influenced the way various nations lived and adjusted to the natural environment, including locations of villages, the distinct structures that they built, and how they obtained food, clothing, tools, and utensils.

2. Describe their varied customs and folklore traditions.

3. Explain their varied economies and systems of government.

5.2 Students trace the routes of early explorers and describe the early explorations of the Americas.

1. Describe the entrepreneurial characteristics of early explorers (e.g., Christopher Columbus, Francisco Vásquez de Coronado) and the technological developments that made sea exploration by latitude and longitude possible (e.g., compass, sextant, astrolabe, seaworthy ships, chronometers, gunpowder).

2. Explain the aims, obstacles, and accomplishments of the explorers, sponsors, and leaders of key European expeditions and the reasons Europeans chose to explore and colonize the world (e.g., the Spanish Reconquista, the Protestant Reformation, the Counter Reformation).

3. Trace the routes of the major land explorers of the United States, the distances traveled by explorers, and the Atlantic trade routes that linked Africa, the West Indies, the British colonies, and Europe.

4. Locate on maps of North and South America land claimed by Spain, France, England, Portugal, the Netherlands, Sweden, and Russia.

5.3 Students describe the cooperation and conflict that existed among the American Indians and between the Indian nations and the new settlers.

1. Describe the competition among the English, French, Spanish, Dutch, and Indian nations for control of North America.

2. Describe the cooperation that existed between the colonists and Indians during the 1600s and 1700s (e.g., in agriculture, the fur trade, military alliances, treaties, cultural interchanges).

3. Examine the conflicts before the Revolutionary War (e.g., the Pequot and King Philip's Wars in New England, the Powhatan Wars in Virginia, the French and Indian War).

4. Discuss the role of broken treaties and massacres and the factors that led to the Indians defeat, including the resistance of Indian nations to encroachments and assimilation (e.g., the story of the Trail of Tears).

5. Describe the internecine Indian conflicts, including the competing claims for control of lands (e.g., actions of the Iroquois, Huron, Lakota [Sioux]).

6. Explain the influence and achievements of significant leaders of the time (e.g., John Marshall, Andrew Jackson, Chief Tecumseh, Chief Logan, Chief John Ross, Sequoyah).

5.4 Students understand the political, religious, social, and economic institutions that evolved in the colonial era.

1. Understand the influence of location and physical setting on the founding of the original 13 colonies, and identify on a map the locations of the colonies and of the American Indian nations already inhabiting these areas.

2. Identify the major individuals and groups responsible for the founding of the various colonies and the reasons for their founding (e.g., John Smith, Virginia; Roger Williams, Rhode Island; William Penn, Pennsylvania; Lord Baltimore, Maryland; William Bradford, Plymouth; John Winthrop, Massachusetts).

3. Describe the religious aspects of the earliest colonies (e.g., Puritanism in Massachusetts, Anglicanism in Virginia, Catholicism in Maryland, Quakerism in Pennsylvania).

4. Identify the significance and leaders of the First Great Awakening, which marked a shift in religious ideas, practices, and allegiances in the colonial period, the growth of religious toleration, and free exercise of religion.

5. Understand how the British colonial period created the basis for the development of political self-government and a free-market economic system and the differences between the British, Spanish, and French colonial systems.

6. Describe the introduction of slavery into America, the responses of slave families to their condition, the ongoing struggle between proponents and opponents of slavery, and the gradual institutionalization of slavery in the South.

7. Explain the early democratic ideas and practices that emerged during the colonial period, including the significance of representative assemblies and town meetings.

5.5 Students explain the causes of the American Revolution.

1. Understand how political, religious, and economic ideas and interests brought about the Revolution (e.g., resistance to imperial policy, the Stamp Act, the Townshend Acts, taxes on tea, Coercive Acts).

2. Know the significance of the first and second Continental Congresses and of the Committees of Correspondence.

3. Understand the people and events associated with the drafting and signing of the Declaration of Independence and the document's significance, including the key political concepts it embodies, the origins of those concepts, and its role in severing ties with Great Britain.

4. Describe the views, lives, and impact of key individuals during this period (e.g., King George III, Patrick Henry, Thomas Jefferson, George Washington, Benjamin Franklin, John Adams).

5.6 Students understand the course and consequences of the American Revolution.

1. Identify and map the major military battles, campaigns, and turning points of the Revolutionary War, the roles of the American and British leaders, and the Indian leaders' alliances on both sides.

2. Describe the contributions of France and other nations and of individuals to the outcome of the Revolution (e.g., Benjamin Franklin's negotiations with the French, the French navy, the Treaty of Paris, The Netherlands, Russia, the Marquis Marie Joseph de Lafayette, Tadeusz Ko'sciuszko, Baron Friedrich Wilhelm von Steuben).

3. Identify the different roles women played during the Revolution (e.g., Abigail Adams, Martha Washington, Molly Pitcher, Phillis Wheatley, Mercy Otis Warren).

4. Understand the personal impact and economic hardship of the war on families, problems of financing the war, wartime inflation, and laws against hoarding goods and materials and profiteering.

5. Explain how state constitutions that were established after 1776 embodied the ideals of the American Revolution and helped serve as models for the U.S. Constitution.

6. Demonstrate knowledge of the significance of land policies developed under the Continental Congress (e.g., sale of western lands, the Northwest Ordinance of 1787) and those policies' impact on American Indians' land.

7. Understand how the ideals set forth in the Declaration of Independence changed the way people viewed slavery.

5.7 Students describe the people and events associated with the development of the U.S. Constitution and analyze the Constitution's significance as the foundation of the American republic.

1. List the shortcomings of the Articles of Confederation as set forth by their critics.

2. Explain the significance of the new Constitution of 1787, including the struggles over its ratification and the reasons for the addition of the Bill of Rights.

3. Understand the fundamental principles of American constitutional democracy, including how the government derives its power from the people and the primacy of individual liberty.

4. Understand how the Constitution is designed to secure our liberty by both empowering and limiting central government and compare the powers granted to citizens, Congress, the president, and the Supreme Court with those reserved to the states.

5. Discuss the meaning of the American creed that calls on citizens to safeguard the liberty of individual Americans within a unified nation, to respect the rule of law, and to preserve the Constitution.

6. Know the songs that express American ideals (e.g., "America the Beautiful," "The Star Spangled Banner").

5.8 Students trace the colonization, immigration, and settlement patterns of the American people from 1789 to the mid-1800s, with emphasis on the role of economic incentives, effects of the physical and political geography, and transportation systems.

1. Discuss the waves of immigrants from Europe between 1789 and 1850 and their modes of transportation into the Ohio and Mississippi Valleys and through the Cumberland Gap (e.g., overland wagons, canals, flatboats, steamboats).

2. Name the states and territories that existed in 1850 and identify their locations and major geographical features (e.g., mountain ranges, principal rivers, dominant plant regions).

3. Demonstrate knowledge of the explorations of the trans-Mississippi West following the Louisiana Purchase (e.g., Meriwether Lewis and William Clark, Zebulon Pike, John Fremont).

4. Discuss the experiences of settlers on the overland trails to the West (e.g., location of the routes; purpose of the journeys; the influence of the terrain, rivers, vegetation, and climate; life in the territories at the end of these trails).

5. Describe the continued migration of Mexican settlers into Mexican territories of the West and Southwest.

6. Relate how and when California, Texas, Oregon, and other western lands became part of the United States, including the significance of the Texas War for Independence and the Mexican-American War.

5.9 Students know the location of the current 50 states and the names of their capitals.

Historical and Social Sciences Analysis Skills

In addition to the standards, students demonstrate the following intellectual, reasoning, reflection, and research skills:

Chronological and Spatial Thinking

1. Students place key events and people of the historical era they are studying in a chronological sequence and within a spatial context; they interpret time lines.

2. Students correctly apply terms related to time, including past, present, future, decade, century, and generation.

3. Students explain how the present is connected to the past, identifying both similarities and differences between the two, and how some things change over time and some things stay the same.

4. Students use map and globe skills to determine the absolute locations of places and interpret information available through a map's or globe's legend, scale, and symbolic representations.

5. Students judge the significance of the relative location of a place (e.g., proximity to a harbor, on trade routes) and analyze how relative advantages or disadvantages can change over time.

Research, Evidence, and Point of View

1. Students differentiate between primary and secondary sources.

2. Students pose relevant questions about events they encounter in historical documents, eyewitness accounts, oral histories, letters, diaries, artifacts, photographs, maps, artworks, and architecture.

3. Students distinguish fact from fiction by comparing documentary sources on historical figures and events with fictionalized characters and events.

Historical Interpretation

1. Students summarize the key events of the era they are studying and explain the historical contexts of those events.

2. Students identify the human and physical characteristics of the places they are studying and explain how those features form the unique character of those places.

3. Students identify and interpret the multiple causes and effects of historical events.

4. Students conduct cost-benefit analyses of historical and current events.